Chef Paul Prudhomme's
Fork in the Road

Chef Paul Prudhomme's
Fork in the Road

A Different Direction in Cooking

Photography by Paul Rico

William Morrow and Company, Inc.
New York

It is the policy of William Morrow and Company, Inc., and its im-
prints and affiliates, recognizing the importance of preserving what
has been written, to print the books we publish on acid-free paper,
and we exert our best efforts to that end.

Library of Congress Cataloging-in-Publication Data

Prudhomme, Paul.
    Chef Paul Prudhomme's fork in the road.—1st. ed.
        p.   cm.
    Includes index.
    ISBN 0-688-12165-9
    1. Cookery, American—Louisiana style. 2. Low-fat diet—
Recipes.
I. Title. II. Title: Fork in the road.
TX715.2.L68P78   1993
641.59763—dc20   93-25836
                                                              CIP

Printed in the United States of America

First Edition

1 2 3 4 5 6 7 8 9 10

BOOK DESIGN BY RICHARD ORIOLO

Certain things in life can only be accomplished as a team—as a unit—where two or more people are working together in the same direction and drawing strength from each other's efforts and commitment to achieving a goal. My late wife, K, and I were such a team with a vision of serving great food to make people happy. Although she was small in frame, she was a giant when it came to her love of good food and good living. She was my partner in business, my friend in life, and I'll miss her as I take another fork in the road. So, K, I'll do just that, and this book is dedicated to you.

Acknowledgments

As soon as I began work on my first cookbook, it was obvious to me that such a venture was beyond the capacity of any one person. Even now, with this fourth book, the task has not really gotten any easier. This project would never have been completed without the talents and loyalty of many very special people.

First, I want to thank the dedicated members of a panel we established to guide our efforts down this *Fork in the Road*. They added immeasurably to this book by contributing creative suggestions and frank opinions. Without input from Deborah Baudoin, Candis Coffee, Amanda Griffin, Julia McSherry, Steve Taylor, and Kathleen Zelman, this book would not have evolved the way it did. I sincerely wish we had had longer to work together.

Patricia Kennedy Livingston, who did the editing in New Orleans, at times drove me crazy with her energy and enthusiasm, but those same qualities were essential to keep the work moving along. A professional writer, she's also a talented amateur cook, and tested each recipe not only for grammar and syntax but also for ease of understanding.

Special thanks are in order to my kitchen assistants. Chef Cannon Wiest endured innumerable interruptions in the test kitchen, frustrating delays, and the difficulties of working with such a weird fat guy. Although James L. Holmes, Jr., arrived on the scene late in the schedule, his unflappable good humor and willingness to test and retest were crucial to the completion of the project. Great job, guys!

Without the computer wizardry of Sean O'Meara, who also assisted me on *Seasoned America*, we'd never have come close to meeting our deadlines. Sean, along with registered dietitian Kathleen Zelman, provided the nutrient analyses that follow each recipe, as well as several useful suggestions for format and content. Their help was invaluable.

My gratitude also goes out to the staff at K-Paul's, without whose cooperation very little could have been accomplished. Thanks to general manager Paul Miller, Andrew Humbert, R. L. Holmes, Janice Rozetcki, Mike Calagna, Claire Bourgeois, and Mary Kay Howland, who sent all those visitors to interrupt us!

Shawn Granger McBride offered her unwavering support of the general idea and the specific applications, encouragement during the difficult times, love and inspiration, and excellent business sense. Couldn't have made it without you Shawn. And my thanks to her husband, John McBride, for accepting with such good grace Shawn's time-consuming involvement in this book.

An enormous thank you is owed to Margie Blaum for keeping track of everything, especially me. Margie, you're a paragon for gracious efficiency.

Ann Bramson, my editor at William Morrow, deserves a medal for her patience in dealing with a hard-headed author. Ann, I truly appreciate your willingness to try new ideas and travel down that unexplored *Fork in the Road*. Thanks also to Ann's assistant, Sarah Rutta—a wonderful go-between.

The beautiful photographs are the result of many hours of hard work by Paul Rico, the incredibly creative man behind the lens, and our wonderful food stylist, Peggy Green. Thanks to both of you for being so willing to keep working until we got just the effects we wanted.

And finally, mere thank yous hardly seem enough for the Simon family in Hawthorne, New Jersey. Sue, who operates professionally under the name SueChef, Inc., tested a number of recipes and offered insightful and complete critiques. Her husband, Brad, and their daughter, Samantha (Sam just happens to be my goddaughter), willingly tasted the dishes Sue cooked and contributed their helpful comments.

Contents

Soups 49

*Nothing is more satisfying to body and spirit than delicious,
nutritious homemade soup. It tells you someone cares
for your well-being (even if you make the soup yourself)!*

Salads 73

*Hearty enough to be served as a main course, they
work well as appetizers or side dishes, too.*

Magic Brightening 95

*Not a new way to cook (it's been enjoyed in the Orient for gener-
ations) but a method that's new to many. In these delicious broths,
meat and vegetables brighten to their peak of color and taste.*

Fish and Seafood 123

*Louisiana waters are famous for the abundance and variety of
good things to eat swimming in them, but if you can't find shrimp,
crawfish, or catfish, use whatever fresh seafood is available
in your area.*

Chicken and Turkey 149

*A boon to low-fat cooking, these recipes demonstrate how versatile
and thrifty poultry can be.*

Meats 197

*Most of these are one-dish meals complete with vegetables and a
starch, so you don't have to prepare anything else except a simple
salad.*

Side Dishes 223

Vegetables, rice, beans, and pasta in numerous combinations can accompany a plain main dish, but if you make the portions a little more generous, the side dishes can suddenly blossom into your principal course.

Desserts 251

For everyone who thinks the meal isn't complete without a sweet finale.

Snacks and Munchies 261

To satisfy that "in-between" craving, tasty things to nibble on. Some of the names may sound funny, but try them first, then see who's laughing.

Index 275

List of Color Photographs

Chef Paul Prudhomme's
Fork in the Road

Introduction

Hi! In this section I want to tell you something about how and why this book came about.

The title, *Fork in the Road,* was chosen because the book represents a different direction in cooking for me. As I travel around this country and talk to people, one of the things that makes a strong impression on me is that so many of you are frustrated at being told you have to learn to eat in a new way. Whether it's for medical or personal reasons, you're supposed to change the way you eat, and that's very, very hard to do.

We're all creatures of habit, and our eating habits are among the hardest to break. Now I'm no scientist, and what follows is just my Cajun philosophy after listening to people and observing how they were raised. I believe the way we like to eat has nothing to do with the way we work today, but relates to the way most people worked in the past.

In the old days, we didn't have machinery to do our heavy work for us, and we didn't have so many cars, so we walked when we had to go somewhere. Most of us didn't have central heating, so our bodies had to work at keeping us warm. All that work required a lot of energy, and food that gives us energy—with high levels of fat and sugar—tastes good. I'm pretty sure Nature designed it that way so that people would eat the foods their bodies needed to keep going.

Although our work habits have changed considerably over the past fifty years or so, our bodies and tastes can't change that quickly, so we want and eat a lot of delicious, high-energy food that we don't need. Then, what happens is that our bodies store all that extra energy as fat. I gain weight very, very fast if I eat more food than I need.

I grew up on a farm in Louisiana, and when I was young I did my share of very heavy work. But that was more than thirty years ago. I've carried this weight since I was very young, and I've been very lucky that it hasn't caused me any serious health problems. I have more energy and endurance than most people you know—ask anyone who works for me! I do, however, feel best when I'm at the low end of my normal weight range.

I'm concerned when people tell me how hard it is to change their cooking and eating habits. As you and I know, a lot of what is called "healthful" food looks and tastes like twigs. Or worse. So I figure what we need to do is select dishes that we've always liked, ones we're used to cooking and eating, and then take out the worst offender—the fat. Unfortunately, it's often the fat that gives foods their textures and flavors.

Nevertheless, my staff and I used as our goal the standard set by the American Heart Association, that not more than 30 percent of the total calories in each dish come from fat. Equally important, however, was our determination that every dish taste as delicious as if it had been created without regard to nutrition. If it doesn't taste good, I don't want to eat it, and I don't think you want to either.

The recipes in this book, with few exceptions, derive fewer than 30 percent of their calories from fat; those that don't conform are clearly indicated. However, they're still useful, since you can always compensate by serving nonfat or low-fat side dishes.

Because I know you don't have unlimited time to spend in your kitchen—no matter how inspired you may be—I also tried to simplify the recipes. Obviously none of them is as easy as popping a frozen dinner into the microwave, but if that's what you like to eat you wouldn't be reading this book!

How we achieved our goals—reducing fat, retaining flavor and textures, as well as a series of ideas to expand your knowledge and expertise—is outlined in the following section. Throughout the book you'll see a great number of dishes you're used to cooking, recipes we've worked on to reduce or eliminate the fat. By looking at these, and noticing what we've done, you can learn to do the same thing with your own favorite dishes. You can get rid of the fat and still make the recipes taste good. Let me show you how.

This is a guidebook. Take a Fork in the Road, and let it lead you toward a new way of more healthful cooking and eating.

Good cooking, Good eating, Good loving!

Notes from the Test Kitchen

Musings . . . and Explanations

There's a lot of information I want to share with you—too much to be written into the individual recipes. Besides, some of these musings and explanations apply to more than one dish, so it seems to make sense to have them all in one place.

Cooking is a lot of fun, and I don't want to do anything or write anything that takes away from having a good time in the kitchen. So the following information is designed to give you more time for the fun stuff!

I also want to say, right here at the start, that I consider this book only a guide. Nothing is carved in stone. If you're not comfortable with a certain ingredient, then for heaven's sake don't use it! I've given you examples of how things can be done, and trust that they'll inspire you to try these recipes and experiment with some of your own. Working on this book has, I think, made me a better cook, and I hope that using it will do the same for you.

So here we go, taking that Fork in the Road!

Ingredients

Nonfat dairy product substitutes. Many of the recipes in this book use nonfat cream cheese, nonfat cottage cheese, and canned evaporated skim milk, either alone or in combination. In the test kitchen we discovered that

3

these products add a wonderful richness and texture to our dishes, without the fat and calories of their whole-milk counterparts. For our purposes, when I combine these products, I call them "creamy mixtures."

A couple of words of caution are in order, though. First, creamy mixtures that contain nonfat dairy products lose their texture and curdle, or "break," if they're heated to more than about 160° or 170°. You'll note that in the recipes we tell you to add the creamers, then either turn off or reduce the heat immediately.

When these mixtures are puréed, they tend to incorporate a good bit of air, making them very frothy. This is no big deal—the bubbles disappear after a minute or two, but it might be disconcerting the first time you see it.

Needless to say, we wouldn't be using nonfat products if we thought any harm could come from them. So far no research has indicated the possibility of any problems with them, and they do offer an advantage in creating rich and creamy dishes. The ingredient that gives nonfat foods this edge is called Simplesse, which is made from dairy protein. Simplesse shouldn't have an adverse effect on anyone who isn't allergic to it.

Artificial sweeteners. Many of our recipes, and not just desserts, call for the optional use of artificial sweeteners. They bring out the natural flavors of other ingredients without adding unnecessary calories. I suggest using equal amounts of two different sweeteners—one with saccharin (Sweet'n Low) and the other with aspartame (Equal), for a balanced taste.

I have read that a tiny percentage of the population is allergic to aspartame; in these few people, it can cause brainwave dysfunction. But for the majority of us, these sweeteners open up endless possibilities for flavor enhancement.

Artificial sweeteners are used in sugarless pudding mixes. You may be surprised to hear that I actually used a pudding mix, but I wanted to experiment with it. All by itself it's not incredible, but if you add things to it, you can make it taste pretty good.

Fruit syrups and juices. I was really having a hard time getting a complete, "round" taste without using butter or oil. Without a "round" taste, I'm not happy or satisfied with a dish. It has to be complete, filling my mouth with all kinds of flavors—sweet, salty, spicy. I couldn't figure out how to get the result I wanted until I hit on the idea of using apple juice.

Obviously there's not a lot of connection between the flavors of butter and apple juice, but by reducing the apple juice, either in the dish itself as it cooks or beforehand by making a syrup, you end up with just a hint of sweetness, a richer color, a slightly fuller texture, and an enormous improvement in overall flavor. We've used the fruit juices and syrups quite a bit—alone or in combination.

Legumes as thickeners. One of our cookbook panel members joked that we ought to call this the Chickpea Cookbook, because they show up in so many different guises. Well, we had a good laugh, and then I explained about legumes, one of our most underrated and underappreciated foods. As any true vegetarian probably knows, legumes—chickpeas, black-eyed peas, navy beans, white beans, and lima beans, to name a few—are a terrific source of protein and are important to people who don't eat meat for health or personal reasons.

The reason we could use these foods in so many recipes is that they are incredibly versatile. Although they have distinctive flavors, they add nutrition and body to a dish without overwhelming the taste of the main ingredients. Along with the creamers, sour creamers, and the fruit juices, legumes are what make many recipes in this book work.

Fresh vs. canned tomatoes. I have specified fresh tomatoes in almost every recipe. If you have access to really good produce, nothing beats the flavor of a fine, fresh tomato. Actually, when we originally cooked many of these dishes, we used a very fine canned product, and considered listing it. However, this particular brand is not available all over the country, so I've simply made the suggestion, leaving the final choice to you.

Whether you choose canned or fresh tomatoes, remember that two cups of peeled, chopped fresh tomatoes approximately equals one 14½-ounce can of Hunt's Choice Cut Diced Tomatoes.

(By the way, do you know the easiest way to peel a tomato? Just immerse it in boiling water until the skin loosens, about one minute, then plunge it into ice water until cool enough to handle. The skin will slip right off.)

Some like it hot—that is, hot chile peppers. If you can't find chile peppers ready-ground, buy them whole and process them in the bowl of a food processor until they are finely ground. If the peppers aren't brittle enough for grinding, first roast them in a preheated 300° oven (it's OK to leave the seeds in—they're full of flavor), then process them.

Some of the varieties we like to use, and which can easily be obtained in New Orleans supermarkets, are New Mexico, ancho, guajillo, habañero, and pasillo chiles. Experiment with the chiles available where you shop—they will vary in heat—but always use a combination for a well-balanced, "round" flavor.

As you know, I like a good bit of heat in my dishes. I use cayenne, chile peppers, and different-colored peppercorns. The amount of heat in chile peppers, such as jalapeño, habañero, New Mexico, etc., is measured in Scoville

Units. Ratings range from 0, or sweet, to hundreds of thousands of heat units. The one we recommend and use most often in our recipes is cayenne, or red pepper, which has a Scoville rating of 20,000 heat units. I hope that someday companies that package peppers and pepper products will indicate heat units on the labels. My mentioning them here is a first step toward encouraging this action.

If you prefer less heat in your dishes, use peppers with a lower heat-unit rating; if you want more heat, then just find peppers with a higher rating.

Turkey and chicken. You can't help but notice that the largest category of recipes is poultry—chicken and turkey. The reason is that poultry is relatively low in fat, especially the white meat, and extremely versatile. I've given you recipes for cooking turkey the way you would other meats—roasting it, as chops, stuffing it, and so forth.

I hope that you'll try substituting chicken or turkey in some of your own favorite recipes, using the guidelines in this book. Again, experiment!

Substitutions. If this is the first cookbook you've ever used, then you'll probably work through a recipe exactly, step by step. And that's great—you have to start somewhere, and I think the recipes in this book are ideal for a beginner because they're not difficult and they all taste wonderful.

The rest of you out there will make your own substitutions whenever necessary or desired. As I said earlier, nothing is carved in stone. If someone at your table is allergic to or plain doesn't like turnips, then leave 'em out, for goodness' sake. The same goes for the artificial sweeteners. Remember, you own this book, it doesn't own you!

Techniques and Equipment

Scrape and clear. Many recipes tell you to "scrape the bottom of the skillet to clear it of all the brown bits." Then you continue cooking for a few minutes and scrape again. What you're doing is caramelizing the vegetables in your dish, and this step is one of the most important directions I have to offer you. Just like a building, the structure of a dish rests on its foundation, and browning the ingredients forms the foundation of flavor for each recipe. By evaporating the surface moisture, you add a wonderful brown color and crispy texture to the food. The flavor that's added after the moisture has evaporated is from the fibers that are left behind. By changing their color, we change their taste to nutty, sweet, slightly smoky—but it's still the same ingredient, only with different levels of taste. The next addition of the same ingredient will give you a different taste and texture.

Browning flour. You can't make a roux without oil, but you can brown the dry flour and use that to add a rich flavor to sauces and gravies. Here's how:

Preheat an 8-inch skillet, preferably nonstick, over high heat to 350°, about 3 minutes. Add the specified amount of flour and stir with a wire whisk to break up all the lumps. When the flour starts to brown, turn the heat to low, shaking and stirring continuously. *Caution: After about 4 or 5 minutes, the flour will burn easily.* As soon as the flour is a milk-chocolate brown color, turn off the heat. This should take approximately 6 minutes. Sift the browned flour and set it aside until it is needed in the recipe.

Scalloping meat. To scallop meat, usually a flank steak, place it in front of you on a firm surface, with the grain of the meat running from left to right. Use a heavy knife—a 6-inch or 8-inch chef's knife works well—and be sure it is very sharp. Working with the knife almost parallel to the surface, slide it through the meat about 1/4 inch below the surface, at about a 30-degree angle from the meat's grain, and cut off a piece about 2 by 3 inches (or as specified in the recipe).

Think of the scallop as a slice of potato for scalloped potatoes—it's thin and more or less oval. That's the shape you're trying for.

Make the next cut right next to the first cut, also at about a 30-degree angle from the meat's grain, but in the opposite direction. Continue down the length of the piece of meat, then through the thickness. You are removing thin ovals from the top of the steak from one end to the other, making the steak thinner with each successive layer of cuts. Don't hurry the process, and try to keep the meat scallops as nearly the same size as possible so that they will all cook in about the same amount of time.

Stocking up on stock. The world's great scientists might not agree, but it seems to me the primary purpose of water on this earth is to diminish the taste of things. OK, so water does have other uses, like floating big ships and such, but you can be sure that if you add it to any dish, water will reduce the flavor. That's why I use stock in my recipes.

Although making your own stock is simple, it does take a little planning. But the difference in flavor between using good stock as opposed to either water or canned soup (which is extremely salty) makes it worth your time and effort. Try cooking rice, potatoes, and pasta in stock—you'll be amazed at how much more flavorful they are.

Start with 2 quarts of *cold* water, and add the vegetable trimmings from the recipe(s) you are cooking, or an unpeeled, quartered onion, an unpeeled and quartered large clove of garlic, and a rib of celery. If you're making beef or poultry stock, add the bones and excess meat, and for seafood stock, add the shells and/or carcasses. There are a very few no-nos when making stock: Don't use bell peppers, spices, or liver.

For richer flavor and color, first roast the meat bones and vegetables in a 350° oven until thoroughly browned, then use them to make your basic stock. Browning the bones and vegetables causes their natural sugars to caramelize on the surface. When preparing a vegetarian dish, simply leave out the meat, poultry, or seafood ingredients.

It's easiest to make stock in a real stockpot—one with a small diameter relative to its height. This is because there will be less evaporation when the liquid has less surface. If you must use a pot with a large diameter, you'll have to check it occasionally, and add water more often.

Place all the ingredients in the pot, and bring to a boil over high heat. Reduce the heat to low, cover, then gently simmer as long as possible, but at least 4 hours, preferably 8. Replenish the water as necessary to keep at least 1 quart of water in the pot at all times. The pot may be uncovered, or partially covered with a lid set askew. Strain, cool, and refrigerate the stock until ready to use.

To defat stock, as called for in our recipes, first refrigerate it overnight. The next day, pack a mesh strainer with ice, preferably crushed, but ice cubes work almost as well. Place the strainer over a pot large enough to hold all the stock, and carefully pour the stock over the ice in a steady, circling stream no thicker than a pencil. To remove all the fat, you may have to repeat this process once or twice.

To make your stock better still, concentrate it. Reduce it down to one third or one fourth over high heat, and you'll have a really rich broth to work with.

The stock will keep up to a week in the refrigerator, and up to 3 months in the freezer.

Finally, if you are short of time, it is far better to use a stock simmered even 20 or 30 minutes than to use water in a recipe.

Bronzing. This is an easy way to cook fish (or chicken or meat), very quickly in a skillet, where high heat seals in the goodness and moisture. It's important to use just the right amount of seasoning and to distribute it evenly. It's critical that the skillet be at the correct temperature (350°). When cooked, the entire surface of the food should be a rich bronze color, the thick parts should be cooked through and the thinner sections crispy and tasty.

Prepping the veggies. We must have some kind of order when we're talking about what size to chop or dice the vegetables, so here goes. We've decided in these recipes that "fine dice" is about ¼ inch, "medium dice" is ½ inch, and "chopped" refers to larger pieces that can be somewhat irregularly shaped.

Some recipes specify julienne vegetables—this means cutting the vegetables in long, thin pieces. For example, julienne bell peppers refers to pieces cut approximately 2½ inches long by about ¼ inch wide.

To roast bell peppers. To remove skin before dicing or chopping, place pepper directly on an open flame—the burner of a gas range works perfectly. Using tongs, turn it until the entire outer skin is blistered and charred black. This will take 3 to 5 minutes, depending upon the pepper's temperature and freshness. Submerge the charred pepper in water with ice in it until cool enough to handle, about 2 minutes, and remove the black outer skin. It should slip off easily, but if any part didn't get charred enough to be loosened, you can peel it off with a knife.

You can also roast peppers in a 500° oven until the skin is charred, about 20 minutes, then cool and remove the outer skin. Keep peppers in the refrigerator until you're ready to roast them, so they will be charred but not cooked.

People often ask me if it's OK to use a **food processor**. Food processors can do a great job if they're in good condition, and if their blades are very sharp. However, I have to be honest, I've seen a lot of bad results from processors whose blades were dull—the food was mashed rather than cut neatly. But if its blades are really sharp, a processor will do a good job. There's a way you can test it—with an onion. After you chop the onion in your processor, smell and taste the result. If the juice is sweet and oniony, then the blades are sharp enough. If the odor and taste are bitter and acid, then the blades need to be sharpened. Or use a good, sharp knife, instead.

Preheating, a Prudhomme signature. We begin almost every recipe by preheating the pot or skillet. A hot container gets the dish off to a great start, and is essential to building the taste. The first five minutes of preparing a dish are the most important, since that's when you're going to set up the conditions for caramelizing, to develop all the taste and excitement the dish can achieve.

Because these recipes are cooked over very high heat, you'll need to use a heavy skillet or pot. If you don't have a sturdy, good-quality skillet and a 5-quart pot, you might consider purchasing them. The investment will pay off many times over in the quality of the dishes you prepare. We also suggest that the skillet or pot have a nonstick surface—it makes the browning and scraping process a lot smoother.

You'll find that many of these recipes work very well in an electric skillet. The advantage is that you have complete control over the temperature.

For a skillet or pot on top of the range, the times shown in the recipes—like 4 minutes over high heat to bring a 10-inch skillet to 350°—will work for 99 percent of all gas ranges in this country. If you want to be absolutely certain that your pan reaches the specified temperature, you can buy a Grille-Temp, a little device available at most kitchen-gadget stores. You just place the device in the pan, turn the heat on, and the Grille-Temp will display the temperature. If you can't find one, ask the store manager to order one for you, or call 1-800-654-6017, and our staff will tell you how to order one.

Dehydrating. Electric dehydrators are used for the jerky and bean snacks in the last chapter. These are simple plug-in appliances, made of lightweight plastic. We suggest choosing a dehydrator that has a temperature control. Depending upon the brand, they come with two to six trays, and you can buy additional trays to increase your appliance's capacity. All models include complete instructions for their use. They can be purchased in the housewares section of large department stores, in specialty kitchen shops, or mail order catalogs.

You can also dehydrate beans and meat in an oven. Set the thermostat at 150°, arrange the food on sheet pans or cookie pans and place in the oven for the specified length of time.

Most ovens, unless they're equipped with a fan, heat unevenly. Therefore, when we use an oven to dehydrate, we move the pans from one shelf to another, so the food will dry evenly, every hour or so.

How Much to Buy?

I imagine that almost every cook keeps fresh onions, garlic, celery, and a few similar items on hand. For those of you who don't, the following guidelines will give you an idea of the quantity you'll need to buy.

Bell pepper	1 medium = 1 cup medium diced
Onion	1 large = 1 cup medium diced
Celery	2 medium ribs = 1 cup medium diced
Garlic	1 medium clove = 1 teaspoon minced
Apple	1 large = 1 cup medium diced
Mushrooms	8 ounce carton = 2 cups chopped

Breakfast and Brunch

*Great ways to get started, whether in the early morning
or much, much later on a lovely, lazy day*

Crawfish Mushroom Omelet

Makes 4 omelets

This is one of my very favorite recipes in the whole book! It's great to look at and fabulous to eat, and drew rave reviews when we were testing it. If you can't get crawfish, you can substitute shrimp or even browned, diced chicken breast.

Seasoning mix
2½ teaspoons sweet paprika
1¾ teaspoons onion powder
1¾ teaspoons garlic powder
1½ teaspoons salt
1½ teaspoons dry mustard
1½ teaspoons dried cilantro
    leaves
1½ teaspoons dried sweet basil
    leaves
1 teaspoon dried thyme leaves
½ teaspoon black pepper
¼ teaspoon white pepper
¼ teaspoon cayenne

Creamy mixture
5 ounces evaporated skim milk
½ cup nonfat cottage cheese

2 tablespoons nonfat cream
    cheese

1 cup chopped onions
1 cup defatted seafood stock
    (page 8), *in all*
2½ cups sliced fresh mushrooms
2 tablespoons all-purpose flour
8 ounces peeled crawfish tails
    (about 2 pounds whole
    crawfish)
4 (8-ounce) cartons egg
    substitute
Vegetable-oil cooking spray

Combine seasoning mix ingredients in a small bowl.

Place the creamy mixture ingredients in a blender and purée until smooth and creamy.

Preheat a 10-inch skillet, preferably nonstick, over high heat to 350°, about 4 minutes.

Add the onions and cook just until they start to brown, about 3 to 4 minutes. Add ¼ *cup* stock, scrape the bottom of the skillet, and cook until the liquid evaporates and the onions start to stick. Add another ¼ *cup* stock and the mushrooms, flour, and *2 tablespoons plus 2 teaspoons* of the seasoning mix. Stir until the flour is completely absorbed. Spread the mixture evenly across the bottom of the skillet and cook, scraping the bottom of the skillet once or twice as crusts form, about 3 to 4 minutes. Add the *remaining ½ cup* stock and clear the bottom of the skillet. Add the creamy mixture and crawfish and cook, stirring constantly, just until the mixture comes to a boil. Be careful at this stage—the mixture may begin to overflow the skillet, and you may have to lower the heat. Turn off the heat and transfer the mixture to another container.

Mix 1½ teaspoons of the seasoning mix into each 8-ounce carton of egg substitute and blend thoroughly.

Clean the skillet and place it back over high heat. Heat it to 300°, about 2 to 2½ minutes. Spray it lightly with vegetable-oil spray and add 1 carton of egg mixture. Turn the heat to medium and cook for 30 seconds. With a spatula push the cooked eggs from the outside rim of the skillet toward the center. When about ¾ of the eggs have cooked, add ½ *cup* of the crawfish mixture across the center, then gently fold the omelet in half. Cook 1 minute, then turn over and cook 1 minute on the other side. Carefully slide the omelet to a plate and top with ¼ *cup* of the crawfish mixture. Repeat the process with the other 3 omelets. Serve immediately.

Per omelet: Calories 413   Protein 70g   Fat 3g
Carbohydrates 23g   7% calories from fat

Eight-Pepper Chicken Omelet

Makes 2 large omelets

The colorful vegetables make this dish really beautiful. And a perfect omelet isn't that hard to make. Just be sure to use a nonstick skillet, and practice a few times before you have an audience. You'll have plenty of volunteers to help dispose of any "mistakes"!

Seasoning mix

1¼ teaspoons salt
¾ teaspoon dry mustard
¾ teaspoon onion powder
¾ teaspoon garlic powder
½ teaspoon sweet paprika
½ teaspoon black pepper
½ teaspoon dried thyme leaves
½ teaspoon dried sweet basil leaves
¼ teaspoon white pepper

2 (8-ounce) cartons egg substitute
½ cup finely diced onions
¼ cup finely diced green bell peppers

1¼ cups defatted chicken stock (page 8), *in all*
2 tablespoons all-purpose flour
¼ cup finely diced red bell peppers
¼ cup finely diced yellow bell peppers
¼ cup finely diced zucchini
¼ cup finely diced yellow squash
¼ cup finely diced fresh mushrooms
6 ounces chicken breast, cut into julienne strips
¼ teaspoon each pink, green, and white peppercorns (see Note)
Vegetable-oil cooking spray

Combine the seasoning mix ingredients in a small bowl.

Mix 1½ teaspoons of the seasoning mix into each 8-ounce carton of egg substitute and blend thoroughly.

Preheat a 10-inch skillet, preferably nonstick, over high heat to 350°, about 4 minutes.

Add the onions and green bell peppers, and cook 2 minutes. Add *1 teaspoon* of the seasoning mix and *¼ cup* of the stock, scrape the bottom of the skillet to clear it of all brown bits, and cook until the liquid evaporates and the vegetables start to stick, about 3 minutes. Add ¼ *cup* stock and the flour and mix until the flour is completely absorbed, and a paste is formed. Add the remaining vegetables, stir, and spread evenly across the bottom of the skillet. Cook 4 minutes, scraping continuously to keep the mixture from burning, then push the mixture outward toward the sides of the skillet.

Place the chicken, the peppercorns, and the *remaining* seasoning mix in the center of the skillet, and cook 3 minutes, turning the chicken to brown it evenly. Add the *remaining ¾ cup* stock, stir, and cook about 3 to 4 minutes. Transfer the contents of the skillet to another container (makes about 1¾ cups).

Clean the skillet and heat it to 300°, about 2 to 2½ minutes.

Lightly spray the skillet with vegetable-oil spray, and add 1 carton of egg mixture. Turn the heat to medium and cook for 30 seconds. With a spatula push the cooked eggs from the outside rim of the skillet toward the center. When about ¾ of the eggs have cooked, add ½ cup of the pepper/chicken mixture across the center, then gently fold the omelet in half. Cook 1 minute, then turn over and cook 1 minute on the other side. Carefully slide the omelet to a plate and top with a generous ¼ cup of the pepper/chicken mixture. Repeat the process with the other omelet. Serve immediately.

Note If separate containers of colored peppercorns are not available where you shop, some stores sell jars with a mixture of pink, white, green, and black peppercorns.

Per omelet: Calories 194   Protein 44g   Fat 4g
Carbohydrates 21g   16% calories from fat

Pan-Roasted Oatmeal

Makes 2 servings

This old-fashioned porridge with a new twist is just right for warming you up on a chilly morning—it will provide plenty of energy to keep you going, and the taste is truly different! And if you stir it very little, the thick starches that you associate with oatmeal will not be there. In their place will be a wonderful nutty crunchiness.

1 cup old-fashioned oats (cooks in 5 minutes)

2 cups water

½ teaspoon salt

4 (1-gram) packets artificial sweetener (page 4)

Preheat a nonstick 10-inch skillet over high heat to 400°, about 4 minutes.

Add the oats, and when they start to turn brown around the edges, stir and cook 1 minute more. Stir and remove from the heat—the oats will continue to brown slightly.

Bring the water and salt to a rolling boil in a 2-quart saucepan over high heat. Stir in the oats, reduce the heat, and simmer for 5 minutes.

Let cool slightly and add the artificial sweetener. Serve warm.

Per serving: Calories 223   Protein 38g   Fat 4g
Carbohydrates 10g   16% calories from fat

Rice Pancakes

Makes about 30 4-inch pancakes

This recipe is a happy blend of the famous calas, or rice cakes, of old New Orleans and the flapjacks of frontier days. Naturally, we've incorporated our innovations, like those wonderful fruit syrups. By the way, the syrups are great to top off your pancakes, and I think nothing goes better with them than plum butter!

1½ cups all-purpose flour
2 tablespoons baking powder
1 teaspoon salt
10 ounces egg substitute
½ cup Prune Syrup (page 46)
¼ cup Apple Syrup (page 47)

¼ cup nonfat cream cheese
1 cup evaporated skim milk
4 cups cooked long-grained white rice
½ cup currants

Mix the 3 dry ingredients in a large bowl and set aside.

Place the eggs in a blender and add the Prune Syrup, Apple Syrup, cream cheese, and skim milk. Process until smooth and creamy, about 30 seconds, and add to the dry ingredients. Mix gently until the dry ingredients are completely absorbed, then fold in the rice and currants.

Preheat a nonstick skillet over high heat to 400°, about 4 minutes. Reduce the heat to medium.

For each pancake, pour ¼ *cup* of the batter into the skillet. When the edges turn light brown and bubbles start to form, flip the pancake to the other side and cook until done. Keep warm and repeat with the *remaining* batter. Serve with White Grape Syrup (page 45), sliced fresh fruit, or low-calorie pancake syrup.

Per serving (3 pancakes): Calories 265   Protein 9g   Fat 0g
Carbohydrates 56g   1% calories from fat

Apples and Cinnamon on Bread Patricia

Makes 4 servings

This recipe is very easy, and it doesn't take long to make. The apple syrup drizzled over the fresh apples is really wonderful. As one of our testers said, "It tastes fattening, but amazingly it isn't!"

Sprinkling mixture

4 (1-gram) packets artificial
    sweetener (page 4)

⅛ teaspoon ground cinnamon

Egg mixture

4 ounces egg substitute

¼ cup apple juice

1½ tablespoons nonfat dry milk

1½ tablespoons White Grape
    Syrup (page 45)

¼ teaspoon ground cinnamon

Topping

4 slices French bread, cut diago-
    nally 1 inch thick by 6
    inches long (see **Note**)

1 small red apple, cored,
    quartered, and cut into
    ¼-inch slices

    Vegetable-oil cooking spray

8 teaspoons Apple Syrup
    (page 47)

Preheat the oven to 350°.

Combine the sprinkling mixture ingredients and set aside.

Combine the egg mixture ingredients thoroughly in a baking pan and soak each piece of bread until it is moist all the way through. The 4 slices of bread should absorb all the egg mixture. Lightly spray a baking sheet with vegetable-oil spray and place the soaked bread on the sheet. Arrange the apple slices evenly across each piece of bread, and top each serving with 2 teaspoons of Apple Syrup. Bake until the apples are done, 20 to 25 minutes. Sprinkle with the cinnamon/sweetener mixture. Serve warm.

Note For best results, use day-old bread—the bread won't absorb the egg mixture very well if it's not dry. If you don't have day-old bread, dry out the bread in a 200° oven. Just be careful not to brown the bread—it should be dry, not toasted.

Per serving: Calories 294   Protein 9g   Fat 2g
Carbohydrates 57g   6% calories from fat

color photograph 2

Not So Plain Pancakes

Makes 18 4-inch pancakes

These pancakes are deceptively simple-looking. They contain neither chunks of fruit nor nuts, yet the fruit syrups add a subtle, distinctive sweetness. You'll never get anything like this out of a box!

1 cup all-purpose flour
1 tablespoon baking powder
½ teaspoon salt
8 ounces egg substitute
1 cup evaporated skim milk

¼ cup Prune Syrup (page 46)
¼ cup White Grape Syrup
  (page 45)
Vegetable-oil cooking spray

Combine the 3 dry ingredients in a large bowl and set aside.

Place the eggs, skim milk, and Prune and White Grape Syrups in a blender and process until well mixed, about 10 to 15 seconds. Pour into the flour mixture and stir gently until well mixed and all the flour is absorbed.

Preheat a nonstick skillet over high heat to 400°, about 4 minutes. Reduce the heat to medium and lightly coat the skillet with vegetable-oil spray.

For each pancake, pour ¼ *cup* of the batter into the skillet. When the edges turn light brown and bubbles start to form, flip the pancake to the other side and cook until done. Keep warm and repeat with the *remaining* batter. Serve with White Grape or Apple Syrup, sliced fresh fruit, or low-calorie pancake syrup.

Per serving (3 pancakes): Calories 176   Protein 9g   Fat 1g
Carbohydrates 33g   3% calories from fat

Different French Toast

Makes 4 servings

What English speakers call French toast, the French call "pain perdu," or "lost bread." That's because it uses stale bread that would otherwise be lost or thrown out. The French, especially those in the country, are thrifty folk and don't like to waste anything. What's different about this recipe? The traditional version is loaded with whole eggs and their cholesterol, and sweetened with sugar, whereas we've used egg substitute and those wonderful fruit syrups.

8 ounces egg substitute	½ teaspoon ground nutmeg
3 tablespoons nonfat dry milk	½ teaspoon ground cardamom
½ cup apple juice	¼ teaspoon salt
¼ cup White Grape Syrup (page 45)	1 loaf French bread (see **Note**), cut into 8 diagonal slices,
¼ cup Prune Syrup (page 46)	approximately 6 inches long
¾ teaspoon ground cinnamon	by 1 inch thick

Place all ingredients except the bread in a blender and blend completely. Pour the mixture into a small baking pan and soak the bread in it until all the liquid is absorbed, turning the bread once.

Preheat a heavy 10-inch skillet, preferably nonstick, to 325°, about 3½ minutes.

Place the soaked bread in the skillet and cook over medium-high heat, turning 3 times, until golden brown on both sides, about 8 minutes in all.

Serve topped with your choice of fresh fruit, artificial sweetener, low-calorie pancake syrup, or one of the fruit syrups on pages 45–48.

Note Bread that's on the dry side soaks up the egg mixture better than fresh, moist bread. So use day-old bread, or dry the bread in a 200° oven for about 15 minutes. Try not to brown the bread—you want it dry, not toasted.

Per serving: Calories 304   Protein 12g   Fat 2g
Carbohydrates 56g   7% calories from fat

Cheese Grits

Makes 7½ cups, enough for 8 servings

In parts of the South, breakfast or brunch can't be served without grits. Literally. I remember going into a coffee shop in Florida to order a late-morning breakfast, but the staff said they were "all out." Upon questioning, they admitted they had bread to make toast, eggs that could be cooked any of a dozen ways, bacon, and coffee. But they were out of grits, so they couldn't offer breakfast. With this recipe you can serve a really great breakfast or brunch.

1 cup grits	½ cup egg substitute
4 cups water	6 tablespoons grated Parmesan
1 teaspoon salt	(or your favorite) cheese, *in all*
¼ cup Prune Syrup (page 46)	1 cup evaporated skim milk
½ cup White Grape Syrup	½ cup all-purpose flour
(page 45)	2 tablespoons baking powder

Preheat a small nonstick skillet over high heat to 400°, about 4 minutes.

Add the dry grits, and when they begin to brown around the edges, stir and cook 1 minute more. Stir again and remove from the heat—the grits will continue to brown slightly.

Bring the water and salt to a rolling boil in a 2-quart saucepan over high heat. Stir in the grits, reduce the heat, and simmer for 15 to 20 minutes, stirring occasionally to be sure the grits do not stick to the bottom of the pan. If the grits seem to be too thick, add up to 1 cup additional water.

Preheat the oven to 350°.

Add the prune and grape syrups to the cooked grits and mix well. Add the eggs, *4 tablespoons* of the Parmesan cheese, and the milk, and mix until thoroughly blended. Add the flour and baking powder, and blend in. Spray a 9 × 9 × 2-inch baking pan with vegetable-oil spray, and pour the grits into it. Sprinkle the *remaining* cheese over the top and bake for 20 minutes or until a knife inserted comes out clean. Serve immediately.

Per 1-cup serving: Calories 206   Protein 9g   Fat 3g
Carbohydrates 37g   11% calories from fat

Couscous

Makes 6 to 8 servings

Hot boudin, cold couscous,
Come on, Cajuns, push-push-push!

That's the battle cry of the Ragin' Cajuns at the University of South-east Louisiana in Lafayette, and it's also the makings of a great meal. Never mind what boudin is, but couscous is . . . well, whip up the recipe and find out for yourself. Most people serve couscous for breakfast—it's great with skim milk and artificial sweetener. Or use it as a side dish, as the starch along with your main course.

1 cup couscous (see **Note**)	¼ cup Apple Syrup (page 47)
2 cups water	1 cup evaporated skim milk
½ teaspoon salt	Vegetable-oil cooking spray

Preheat a nonstick 10-inch skillet over high heat to 400°, about 4 minutes.

Add the couscous, and when it starts to turn brown around the edges, stir and cook 1 minute more. Stir and remove from the heat—the couscous will continue to brown slightly.

Bring the water and salt to a rolling boil in a 2-quart saucepan over high heat. Stir in the couscous, reduce the heat, and simmer, stirring occasionally, for 5 minutes. As the couscous cooks, if it starts to thicken too much, gradually add up to 1 cup additional water. Remove from the heat, add the Apple Syrup and skim milk, and combine thoroughly.

Preheat the oven to 350°.

Spray a 9 × 9 × 2-inch baking pan with vegetable-oil spray, and pour the couscous into it. Bake 15 minutes. Serve immediately.

Note Couscous, which looks like very grainy yellow cornmeal, is actually made of steamed semolina, a fine, hard-wheat pasta of North African origin. Couscous is readily available in Cajun country, and can often be obtained in specialty markets throughout the U.S.

Per serving: Calories 406   Protein 15g   Fat 3g
Carbohydrates 82g   7% calories from fat

Bread

The staff of life, the stuff of satisfaction. Some of these loaves and muffins have unusual and exciting tastes and textures.

Pear Bran Muffins

Makes about 12 muffins

While these muffins are baking they smell so divine (and even more so when they come out of the oven) that you're going to have a hard time waiting until they're cool enough to eat! And the muffins are so moist they won't need to be buttered.

Some bran is more bitter than others, so taste it before cooking to make sure it's sweet. Otherwise, your muffins may have a bitter taste.

1 cup raw wheat bran (see Note)	¼ cup White Grape Syrup (page 45)
2 cups all-purpose flour	¼ cup nonfat cream cheese
3 tablespoons baking powder	1 tablespoon vanilla extract
½ teaspoon salt	2 cups pears, peeled and diced into ¼-inch cubes
4 (1-gram) packets artificial sweetener (page 4)	½ cup plus 2 tablespoons evaporated skim milk
¼ cup Prune Syrup (page 46)	Vegetable-oil cooking spray
¼ cup Apple Syrup (page 47)	

Preheat a heavy nonstick 10-inch skillet over high heat to 300°, about 3 minutes.

Add the wheat bran, and when it begins to turn brown around the edges, stir continuously while cooking 1 minute more. Turn off the heat; the bran will continue to brown slightly.

Place all the dry ingredients in a bowl—no need to sift—and mix thoroughly. Pour the fruit syrups in a circular pattern over the dry mixture, then add the cream cheese and vanilla.

Stand with the mixing bowl in front of you, and mix by sliding your hands, palms up, under the mixture from the near side to the far side. Fold the mixture over and squeeze it to blend the ingredients. Continue this process until all the ingredients are well blended.

Add the pears, and repeat the folding and squeezing process until the pears are thoroughly mixed in. Add the milk, and with a rubber spatula fold the batter until it is completely blended.

Preheat the oven to 325°.

Spray the cups of a 12-muffin tin with vegetable-oil spray, and spoon the batter into them, filling the cups to the top. Bake until done, about 45 minutes. Remove from the tin and let cool slightly before serving.

Note Whole bran can be found in the baking section of your market (near the flour, cornmeal, etc.), as well as in health food stores.

Per muffin: Calories 170   Protein 5g   Fat 0g
Carbohydrates 37g   2% calories from fat

color photograph 4

Apple Raisin Muffins

————————————————————————————————

Makes about 12 muffins

If there are sleepyheads at your house who never want to get up in the morning, try slipping these in the oven as a wake-up call. The fragrance is incredibly tempting, and the taste is worth getting up for!

3 cups all-purpose flour

3 tablespoons baking powder

½ teaspoon salt

1 teaspoon ground cinnamon

¼ teaspoon ground allspice

6 (1-gram) packets artificial
   sweetener (page 4)

¼ cup White Grape Syrup
   (page 45)

¼ cup Apple Syrup (page 47)

¼ cup Prune Syrup (page 46)

¼ cup nonfat cream cheese, cut
   into pieces

2 cups apples, peeled, cored,
   and diced into ¼-inch cubes

1 cup raisins

1 cup evaporated skim milk
   Vegetable-oil cooking spray

Place the 6 dry ingredients in a bowl—no need to sift—and mix thoroughly. Pour the Grape, Apple, and Prune Syrups in a circular pattern over the dry mixture, then add the cream cheese.

Stand with the mixing bowl in front of you and mix by sliding your hands, palms up, under the mixture from the near side to the far side. Fold the mixture over and squeeze it to blend the ingredients. Continue this process until all the ingredients are well blended.

Add the apples and raisins, and repeat the folding and squeezing process until they are thoroughly mixed in. Add the milk, and with a rubber spatula fold the batter until completely blended.

Preheat the oven to 300°.

Spray the cups of a 12-muffin tin with vegetable-oil spray, and divide the batter evenly among them, filling the cups to the top. Bake until done, about 55 minutes. Serve warm.

Per muffin: Calories 227   Protein 6g   Fat 1g

Carbohydrates 50g   2% calories from fat

Rice Flour Muffins

Makes 18 to 24 muffins

You may not be familiar with some of these ingredients, but probably can find them in your local health food store. These grains add a truly unusual goodness to the muffins, and the result will be worth the effort it takes to locate them!

½ cup raw wheat germ

¼ cup alfalfa seeds

½ cup cracked wheat cereal

1 cup all-purpose flour

2 cups brown rice flour

¼ cup baking powder

¾ teaspoon salt

¼ cup nonfat mayonnaise

¼ cup Prune Syrup (page 46)

¼ cup Apple Syrup (page 47)

¼ cup White Grape Syrup
  (page 45)

2 cups evaporated skim milk
  Vegetable-oil cooking spray

Preheat the oven to 350°.

Place a 10-inch skillet, preferably nonstick, over high heat and add the wheat germ, alfalfa seeds, and wheat cereal. Cook, shaking the skillet occasionally, until the seeds start to pop and the mixture starts to brown, about 3 to 4 minutes. Remove from the heat and set aside.

Place the dry ingredients in a bowl—no need to sift—and mix thoroughly. Add the mayonnaise and syrups, and combine with your hands until they are incorporated into the dry mixture and the batter has formed little balls. Add the toasted mixture and blend in. With a rubber spatula fold in the evaporated milk until the batter is completely blended.

Spray the cups of two 12-muffin tins with vegetable-oil spray, and fill the cups about ¾ full. Bake until done, about 25 minutes. Serve warm.

Per muffin: Calories 147   Protein 5g   Fat 1g
Carbohydrates 29g   4% calories from fat

Sunflower Sprout Muffins

Makes 18 to 24 muffins

Sunflower sprouts are fat and crunchy, and add an exciting texture to these muffins. You should be able to find them in health food stores or markets that specialize in organically grown produce.

2 tablespoons sesame seeds
2 tablespoons sunflower seeds
1½ cups whole wheat flour
1½ cups all-purpose flour
¼ cup baking powder
½ teaspoon salt
¼ cup Prune Syrup (page 46)

¼ cup White Grape Syrup (page 45)
½ cup chopped sunflower sprouts
2 cups evaporated skim milk
Vegetable-oil cooking spray

Preheat the oven to 350°.

Place a 10-inch skillet, preferably nonstick, over high heat and add the sesame and sunflower seeds. Cook, shaking the pan occasionally, until the seeds start to pop and turn brown, about 3 to 4 minutes. Remove from the heat and set aside.

Place the flours, baking powder, and salt in a bowl—no need to sift—and mix thoroughly. Add the Prune and Grape Syrups, and mix with your hands until the syrups are completely incorporated into the flour mixture and the batter has formed little balls. Add the toasted seeds and chopped sprouts, and mix in. Using a rubber spatula, fold in the evaporated milk until completely blended. The batter will be very thick and wet-looking.

Spray the cups of a 12-muffin tin with vegetable-oil spray, and divide the batter evenly among them. Bake until done, about 25 minutes. Serve warm.

Per muffin: Calories 107   Protein 3g   Fat 2g
Carbohydrates 19g   18% calories from fat

Sunflower Bread

Sunflower seeds are such a popular snack that most supermarkets carry them. Sunflower sprouts, on the other hand, may be harder to find; we get ours from a local health food store. Persevere—if you can't find them easily, ask the produce manager to order them. If that fails, try some other variety of sprouts—your favorite kind.

2 packages dry yeast	¼ cup White Grape Syrup
1¼ cups hot (105°–110°) water	(page 45)
½ cup untoasted sunflower	½ cup chopped sunflower
seeds	sprouts
3 cups all-purpose flour, *in all*	½ cup currants
¾ teaspoon salt	Vegetable-oil cooking spray
¼ cup Prune Syrup (page 46)	

Add the yeast to the hot water, stir gently until the yeast dissolves and set aside.

Place a 10-inch skillet, preferably nonstick, over high heat and add the sunflower seeds. Heat, shaking occasionally, until the seeds start to turn brown, about 3 to 4 minutes. Remove from the heat and set aside.

Place 2½ *cups* of the flour and the salt in the bowl of an electric food mixer equipped with a dough hook, and stir with a rubber spatula until well combined. Add the fruit syrups, and mix at low speed until the ingredients are well blended. Add the yeast/water mixture and mix about 1 minute. Turn the control to high and mix for 5 minutes, add the *remaining ½ cup* flour, and continue mixing at high speed 10 minutes more. Add the seeds, sprouts, and currants, and process just until evenly distributed.

Place the dough on a lightly floured surface and separate it into 4 pieces. Knead each piece 6 to 8 times.

Spray 4 loaf pans (5¾ × 3 × 2¼ inches) with vegetable-oil spray. Roll each piece of dough into a cylinder, stretch each cylinder to the size of a

(*continued*)

pan, place them in the pans and lightly spray the tops. Let rise in a warm, draft-free place (approximately 80°) about 1 hour or until doubled in bulk (see Note).

Preheat the oven to 300°. Bake until done, about 30 minutes, and remove from the pans to cool, preferably on a wire rack, before slicing.

Note A gas oven with a pilot light makes an ideal place to let bread rise. Don't turn the heat on; the pilot light will supply just enough warmth to encourage the rising process.

Per serving (2 slices): Calories 93   Protein 3g   Fat 2g
Carbohydrates 17g   15% calories from fat

Pepper Cornbread

Makes about 18 muffins

When we worked on this recipe, we didn't know whether to call it "Peppercorn Bread" or "Pepper Cornbread." Whatever you call it, these muffins are colorful and pack quite a wallop!

1 cup all-purpose flour
1 cup corn flour
1 cup yellow cornmeal
¼ cup baking powder
1 teaspoon salt
1 tablespoon crushed red pepper
1 tablespoon pink peppercorns
   (see Note)
1 tablespoon green peppercorns
   (see Note)

¼ cup nonfat mayonnaise
¼ cup nonfat cream cheese
¼ cup White Grape Syrup
   (page 45)
¼ cup Prune Syrup (page 46)
2 cups evaporated skim milk
2 tablespoons olive oil
1 cup currants
   Vegetable-oil cooking spray

Preheat the oven to 350°.

Place the 8 dry ingredients in a bowl—no need to sift—and mix thoroughly. Add the mayonnaise, the cream cheese, and the syrups, and mix with your hands until they are completely incorporated into the dry ingredients and the batter has formed little balls. Add the evaporated milk, the olive oil, and the currants, and with a rubber spatula fold together until the batter is completely blended.

Spray the cups of two 12-muffin tins with vegetable-oil spray, and spoon the batter into them, filling the cups about ⅔ full. Bake until done, about 25 minutes. Serve warm.

Note If you cannot find separate containers of pink and green peppercorns where you shop, you may be able to find peppercorn medleys that are pink and green as well as black and white.

Per muffin: Calories 159   Protein 5g   Fat 2g
Carbohydrates 31g   12% calories from fat

color photograph 6

Seasoned Bread

━━━ ━━━ ━━━ ━━━ ━ ━━ ━━ ━━ ━━ ━━ ━━ ━━ ━ ━━ ━━ ━ ━━

Makes 4 small loaves

Yes, yes, I know all bread is seasoned, even if it's just with salt. But this bread is *seasoned*. It's not for your four-year-old's peanut butter sandwich. Like a lot of other wonderful things, this one's strictly for adults. It goes well with soups and salads, and can be toasted for a crunchy snack.

½ cup dried chickpeas

½ cup dried white beans

½ teaspoon white pepper

¼ teaspoon cayenne

Seasoning mix

2 teaspoons dry mustard

1 teaspoon sweet paprika

1 teaspoon garlic powder

1 teaspoon dried sweet basil
   leaves

¾ teaspoon salt

¾ teaspoon onion powder

½ teaspoon black pepper

2 packages dry yeast

½ cup warm (105°–110°) water

2½ cups plus 2 tablespoons
   all-purpose flour, *in all*

¼ cup White Grape Syrup
   (page 45)
   Vegetable-oil cooking spray

Day 1: Place the chickpeas and white beans in separate containers, add water to cover by 3 to 4 inches, and soak overnight in the refrigerator. As they absorb the water, they will more than double their volume.

Day 2: Combine the seasoning mix ingredients in a small bowl.

Add the yeast to the warm water, stir gently until the yeast dissolves, and set aside.

Drain the chickpeas and white beans, place them in a food processor, and purée.

Place *2 cups* of the flour and the seasoning mix in the bowl of an electric food mixer equipped with a dough hook, and stir with a rubber spatula until well combined. Add the puréed chickpeas and white beans and the White

Grape Syrup. Mix at low speed until the ingredients are well blended, then add the yeast/water mixture and mix about 1 minute. Turn the control to high and mix for 5 minutes, add ½ *cup* flour, and continue mixing at high speed 10 minutes more.

Place the dough on a lightly floured surface and separate it into 4 pieces. Knead each piece 6 to 8 times.

Spray 4 loaf pans (5¾ × 3 × 2¼ inches) with vegetable-oil spray. Roll each piece of dough into a cylinder, stretch cylinders to the size of the pans, place them in the pans and lightly spray the tops. Let rise in a warm place (approximately 80°) for about 1 hour or until doubled in bulk (see **Note**).

Preheat the oven to 300°. Bake until done, about 30 minutes, and remove from the pans to cool, preferably on a wire rack, before slicing.

Note A gas oven with a pilot light makes an ideal place to let bread rise. Don't turn the heat on; the pilot light will supply just enough warmth to encourage the rising process.

Per serving (2 slices): Calories 80   Protein 3g   Fat 0g
Carbohydrates 16g   5% calories from fat

color photograph 7

Three-Seed Bread

Makes 4 small loaves

In this recipe three kinds of seed add a pleasant crunch to the bread; the blue cornmeal (although you could use yellow or white cornmeal if you can't find blue) gives it a hint of southwestern flavor; and the fruit syrups provide sweetness without refined sugar.

¼ cup pumpkin seeds	¾ teaspoon salt
2 tablespoons poppy seeds	¼ cup Prune Syrup (page 46)
2 tablespoons sesame seeds	¼ cup White Grape Syrup
2 packages dry yeast	(page 45)
¾ cup warm (105°–110°) water	3 tablespoons unsalted butter
2¼ cups all-purpose flour, *in all*	Vegetable-oil cooking spray
1 cup blue cornmeal	

Place a 10-inch nonstick skillet over high heat and add the pumpkin, poppy, and sesame seeds. Cook, shaking skillet occasionally, until the seeds start to pop and turn brown, about 3 to 4 minutes. Remove from the heat and set aside.

Add the yeast to the warm water, stir gently until the yeast dissolves, and set aside.

Place 2 *cups* of the flour, the cornmeal, and salt in the bowl of an electric mixer equipped with a dough hook, and combine with a rubber spatula until well blended. Fold in the toasted seeds with the spatula. Add the fruit syrups and butter, turn the mixer to low speed, and mix until the ingredients reach the crumbly stage. Add the yeast mixture, raise the mixer speed to medium, and mix 5 minutes. Add the *remaining ¼ cup* flour and mix at medium speed for 10 minutes more.

Place the dough on a lightly floured surface and separate it into 4 pieces. Knead each piece 6 to 8 times.

Spray 4 loaf pans (5¾ × 3 × 2¼ inches) with vegetable-oil spray. Roll each piece of dough into a cylinder, stretch cylinders to the size of the pans, place in the pans, and lightly spray the tops. Let rise in a warm place (approximately 80°) for about 1 hour or until doubled in bulk (see Note).

Preheat the oven to 300°. Bake until done, about 45 minutes, and remove from the pans to cool, preferably on a wire rack, before slicing.

Note A gas oven with a pilot light makes an ideal place to let bread rise. Don't turn the heat on—the pilot light alone will supply just enough warmth to encourage the rising process.

Per serving (2 slices): Calories 101   Protein 2g   Fat 3g
Carbohydrates 16g   27% calories from fat

No-Name Bread

Makes 4 small loaves

 This is a fairly dense bread that goes well with fruit and cheese (nonfat, of course)—it makes a great snack because it's filling.

¼ cup dried chickpeas

¼ cup dried white beans

3 packages dry yeast

¾ cup warm (105°–110°) water

1¼ cups all-purpose flour

1 cup stone-ground whole wheat flour

⅓ cup yellow cornmeal

¾ teaspoon salt

3 tablespoons Prune Syrup (page 46)

2 tablespoons White Grape Syrup (page 45)

½ cup currants

Vegetable-oil cooking spray

Day 1: Place the chickpeas and white beans in separate containers, add water to cover by 3 or 4 inches, and soak overnight in the refrigerator. As they absorb the water, they will more than double their volume.

Day 2: Add the yeast to the warm water, stir gently until the yeast dissolves, and set aside.

Drain the chickpeas and white beans and set them aside.

Place the flours, cornmeal, and salt in the bowl of an electric food mixer equipped with a dough hook, and stir until thoroughly mixed. Add the chickpeas, white beans, syrups, and currants, and mix at low speed for 1 minute. Add the yeast/water mixture and mix at medium speed for 15 minutes.

Place the dough on a lightly floured surface and separate it into 4 pieces. Knead each piece 6 to 8 times.

Spray 4 loaf pans (5¾ × 3 × 2¼ inches) with vegetable-oil spray. Roll each piece of dough into a cylinder, stretch cylinders to the size of the pans, place in the pans and lightly spray the tops. Let rise in a warm place (approximately 80°) for about 1 hour or until doubled in bulk (see **Note**).

Preheat the oven to 300°. Bake until done, about 45 minutes, and remove from the pans to cool, preferably on a wire rack before slicing.

Note A gas oven with a pilot light makes an ideal place to let bread rise. Don't turn the heat on; the pilot light alone will supply just enough warmth to encourage the rising process.

Per serving (2 slices): Calories 80   Protein 3g   Fat 0g
Carbohydrates 17g   4% calories from fat

Prune Date Bread

Makes 4 small loaves

You can guess from the name that this bread is super-nutritious, but it is also moist and delicious. I especially like it spread with softened, nonfat cream cheese. Yum!

3 packages dry yeast
1 cup warm (105°–110°) water
2 cups unsifted all-purpose
   flour
1 cup yellow cornmeal
1 cup blue cornmeal
¾ teaspoon salt
¼ cup mixed bean sprouts

12 pitted prunes, diced into
   ¼-inch pieces
12 pitted dates, diced into
   ¼-inch pieces
¼ cup White Grape Syrup
   (page 45)
   Vegetable-oil cooking spray

(continued)

Add the yeast to the warm water, stir gently until the yeast dissolves, and set aside.

Place the flour, yellow and blue cornmeal, and salt in the bowl of a food mixer equipped with a dough hook, and mix with a rubber spatula until well combined. Add the bean sprouts, prunes, and dates, and mix with the spatula. Add the White Grape Syrup and mix at low speed until ingredients are blended and reach the crumbly stage. Add the yeast mixture and mix at medium speed for 15 minutes.

Place the dough on a lightly floured surface and separate it into 4 pieces. Knead each piece 6 to 8 times.

Spray 4 loaf pans (5¾ × 3 × 2¼ inches) with vegetable-oil spray. Roll each piece of dough into a cylinder, stretch cylinders to the size of the pans, place in the pans, and lightly spray the tops. Let rise in a warm place (approximately 80°) for about 1 hour or until doubled in bulk (see Note).

Preheat the oven to 300°.

Bake until done, about 40 minutes, and remove from the pans to cool, preferably on a wire rack, before slicing.

Note A gas oven with a pilot light makes an ideal place to let bread rise. Don't turn the heat on; the pilot light alone will supply just enough warmth to encourage the rising process.

Per serving (2 slices): Calories 104   Protein 2g   Fat 1g
Carbohydrates 23g   5% calories from fat

Spreads and Syrups

*Spread on bread and plain cake, pour over fruit and vegetables,
and use as ingredients in other recipes.*

This section contains some new ideas about spreads and syrups, which can be used to enhance and enrich many different kinds of foods. The spreads can be used to add an extra dimension to soups, as well as sandwiches, sauces, and baked potatoes. Use these recipes as a springboard to develop your own favorites.

The syrups add an exciting flavor boost to sauces and breads, soups and salads. Try combining ½ cup White Grape Syrup with ¼ cup Apple Syrup or a little citrus juice to add to something special. Use your imagination—experiment with different flavors and enjoy!

Citrus Sweet Potato Spread

Makes about 1 cup

 Great on bread or muffins, or over plain cake or custard.

2 cups sweet potatoes (see Note), peeled and diced into 1-inch cubes (about 2 medium or 1 large)

3 cups apple juice

½ lemon, peeled, seeded, sectioned, each section cut into 3 pieces

½ medium orange, peeled, seeded, sectioned, each section cut into 3 pieces

12 (1-gram) packets artificial sweetener (page 4)

Place sweet potatoes and apple juice in a 3-quart pot over high heat. Bring to a boil, reduce the heat slightly, and simmer until sweet potatoes are fork tender and almost all the apple juice evaporates, about 30 to 35 minutes. Transfer the mixture from the pot to a blender or food processor along with all the remaining ingredients and purée until smooth. Cover and refrigerate.

Note The sweet potatoes should be the light orange variety rather than the light yellow kind.

Per 1-tablespoon serving: Calories 49   Protein 1g   Fat 0g
Carbohydrates 12g   0% calories from fat

Butternut Squash Marmalade

Makes about 2¾ cups

 This spread is wonderful on croissants, and great with toasted, very crunchy breads!

4 cups butternut squash, peeled
   and diced into 1-inch cubes
1 cup chopped onions
3 cups apple juice
¼ teaspoon dillweed
¼ teaspoon salt
¼ teaspoon ground nutmeg

⅛ teaspoon white pepper
2 tablespoons lemon juice
2 tablespoons orange juice
   concentrate
12 (1-gram) packets artificial
   sweetener (page 4)

Place the butternut squash, onions, and apple juice in a 3-quart pot over high heat. Bring to a boil, reduce the heat slightly, and cook until the squash is fork tender and almost all the apple juice evaporates, about 25 to 30 minutes. Transfer the mixture from the pot to a blender or food processor, along with remaining ingredients, and purée until smooth. To keep, refrigerate in a covered container.

Per 1-tablespoon serving: Calories 19   Protein 0g   Fat 0g
Carbohydrates 5g   4% calories from fat

Plum Butter

 Use this butter anytime you would apple butter. I enjoy it spread on bread or muffins with dinner.

4 plums, unpeeled, each cut into
   6 wedges
2 cups butternut squash, peeled
   and diced into 1-inch cubes
3 cups apple juice

½ cup nonfat cream cheese
½ cup nonfat mayonnaise
1 tablespoon lemon juice
8 (1-gram) packets artificial
   sweetener (page 4)

Place plums, butternut squash, and apple juice in a 3-quart pot over high heat, bring to a boil, reduce the heat slightly, and cook until the squash is fork tender and almost all the apple juice evaporates, about 25 to 30 minutes. Transfer the mixture from the pot to a blender or food processor along with the remaining ingredients and purée. To store, refrigerate in a covered container.

Per 1-tablespoon serving: Calories 12   Protein 0g   Fat 0g
Carbohydrates 3g   2% calories from fat

Sweet and Tart Spread

 I'm still looking for a spot where I don't like this spread!

2 cups sweet potatoes, peeled
    and diced into 1-inch cubes
    (about 2 medium or 1 large)
3 cups apple juice
4 cups apples, unpeeled and
    diced into 1-inch cubes

¼ teaspoon ground mace
½ teaspoon ground cinnamon
½ teaspoon dry mustard
¼ cup White Grape Syrup
    (page 45)

Place sweet potatoes, apple juice, and apples in a 3-quart pot over high heat, bring to a boil, reduce the heat slightly, and simmer until sweet potatoes are fork tender and almost all the apple juice evaporates, about 30 to 35 minutes. Transfer the mixture from the pot to a blender or food processor along with the remaining ingredients and process until puréed. To store, refrigerate in a covered container.

Per 1-tablespoon serving: Calories 26   Protein 0g   Fat 0g
Carbohydrates 6g   1% calories from fat

White Grape Syrup

Makes 1½ cups

Try this syrup over pancakes or waffles, plain cake, or fresh fruit—wherever you want an unusual, sweet accent. I don't want to mention names, but I know someone who sometimes "accidentally" spills some so she can scrape it up and lick the spatula.

Place 2 (12-ounce) cans of white grape juice concentrate in a 10-inch non-stick skillet over high heat and cook until the juice comes to a boil and foamy bubbles cover the entire surface, about 10 to 15 minutes. **Caution:** Once the juice starts to foam, the bubbles will rise above the level of the skillet. Immediately reduce the heat to medium, and continue to cook until the juice is reduced to 1½ cups, about 20 minutes more. Let cool, then place in a covered container and refrigerate.

Before using the syrup in a recipe, remove it from the refrigerator as you start your preparation, so it will have time to come to room temperature. The syrup will be thinner and easier to pour and measure.

Per 1-tablespoon serving: Calories 38   Protein 1g   Fat 0g
Carbohydrates 9g   3% calories from fat

Purple Grape Syrup

Makes 1 cup

Place 1 (12-ounce) can of purple grape juice concentrate in a 10-inch nonstick skillet over high heat. Bring to a boil and cook for 5 minutes. Reduce the heat to medium and continue to cook until the juice is reduced to 1 cup, about 10 minutes more. **Caution:** Because of the consistency of the grape juice concentrate, occasional light sticking may occur, so use a wooden spoon to check and clear the bottom of the skillet two or three times during the reduction. Let cool, then place in a covered container and refrigerate.

Remove the syrup from the refrigerator as you start your preparation, so it will have time to come to room temperature. The syrup will be thinner and easier to pour and measure.

Per 1-tablespoon serving: Calories 38   Protein 1g   Fat 0g
Carbohydrates 9g   3% calories from fat

Prune Syrup

Makes 1½ cups

Place 1 (48-ounce) bottle of prune juice, preferably with pulp, in a 5-quart nonstick pot over high heat and bring to a boil. Cook until the liquid is reduced to 1½ cups about 50 to 55 minutes. Let cool, then place in a covered container and refrigerate.

Remove the syrup from the refrigerator as you start your preparation, so it will have time to come to room temperature. The syrup will be thinner and easier to pour and measure.

Per 1-tablespoon serving: Calories 3   Protein 0g   Fat 0g
Carbohydrates 1g   1% calories from fat

1. Crawfish Mushroom Omelet
page 12

2. Not So Plain Pancakes
page 19

3. Different French Toast
page 20

4. Apple Raisin Muffins
page 26

White Grape Syrup
page 45

5. Pepper Cornbread
page 31

6. Seasoned Bread
page 32

7. Three-Seed Bread
page 34

8. No-Name Bread
page 36

9. New Turkey and Andouille Gumbo
page 50

10. Shrimp and Corn Bisque
page 68

Apple Syrup

Makes 1½ cups

Place 2 (12-ounce) cans of apple juice concentrate in a 10-inch nonstick skillet over high heat and cook until the juice comes to a boil and foamy bubbles cover the entire surface, about 10 to 15 minutes. *Caution: Once the juice starts to foam, the bubbles will rise above the level of the skillet.* Immediately reduce the heat to medium, and continue to cook until the juice is reduced to 1½ cups, about 20 minutes more. Let cool, then place in a covered container and refrigerate.

Before using the syrup in a recipe, remove it from the refrigerator as you start your preparation, so it will have time to come to room temperature. The syrup will be thinner and easier to pour and measure.

Per 1-tablespoon serving: Calories 44   Protein 0g   Fat 0g
Carbohydrates 11g   0% calories from fat

Pineapple Syrup

Makes 1 cup

Place 1 (12-ounce) can of pineapple juice concentrate in a 10-inch non-stick skillet over high heat. Bring to a boil and cook for 5 minutes. Reduce the heat to medium and continue to cook until the juice is reduced to 1 cup, about 10 minutes longer. *Caution: Because of the consistency of the pineapple juice concentrate, occasional light sticking may occur, so use a wooden spoon to check and clear the bottom of the skillet two or three times during the reduction.* Let cool, then place in a covered container and refrigerate.

Remove the syrup from the refrigerator as you start your preparation, so it will have time to come to room temperature. The syrup will be thinner and easier to pour and measure.

Per 1-tablespoon serving: Calories 53   Protein 0g   Fat 0g
Carbohydrates 13g   0% calories from fat

Soups

Nothing is more satisfying to body and spirit than delicious,
nutritious homemade soup. It tells you someone cares
for your well-being (even if you make the
soup yourself)!

New Turkey and Andouille Gumbo

Makes about 7 cups, enough for 6 appetizer or 4 main-dish servings

The name "gumbo" is said to come from the Bantu tribe's word for okra, the seeds of which were imported into this country by African slaves, who wove them into their hair. Okra was used to thicken soups and sauces, and over the years the word came to represent a particular type of wonderfully flavored soup. There are probably 25 or 30 kinds of gumbo, but we chose three that are representative. They work well with our no-oil method, and they're especially delicious! This recipe contains turkey and turkey sausage, but not a pod of "gumbo"!

Seasoning mix

2 teaspoons salt
1 teaspoon sweet paprika
1 teaspoon onion powder
1 teaspoon garlic powder
1 teaspoon dry mustard
½ teaspoon black pepper
½ teaspoon white pepper

1 pound turkey breast, diced ½ inch
8 ounces turkey andouille sausage (see **Note**), diced ½ inch

8 ounces turkey tasso (see **Note**), diced ¼ inch
1 cup chopped green bell peppers
1 cup chopped celery
7¾ cups defatted chicken stock (page 8), *in all*
8 tablespoons all-purpose flour, browned (page 7)
2 cups cooked long-grain white rice

Combine the seasoning mix ingredients in a small bowl.

Preheat the oven to 400°.

Sprinkle all surfaces of the diced turkey evenly with *1 tablespoon* of the seasoning mix and rub it in well. Place the seasoned turkey in a baking pan, bake for 15 minutes, remove from the oven, and set aside.

Place the andouille and tasso in a separate baking pan, bake for 25 minutes, remove from the oven, and set aside.

Meanwhile, preheat a heavy 5-quart pot, preferably nonstick, over high heat to 350°, about 4 minutes.

Add the bell peppers, celery, and the *remaining* seasoning mix. Cook for 15 minutes, occasionally scraping up the brown crust as it forms on the bottom of the pot—it is this browning that gives the vegetables a naturally sweet touch and forms the basis for the gumbo's final flavor.

Add ½ *cup* of the stock and scrape the bottom of the pot to clear it. Cook for 20 minutes, scraping occasionally, until most of the liquid evaporates. (The vegetables will look pretty, and the sauce will be a rich reddish-brown.) Add ¾ *cup* stock and the browned flour; mix thoroughly (now the vegetables will be light brown and pasty-looking), then add the *remaining 6½ cups* stock. Stir well and cook 10 minutes more.

Remove ½ cup gumbo base from the pot and deglaze the pan in which the andouille and tasso were cooked. To the pot add the andouille, tasso, and liquid from the baking pan, and cook 10 minutes more. Add the turkey, turn off the heat, and serve over the rice.

Note If you cannot find turkey andouille, substitute well-seasoned smoked turkey sausage, and if you cannot find turkey tasso, use smoked turkey thighs or wings. These south Louisiana favorites give gumbo the kind of flavor we expect and are used to, but your dish can be rich and well-seasoned too, so don't be afraid to try this recipe!

Per 1-cup serving: Calories 558   Protein 67g   Fat 13g
Carbohydrates 42g   26% calories from fat

New Chicken and Shrimp Gumbo

Makes 12 cups, enough for 12 appetizer or 6 to 8 main-dish servings

This wonderful gumbo does have "gumbo" (the Bantu word for okra) in it. We've also used some southern country favorites—mustard and collard greens. The vegetables make this dish nutritious, and the combination of flavors makes it delicious. Best of all, it's quick and easy to prepare.

Seasoning mix
- 1 tablespoon sweet paprika
- 1 tablespoon dry mustard
- 2½ teaspoons dried sweet basil leaves
- 2 teaspoons salt
- 2 teaspoons onion powder
- 2 teaspoons garlic powder
- 1½ teaspoons dried thyme leaves
- 1¼ teaspoons dried oregano leaves
- ¾ teaspoon black pepper
- ½ teaspoon white pepper
- ½ teaspoon cayenne

- 1 pound chicken breast, diced into ½-inch cubes
- 1 pound peeled medium shrimp

- 6 cups chopped mustard greens, *in all*
- 3 cups chopped onions, *in all*
- 2 cups chopped green bell peppers
- 2 cups chopped celery
- 3 cups sliced okra, *in all*
- 3 bay leaves
- 1 cup apple juice
- 6 tablespoons all-purpose flour, browned (page 7)
- 3 cups defatted chicken stock (page 8)
- 2 cups defatted seafood stock (page 8)
- 3 cups chopped collard greens
- 6 cups cooked long-grain white rice

Combine the seasoning mix ingredients in a small bowl.

Sprinkle the diced chicken with *1 tablespoon* of the seasoning mix, and sprinkle the shrimp with *another tablespoon* of the seasoning mix.

Preheat a heavy 5-quart pot, preferably nonstick, over high heat to 350°, about 4 minutes.

Add *3 cups* of the mustard greens, *2 cups* of the onions, all of the bell peppers and the celery, *1 cup* of the okra, and the bay leaves. Cook, stirring occasionally to check for sticking, about 8 minutes.

Add the apple juice and *remaining* seasoning mix, stir, and cook until most of the liquid is absorbed, about 6 to 8 minutes. Add the seasoned chicken, cover the pot, and cook 2 minutes. Add the browned flour and stir until it is completely absorbed and a paste forms. Cover and cook 1 minute. Add both the stocks, stir well, cover, bring to a boil, and cook 3 minutes. Add the collard greens, the *remaining* mustard greens, onions, and okra, and mix thoroughly. Cover the pot and bring to a boil, about 5 minutes. Add the seasoned shrimp, stir, bring to a boil, and cook until shrimp turn pink and plump, about 3 to 4 minutes. Serve over the rice.

Per 1-cup serving: Calories 289   Protein 26g   Fat 3g
Carbohydrates 40g   8% calories from fat

New Okra and Meat Gumbo

Makes 9 cups, enough for 9 appetizer or 5 main-dish servings

Here's yet another version of gumbo—we sometimes think of it as "Louisiana's Official State Soup." In central Louisiana, especially in Acadiana, lots of different meats are included in the gumbo, while on the coastline and in the marshlands, seafood is more frequently used.

Seasoning mix
- 2 teaspoons sweet paprika
- 2 teaspoons onion powder
- 2 teaspoons dried sweet basil leaves
- 1½ teaspoons salt
- 1½ teaspoons garlic powder
- 1½ teaspoons dry mustard
- 1 teaspoon dried thyme leaves
- ½ teaspoon black pepper
- ½ teaspoon white pepper
- ½ teaspoon ground cumin
- ¼ teaspoon cayenne

- 3 cups chopped onions, *in all*
- 2 cups chopped green bell peppers, *in all*
- 4 cups sliced okra, *in all*
- 2 cups chopped celery
- 1 cup apple juice
- 4 cups defatted beef stock (page 8), *in all*
- ½ cup all-purpose flour, browned (page 7)
- 1 teaspoon minced fresh garlic
- 4½ cups cooked long-grain white rice

- 1 pound flank steak, all visible fat removed and cut into ½-inch cubes

Combine the seasoning mix ingredients in a small bowl.

Sprinkle all surfaces of the diced flank steak evenly with *1 tablespoon* of the seasoning mix and set aside.

Preheat a heavy 5-quart pot, preferably nonstick, over high heat to 350°, about 4 minutes.

Add *2 cups* of the onions, *1 cup* of the bell peppers, *2 cups* of the okra, and all of the celery. Cook, scraping the bottom of the pot occasionally to clear it of brown bits, until the vegetables start to stick, about 8 minutes. Add the apple juice and *remaining* seasoning mix. Stir and cook, checking the bottom of the pot occasionally for sticking, until all the liquid evaporates, about 8 minutes. Add *1 cup* of the stock and the browned flour, and mix until the flour is completely absorbed, the browned flour is no longer visible, and a loose paste forms, about 2 minutes.

Add the seasoned beef, stir, and cook, scraping the bottom occasionally as sticking occurs, for 2 minutes. Add the *remaining* onions, bell peppers, okra, and the garlic. Stir and continue to cook and scrape the bottom for 3 minutes. Add the *remaining* 3 cups of stock, stir until well blended, and cook 10 minutes. Serve over the rice.

Per 1-cup serving: Calories 332   Protein 20g   Fat 8g
Carbohydrates 44g   23% calories from fat

Oyster Soup

Makes 7 cups, enough for 7 appetizer or 4 main-dish servings

If you've ever thought that oyster soup was too much trouble to make, here's the recipe for you! This version is much easier and quicker than those prepared by traditional methods, yet it tastes every bit as delicious.

Seasoning mix

1½ teaspoons salt
1½ teaspoons dried sweet basil
      leaves
  1 teaspoon sweet paprika
  1 teaspoon onion powder
  1 teaspoon garlic powder
  1 teaspoon dried thyme leaves
  ½ teaspoon dry mustard
  ½ teaspoon dried oregano
      leaves
  ¼ teaspoon white pepper
  ⅛ teaspoon black pepper

Creamy mixture

  1 (5-ounce) can evaporated
      skim milk
  ¼ cup nonfat cream cheese

  1 cup chopped onions
  ½ cup chopped celery
  1 cup apple juice
  4 tablespoons all-purpose flour
  3 cups oyster liquor
48 medium oysters, about 3½
      pints
  2 tablespoons finely chopped
      fresh parsley
  ½ cup thinly sliced green onions
  2 tablespoons unsalted butter,
      optional

Combine the seasoning mix ingredients in a small bowl.

Place the canned milk and cream cheese in a blender and process until smooth and creamy; set aside.

Preheat a heavy 5-quart pot, preferably nonstick, over high heat to 350°, about 4 minutes.

Add the onions, celery, and *2 tablespoons* of the seasoning mix. Stir, and cook until the vegetables start to stick, about 3 to 4 minutes. Add the apple juice, scrape the bottom of the pot to clear the browned bits, and cook until most of the liquid evaporates, leaving just enough to cover the vegetables, about 5 to 6 minutes. Add the flour and mix until it is completely absorbed, a paste forms, and no flour is visible. Smooth the mixture evenly across the bottom of the pot and cook until a crust starts to form, about 1 minute. Add the oyster liquor and *remaining* seasoning mix, and whisk until all the ingredients are thoroughly blended. Cook, whisking occasionally, for 5 minutes. Whisk in the creamy mixture and add the oysters. Stir and cook 1 minute. Add the parsley and green onions, then stir and cook just until the soup comes to a boil. **Caution:** These creamy blended mixtures can "break" or curdle easily if they are brought to a full boil. Therefore, bring the liquid just to a gentle boil and stir immediately. Remove from the heat and, if desired, gently stir in the butter until completely blended. (This soup is wonderful without the butter, but even better with it.) Serve immediately.

Per 1-cup serving (without butter): Calories 241   Protein 21g   Fat 7g
Carbohydrates 21g   26% calories from fat

Mike's Vegetable Soup

Makes 20 cups, enough for 10 main-dish servings

This hearty vegetable soup makes a delicious and nutritious vegetarian meal served with a tossed green salad and crusty French bread. Mike liked it so much we named it for him. You don't mess with someone named Mike who's six feet two and weighs three hundred pounds!

Seasoning mix

 3 teaspoons salt

1¾ teaspoons dried savory leaves

1¼ teaspoons garlic powder

1¼ teaspoons onion powder

1¼ teaspoons dry mustard

1¼ teaspoons dried cilantro leaves

1¼ teaspoons dried parsley leaves

1¼ teaspoons dried chervil

 1 teaspoon white pepper

¾ teaspoon black pepper

¾ teaspoon ground sage

---

10 cups vegetable stock (page 8), *in all*

 1 large onion, peeled and cut into 8 to 10 wedges, *in all*

 1 large potato, peeled, cut into 1-inch rounds, and quartered, *in all*

 2 large carrots, peeled, cut lengthwise; then into 1-inch pieces, *in all*

½ small green cabbage, cut into 4 to 5 wedges, *in all*

 1 large red bell pepper, cut into 1-inch pieces, *in all*

 1 large yellow bell pepper, cut into 1-inch pieces, *in all*

 1 medium turnip, peeled and cut into 10 wedges, *in all*

 1 medium rutabaga, peeled and cut into 10 wedges, *in all*

 4 ribs bok choy, cut into 1-inch diagonal pieces, *in all*

 2 cups apple juice

Combine the seasoning mix ingredients in a small bowl.

Place a heavy 10-quart pot, preferably nonstick, over high heat and add 6 *cups* of the stock. Bring to a full boil, add all the seasoning mix and ¼ of each vegetable. Cook until the vegetables are tender, about 14 to 16 minutes. Strain the cooked vegetables and, reserving the broth, transfer them to a food processor. Purée the vegetables, adding a little of the reserved broth if necessary, until they are liquefied, about 2 to 3 minutes. Return the puréed mixture to the pot, add the *remaining 4 cups* of stock and the apple juice, mix together, and bring to a boil. Add the *remaining* vegetables and return the mixture to a boil over high heat. Reduce the heat to medium, cover, and simmer until the vegetables are fork tender, about 25 to 30 minutes.

Per 2-cup serving: Calories 96   Protein 3g   Fat 0g
Carbohydrates 22g   1% calories from fat

Crowley Rice Soup

Makes 8 cups, enough for 8 appetizer or 4 main-dish servings

Crowley, just off Interstate 10 between Lafayette and Lake Charles, might be called the Rice Capital of Louisiana. Rice grows in every direction, and there are rice mills rising from the flat land all around the town. Crowley is also famous as the hometown of our four-term governor Edwin Edwards.

In Louisiana we eat a lot of rice in a lot of different ways. And, as you can see, there are many ingredients in this soup besides rice.

Seasoning mix
1¾ teaspoons salt
1¼ teaspoons onion powder
1¼ teaspoons garlic powder
1¼ teaspoons dry mustard
1¼ teaspoons ground cumin
1¼ teaspoons dried thyme leaves
¾ teaspoon sweet paprika
¾ teaspoon white pepper
¼ teaspoon black pepper

2½ cups chopped onions, *in all*
2½ cups chopped celery, *in all*
3 bay leaves
1 cup apple juice
¼ cup tamari (see Note)

4 tablespoons balsamic vinegar, *in all*
4 tablespoons Worcestershire sauce, *in all*
11 cups vegetable stock (page 8), *in all*
1 cup long-grain brown rice
½ cup chopped green bell peppers
½ cup small diced zucchini
½ cup small diced yellow squash
½ cup small diced carrots
4 (1-gram) packets artificial sweetener (page 4), optional

Combine the seasoning mix ingredients in a small bowl.

Preheat a heavy 5-quart pot, preferably nonstick, over high heat to 350°, about 4 minutes.

Add 2 *cups* of the onions, 2 *cups* of the celery, the bay leaves, and all the seasoning mix. Stir and cook about 5 minutes, then add the apple juice, tamari, *3 tablespoons* of the vinegar, and *3 tablespoons* of the Worcestershire sauce. Stir and cook, checking the bottom of the pot occasionally for sticking, until all the liquid evaporates and the vegetables start to stick to the bottom, about 20 minutes. Stir in *9 cups* of stock, bring to a full boil, and cook for 25 minutes. Add the *remaining 2 cups* of stock, the *remaining* vinegar and Worcestershire sauce, and the rice. Stir and cook for 30 minutes. Add the remaining ingredients, including the artificial sweetener if desired, and cook until the vegetables are tender, about 4 to 6 minutes. Serve immediately.

Note Tamari is a very rich, flavorful soy sauce, available in specialty markets and in the international or ethnic food sections of many supermarkets. If you cannot find tamari where you shop, use any good quality soy sauce.

Per 1-cup serving: Calories 375   Protein 12g   Fat 1g
Carbohydrates 85g   2% calories from fat

Lentil Soup

Lentils are an excellent source of protein, and should be in the pantry of every vegetarian. Notice that our recipe uses vegetable stock rather than chicken stock, but the result isn't just for those who abstain from animal products. This soup is so flavorful and hearty that no one will want to be left out, and the seasonings give it an extra zing.

Seasoning mix
- 2 teaspoons sweet paprika
- 1½ teaspoons salt
- 1½ teaspoons garlic powder
- 1½ teaspoons dry mustard
- 1½ teaspoons dried thyme leaves
- 1 teaspoon onion powder
- 1 teaspoon ground cumin
- 1 teaspoon dried cilantro leaves
- ¾ teaspoon black pepper
- ½ teaspoon white pepper
- ¼ teaspoon cayenne

- 2 cups chopped onions, *in all*
- 2 cups chopped green bell peppers, *in all*
- 2 cups chopped celery, *in all*
- 3 bay leaves
- 1 cup apple juice
- 2 teaspoons minced fresh garlic
- 2 cups dried lentils
- 10 cups vegetable stock (page 8), *in all*
- ¼ cup tamari (see **Note**)
- 1 cup medium diced carrots
- 1 cup medium diced parsnips
- 1 cup medium diced zucchini
- 1 cup medium diced yellow squash
- 1 cup medium diced fresh mushrooms

Combine the seasoning mix ingredients in a small bowl.

Preheat a heavy 8-quart pot, preferably nonstick, over high heat to 350°, about 4 minutes.

Add *1 cup* of the onions, *1 cup* of the bell peppers, *1 cup* of the celery, and the bay leaves. Stir and cook, scraping the bottom of the pot occasionally to clear, about 5 minutes. Add the apple juice and *2 tablespoons* of the seasoning mix, check the bottom of the pot for sticking, and cook until all the liquid evaporates, about 10 minutes.

Add the *remaining* onions, bell peppers, celery, and seasoning mix, and the garlic and lentils. Stir and cook 1 minute, then add *6 cups* of the stock and the tamari. Stir and cook 30 minutes, checking the bottom of the pot occasionally for sticking. Stir in *2 cups* stock and cook 10 minutes. Stir in the *remaining 2 cups* stock and cook 5 minutes. Add the carrots and parsnips, stir and cook 6 minutes. Add all the remaining vegetables, stir, and bring the soup back to a boil, about 5 minutes. Serve immediately.

Note Tamari is a very rich, flavorful soy sauce, available in specialty markets and the international or ethnic food sections of many supermarkets. If you cannot find tamari where you shop, use any good quality soy sauce.

Per 1-cup serving: Calories 106   Protein 6g   Fat 1g
Carbohydrates 21g   4% calories from fat

Jazzy Potato Soup

Makes 9 cups, enough for 9 appetizer servings

What a great rendition of an old standard this is—the seasoning is so jazzed up you'll forget the dish is low in fat. Because the amount of starch in potatoes varies greatly, the soup may be a little too thick or too thin. Add more or less stock to get the consistency you want.

Seasoning mix
- 2 teaspoons salt
- 2 teaspoons onion powder
- 2 teaspoons dry mustard
- 1 teaspoon garlic powder
- 1 teaspoon dried rosemary leaves
- ¾ teaspoon white pepper
- ½ teaspoon paprika
- ½ teaspoon ground cumin

Creamy mixture
- 1 (12-ounce) can evaporated skim milk, *in all*
- ½ cup nonfat cottage cheese

- 2 tablespoons all-purpose flour

- ½ cup chopped onions
- 1 cup chopped celery
- 2 cups small diced potatoes
- 5 cups large diced potatoes, *in all*
- 1 cup apple juice
- 3 cups vegetable stock (page 8), *in all*
- ¼ cup chopped fresh parsley
- ½ cup thinly sliced green onions

Combine the seasoning mix ingredients in a small bowl.

Place ¼ *cup* of the skim milk, the cottage cheese, and the flour in a blender, and blend until smooth and creamy. Add the *remaining* skim milk, blend until thoroughly mixed, remove from blender, and set aside.

Preheat a heavy 5-quart pot, preferably nonstick, over high heat to 350°, about 4 minutes.

Add the onions, celery, small diced potatoes, 2 *cups* of the large diced potatoes, and 2 *tablespoons* of the seasoning mix. Stir and cook, scraping the bottom of the pot as brown crusts form, for 5 minutes. Add the apple juice, scrape the bottom of the pot free of crusts, and continue to cook until all of the liquid evaporates, about 10 minutes. Add *1 cup* of the stock and the *remaining* seasoning mix. Scrape the bottom of the pot to clear all the crusts, and transfer the ingredients from the pot to a blender. Purée until smooth and return to the pot. Cook over high heat until a nice brown crust forms on the bottom of the pot, about 8 minutes. Add *1 cup* of the stock and stir to clear the bottom of the pot of crusts. Stir in the *remaining 1 cup* of stock and cook 1 minute. Add the *remaining 3 cups* large diced potatoes, cover, bring to a boil, reduce the heat to medium, and cook for 12 minutes, checking the bottom of the pot occasionally for sticking.

Whisk in the creamy mixture, bring just to a gentle boil to prevent curdling, remove from the heat, and blend in the parsley and green onions. Serve immediately.

Per 1-cup serving: Calories 129   Protein 6g   Fat 0g
Carbohydrates 26g   2% calories from fat

Butternut Squash Soup

Makes about 6 cups, enough for 6 appetizer or 3 main-dish servings

This fragrant, pretty soup would make a wonderful meal served with plenty of dark bread—just the thing to warm you up on a cold day. For a very special occasion, you could serve it in the hollowed-out squash shells. Top the soup with a dollop of meringue, dust with nutmeg, and run under the broiler just until the meringue starts to brown. Or try a spoonful of cool, nonfat yogurt.

Seasoning mix
1½ teaspoons onion powder
1¼ teaspoons salt
 1 teaspoon garlic powder
 ¾ teaspoon sweet paprika
 ¾ teaspoon black pepper
 ¾ teaspoon white pepper
 ½ teaspoon ground cinnamon
 ¼ teaspoon ground nutmeg
 ⅛ teaspoon ground coriander

 1 (12-ounce) can evaporated skim milk
10 tablespoons nonfat dry milk
3½ cups medium diced butternut squash (see Note)
 3 cups defatted chicken stock (page 8), *in all*
1½ cups finely diced butternut squash
 1 to 4 (1-gram) packets artificial sweetener (page 4), optional

Combine the seasoning mix ingredients in a small bowl.

Place the evaporated milk and dry milk in a blender or food processor and process until smooth and creamy; set aside.

Place the medium diced squash and *2 cups* of stock in a blender or food processor and purée as finely as possible to a very thick paste. If the blending process stops because the mixture is too thick, add small amounts of stock as necessary to allow the process to continue. When the mixture is completely puréed, add any *remaining* stock, along with all of the seasoning mix, and blend thoroughly.

Preheat a heavy 5-quart pot, preferably nonstick, over high heat to 350°, about 4 minutes.

Place the puréed squash in the pot and cook, frequently scraping up the brown bits on the bottom of the pot, until the mixture thickens and comes to a full, rolling boil, creating many "volcanoes" that bubble constantly. Add the milk mixture and the finely diced squash, reduce the heat to low, and stir well. **Caution:** Dishes using creamy blended mixtures can "break" or curdle easily if they are brought to a full boil. Therefore, bring the liquid just to a gentle boil, and stir immediately. Simmer, stirring frequently, for 8 minutes. Turn off the heat, taste, and if desired, add up to 4 packets of your favorite artificial sweetener.

Note This is the size you'll need to dice the squash if you use a blender. With a food processor, the pieces don't have to be so small, but if the mixture does not become completely puréed, use a blender.

Per 1-cup serving: Calories 158   Protein 10g   Fat 2g
Carbohydrates 28g   10% calories from fat

color photograph 10

Shrimp and Corn Bisque

Makes 12 cups, enough for 12 appetizer or 6 main-dish servings

 This bisque is so fragrant, you may have a hard time keeping your family away from the pot while it's cooking!

Seasoning mix

2 teaspoons dry mustard

1½ teaspoons salt

1½ teaspoons sweet paprika

1½ teaspoons garlic powder

1¼ teaspoons onion powder

½ teaspoon white pepper

½ teaspoon dried thyme leaves

½ teaspoon dried sweet basil leaves

¼ teaspoon black pepper

¼ teaspoon cayenne

¼ teaspoon dried oregano leaves

Creamy mixture

2 cups evaporated skim milk

6 tablespoons nonfat dry milk

¼ cup nonfat mayonnaise

¼ cup nonfat cream cheese

2½ cups chopped onions, *in all*

4 cups fresh-cut corn, *in all* (about 6 to 8 ears)

2 cups apple juice, *in all*

1½ cups defatted shrimp stock (page 8), *in all*

1 cup chopped celery

1 teaspoon minced fresh garlic

1½ pounds medium peeled shrimp

2 tablespoons minced fresh parsley

Combine the seasoning mix ingredients in a small bowl.

Place the creamy mixture ingredients in a blender and purée until smooth and creamy. Set aside.

Purée *1 cup* of the onions, *2 cups* of the corn, *½ cup* of the apple juice, and *1 tablespoon* of the seasoning mix in a blender or food processor.

Preheat a heavy 5-quart pot, preferably nonstick, over high heat to 350°, about 4 minutes.

Place the puréed ingredients in the pot, add *1 tablespoon* seasoning mix, and cook, scraping occasionally, until a brown crust forms over the entire bottom, approximately 12 minutes. (**Note:** This is a very important step, for each time a crust forms and browns slightly, it adds an enormous amount of flavor to the bisque, and it is as important to the final result as a foundation is to a house. Also, you'll notice that the volume of the mixture reduces as the liquid cooks out of it, and the color changes from a bright gold to a richer, brownish gold. Taste the mixture at this point and you will discover that it has a natural sweetness.)

Add the celery, garlic, *½ cup* apple juice, *½ cup* stock, and the *remaining* onions, corn, and seasoning mix, and mix thoroughly. Add the *remaining 1 cup* apple juice, scrape the bottom of the pot, and cook for 15 minutes, occasionally checking the bottom of the pot for sticking. Add the shrimp and cook 3 minutes. Stir in the creamy mixture and the *remaining 1 cup* stock, mix thoroughly, and cook just until it starts to boil, about 3 minutes. **Caution:**Dishes using these creamy mixtures can "break" or curdle easily if they are brought to a full boil. Therefore, bring the liquid just to a gentle boil and stir immediately. Remove from the heat, stir in the parsley, and serve immediately.

Per 1-cup serving: Calories 193   Protein 18g   Fat 2g
Carbohydrates 29g   8% calories from fat

color photograph 11

Shrimp and Hot Curry Cream Soup

Makes 8 cups, enough for 8 appetizer or 4 main-dish servings

The hot curry powder we use is available in specialty markets or in the international or ethnic foods sections of many supermarkets. If you cannot find it where you shop, use the best-quality curry powder available, and if you prefer more heat, just increase the amount of cayenne. The combination of spices with the creamy soup and shrimp is just wonderful!

1 cup dried chickpeas

Seasoning mix
1½ teaspoons salt
1½ teaspoons onion powder
1½ teaspoons garlic powder
1½ teaspoons dry mustard
1 teaspoon sweet paprika
1 teaspoon dried sweet basil leaves
1 teaspoon dried oregano leaves
½ teaspoon black pepper
¼ teaspoon white pepper
¼ teaspoon cayenne

2 pounds peeled headless medium shrimp
2 cups chopped onions
1 cup chopped celery
1 cup cauliflower florets
1 teaspoon minced fresh garlic
1 cup apple juice
3 cups defatted seafood stock (page 8)
2 teaspoons ground ginger
2 teaspoons hot curry powder (see **Note**)
2 (12-ounce) cans evaporated skim milk
3 tablespoons unsalted butter, optional

Day 1: Add enough water to the chickpeas to cover them by 3 or 4 inches, and soak overnight in the refrigerator. As the chickpeas absorb the water, they will more than double in volume.

Day 2: Drain the chickpeas, measure 2 cups, and set them aside.

Combine the seasoning mix ingredients in a small bowl. Sprinkle the shrimp with *1 tablespoon* of this mixture and set aside.

Preheat a heavy 5-quart pot, preferably nonstick, over high heat to 350°, about 4 minutes. Add the onions, celery, cauliflower, the drained chickpeas, and the *remaining* seasoning mix. Stir and cook, scraping the bottom of the pot as sticking occurs, for 6 minutes. Add the garlic and apple juice, clear the bottom, and cook until most of the liquid evaporates, about 7 minutes.

Transfer all the ingredients from the pot to a blender and purée, adding *2 cups* of the stock a little at a time, until the mixture is smooth and well blended. Add the *remaining* cup of stock, blend, and set aside. Clean the pot and place it back over high heat. Add the blended mixture, the shrimp, ginger, and curry, and cook until small "volcanoes" start erupting from the bottom of the pot, about 2 to 3 minutes. Stir in both cans of skim milk and bring just to a gentle boil, stir, bring just to a boil again, and stir. When the liquid boils for the third time, remove the pot from the heat, and, if desired, gently stir in 3 tablespoons unsalted butter until completely blended. (This is a great dish without the butter, but tastes even better with it!)

Note We use McCormick-brand curry powder—hot or Madras style.

Per 1-cup serving (without butter): Calories 339   Protein 34g   Fat 9g
Carbohydrates 32g   23% calories from fat

Salads

*Hearty enough to be served as a main course, they
work well as appetizers or side dishes, too.*

C. D. Potato Salad

Makes about 7 cups, enough for 10 to 12 side servings

 Seeds add great taste and a nice crunchiness to this unusual potato salad. I like the contrast in texture as well as the flavor and color.

Seasoning mix

1½ teaspoons salt
1 teaspoon onion powder
1 teaspoon dry mustard
¾ teaspoon garlic powder
½ teaspoon sweet paprika
½ teaspoon white pepper
¼ teaspoon black pepper
¼ teaspoon cayenne

2 large Idaho potatoes
1 tablespoon poppy seeds

1 tablespoon sesame seeds
8 ounces egg substitute
1 teaspoon prepared yellow mustard
1½ cups nonfat mayonnaise
1 (5-ounce) can evaporated skim milk
¼ cup finely diced celery
½ cup thinly sliced green onions
2 tablespoons chopped fresh parsley

Combine the seasoning mix ingredients in a small bowl and set aside.

Cook the potatoes in enough water to cover over high heat until tender, about 45 minutes. Drain, cool, peel, and dice into ½-inch cubes.

While the potatoes are cooking, place a small skillet over high heat. Add all the seeds, and cook until the poppy seeds start to pop and the sesame seeds start to brown. Remove from the heat, set aside to cool, then add to the seasoning mix and stir to combine thoroughly.

Preheat a heavy 10-inch skillet, preferably nonstick, over high heat to 300°, about 2 to 3 minutes.

Add the eggs and cook, stirring occasionally, until firm but still moist-looking—they should look like scrambled eggs. Turn off the heat, let the eggs cool, and break them up into small pieces.

Combine the seed/seasoning mix, mustard, mayonnaise, and evaporated milk, and blend thoroughly. Place the cubed potatoes in a large bowl and add the celery, green onions, parsley, and cooked eggs, and gently mix together. Then gently fold in the mayonnaise mixture until well blended.

Per 1-cup serving: Calories 90   Protein 4g   Fat 1g
Carbohydrates 19g   9% calories from fat

Freed Egg Salad

Makes 4 to 6 cups, enough for 4 to 6 side servings

 If you're watching your cholesterol, this recipe will be a very welcome alternative to regular egg salad.

The real challenge in creating this recipe was to achieve a great flavor. I hope you'll think it's as good as I do.

Seasoning mix

1½ teaspoons salt

1½ teaspoons dried sweet basil leaves

1 teaspoon sweet paprika

1 teaspoon onion powder

¾ teaspoon garlic powder

½ teaspoon dry mustard

½ teaspoon black pepper

½ teaspoon white pepper

¼ teaspoon cayenne

2 tablespoons olive oil

½ cup finely diced onions

½ cup finely diced green bell peppers

½ cup finely diced celery

3 (8-ounce) cartons egg substitute

1 cup finely chopped green cabbage

1 cup finely chopped red leaf lettuce

1 cup finely chopped green leafy tops of bok choy

½ cup finely diced white stalks of bok choy

1 cup nonfat whipped mayonnaise

½ cup thinly sliced green onions

1 teaspoon balsamic vinegar

1 teaspoon Worcestershire sauce

2 (1-gram) packets artificial sweetener (page 4)

Combine seasoning mix ingredients in a small bowl and set aside.

Preheat a heavy 10-inch skillet, preferably nonstick, over high heat to 350°, about 4 minutes. Add the oil, diced onions, bell peppers, celery, and 2 *tablespoons* of the seasoning mix. Stir and cook, scraping the bottom of the skillet as sticking occurs, for 4 minutes. Add the eggs, turn down the heat to medium, and cook, turning over the eggs as they begin to form. Once the eggs are cooked—they should still look moist, just like regular scrambled eggs—turn off the heat, let the eggs cool, and break them up into small pieces. Place all the remaining ingredients in a large bowl, add the cooled eggs, and gently fold until well mixed. Use in sandwiches or serve on a bed of lettuce.

Per 1-cup serving: Calories 221   Protein 18g   Fat 7g
Carbohydrates 26g   29% calories from fat

color photograph 12

Macaroni Salad

Makes about 8 cups, enough for 12 side or 8 main-dish servings

Every cook's repertoire ought to contain a recipe for macaroni salad—it goes so well with barbecue and other spicy meat dishes, and makes a nice light lunch all by itself. Serve the salad at room temperature or chilled, but refrigerate any leftovers.

Seasoning mix
  1 teaspoon salt
  1 teaspoon dry mustard
  ¾ teaspoon garlic powder
  ½ teaspoon sweet paprika
  ½ teaspoon onion powder
  ¼ teaspoon white pepper
  ¼ teaspoon black pepper
  ⅛ teaspoon cayenne

  3 cups dry elbow macaroni

  1½ cups nonfat mayonnaise
  ½ cup low-fat sour cream
  1 (5-ounce) can evaporated skim milk
  1 tablespoon tamari (see Note)
  ½ cup finely chopped onions
  ½ cup finely chopped green bell peppers
  ½ cup finely chopped celery
  ½ cup finely chopped carrots
  ½ cup finely chopped green cabbage

Combine the seasoning mix ingredients in a small bowl.

Cook the macaroni according to package directions, rinse, drain, and set aside to cool. Place the mayonnaise, sour cream, and skim milk in a large bowl, and add the tamari and seasoning mix. Whip together until completely blended. Then add the cooled macaroni and the remaining ingredients, and toss gently until well mixed.

Note Tamari is a very rich, flavorful soy sauce, available in specialty markets and the international or ethnic food sections of many supermarkets. If you cannot find tamari where you shop, use any good quality soy sauce.

Per 1-cup serving: Calories 213   Protein 8g   Fat 2g
Carbohydrates 45g   8% calories from fat

11. Shrimp and Hot Curry Cream Soup
page 70

12. Macaroni Salad
page 78

13. Bronzed Tuna Salad
page 80

Shrimp and Artichoke Salad
page 92

14. Bronzed Chicken Salad
page 82

15. Chickpea Salad Evelyn
page 86

16. Tijuana Pinto Bean Salad
page 90

17. Oven-Fried Catfish
page 124

18. Magic Brightening
page 95

When we make our stocks for Magic Brightening
Broths we first brown the bones (chicken necks and
backs, top left) in a 350° oven to make the broth rich
in color and flavor.

We use all kinds of vegetables—yellow summer squash,
carrots, parsnips, acorn squash, mirlitons, mushrooms,
potatoes, turnips—except for those like tomatoes,
which are very soft or pulpy.

Offer different colors of bell pepper just because they're so beautiful.

Low-fat, delicious, go-with-anything turkey breasts (bottom right) are sliced into strips for "brightening."

Cast-iron pots and wire baskets work beautifully for us, but the results will be great whatever you use.

19. New Shrimp Remoulade
page 130

20. Shrimp Bascom
page 134

21. Sweet Pepper Cream Shrimp
page 136

22. Shrimp-Stuffed Acorn Squash
page 138

23. Crawfish in Cream Sauce with Pasta
page 142

24. Chicken Brassica
page 150

25. Chicken with Mushrooms and Chickpeas
page 154

26. Lemon Dill Chicken
page 162

27. Slow-Roasted Hen
page 164

28. Stuffed Turkey Roast
page 168

29. Stuffed Turkey Chops
page 170

Sweet and Creamy Cole Slaw

Makes 6 cups, enough for 10 to 12 side servings

 This light and tangy salad goes well with many kinds of meat, and is almost a necessity for a picnic. It's another one of my favorites.

1 tablespoon poppy seeds
1 tablespoon sesame seeds

Seasoning mix
1½ teaspoons dry mustard
1 teaspoon salt
¾ teaspoon onion powder
¾ teaspoon garlic powder
½ teaspoon sweet paprika
½ teaspoon white pepper
½ teaspoon dried sweet basil
   leaves
½ teaspoon dillweed
¼ teaspoon black pepper
⅛ teaspoon cayenne

Creamy dressing
1 (5-ounce) can evaporated
   skim milk
½ cup nonfat cottage cheese
½ cup nonfat mayonnaise
¼ cup Apple Syrup (page 47)

6 cups medium chopped green
   cabbage
1½ cups grated unpeeled red
   apple
¾ cup currants
¼ cup finely diced onions

Place a small, heavy nonstick skillet over high heat and add the poppy seeds and sesame seeds. Toss and cook until the seeds start to pop, then remove them and set aside.

Combine the seasoning mix ingredients in a small bowl, and purée the dressing ingredients in a blender until smooth and creamy. Place the remaining ingredients in a large bowl, add the seasoning mix, and toss to mix. Add the dressing and stir gently until it is evenly distributed.

Per 1-cup serving: Calories 185   Protein 5g   Fat 2g
Carbohydrates 41g   7% calories from fat

color photograph 13

Bronzed Tuna Salad

Makes 4 cups, enough for 4 main-dish servings

This is my absolute favorite recipe in this book! Put aside any prejudice you might have about ho-hum tuna salad. This one, made with fresh fish bronzed to perfection, is sophisticated and exciting.

Seasoning mix

1½ teaspoons salt

¾ teaspoon onion powder

¾ teaspoon dry mustard

½ teaspoon sweet paprika

½ teaspoon garlic powder

½ teaspoon black pepper

½ teaspoon ground cumin

¼ teaspoon white pepper

⅛ teaspoon cayenne

½ cup pumpkin seeds

½ cup raw wheat germ

2 (8-ounce) pieces of fresh tuna

Vegetable-oil cooking spray

¼ cup nonfat cream cheese

½ cup nonfat cottage cheese

½ cup nonfat sour cream

1 (5-ounce) can evaporated skim milk

2 (1-gram) packets artificial sweetener (page 4), optional

2 cups finely chopped green cabbage

½ cup thinly sliced green onions

¼ cup finely chopped red bell peppers

Combine the seasoning mix ingredients in a small bowl.

Place a heavy 10-inch skillet, preferably nonstick, over high heat, and add the pumpkin seeds and wheat germ. Toss and cook until the seeds and wheat germ start to brown, remove from heat and set aside.

Wipe the skillet clean and place it back over high heat to 400°, about 5 minutes. While the skillet is heating, sprinkle each side of the tuna with a liberal ¼ *teaspoon* of the seasoning mix. When the skillet reaches 400°, spray it lightly with vegetable-oil spray. Place the tuna in the skillet and cook until it turns a nice brown color, about 2 minutes on each side. Remove the tuna from the skillet and set it aside to cool. The tuna will be rare at this point, but out of the skillet it will continue to cook to medium in about 5 minutes. Once the tuna has cooled, flake it into bite-size pieces and set it aside.

Place the cream cheese, cottage cheese, sour cream, and evaporated milk in a large bowl, add the *remaining* seasoning mix and, if desired, the artificial sweetener. Whip to blend thoroughly. Fold in the cabbage, green onions, bell peppers, reserved pumpkin seeds, and wheat germ. Gently fold in the flaked tuna until well mixed. Serve immediately.

Per 1-cup serving: Calories 378   Protein 43g   Fat 11g
Carbohydrates 25g   25% calories from fat

color photograph 14

Bronzed Chicken Salad

▬ ▬ ▬ ▬ ▬ ▬ ▬ ▬ ▬ ▬ ▬ ▬ ▬ ▬ ▬ ▬ ▬ ▬

Makes 8 cups, enough for 8 main-dish servings

Bronzing the chicken gives this salad an exciting flavor that you can't get any other way—and it's fast, too! Good served warm, at room temperature, or cold, it's one of the most satisfying combinations around!

Seasoning mix

1½ teaspoons salt

1½ teaspoons sweet paprika

1 teaspoon garlic powder

1 teaspoon dry mustard

1 teaspoon dried thyme leaves

¾ teaspoon onion powder

½ teaspoon white pepper

½ teaspoon dried marjoram leaves

½ teaspoon ground sage

¼ teaspoon black pepper

⅛ teaspoon cayenne

▬

1½ pounds boneless, skinless chicken breast halves, all visible fat removed

1 tablespoon plus 1 teaspoon cornstarch

3 tablespoons dry sherry

5 cups defatted chicken stock (page 8)

¼ cup Apple Syrup (page 47)

25 whole peeled garlic cloves

2 large carrots, peeled and cut diagonally into ¼-inch to ½-inch pieces

1 small onion, peeled and cut into 8 wedges

12 medium fresh mushrooms, quartered

1 large green bell pepper, cored, seeded, and cut into bite-size pieces

¼ medium head green cabbage, cut into bite-size pieces

2 cups broccoli florets

2 cups cauliflower florets

¼ cup tamari (see **Note**)

¼ cup balsamic vinegar

4 (1-gram) packets artificial sweetener (page 4), optional

Combine the seasoning mix ingredients in a small bowl, and sprinkle each side of each chicken breast with ¼ *teaspoon* of this mixture.

Preheat a heavy 10-inch skillet, preferably nonstick, over high heat to 400°, about 5 minutes.

Place the seasoned chicken breasts in the skillet, 2 or 3 at a time, and cook until they are bronze-colored, about 1½ minutes per side. This will probably have to be done in two batches. When the chicken is cooked, set it aside to cool, then cut it into bite-size pieces.

While the chicken is cooling, combine the cornstarch and sherry and stir to dissolve. Set aside.

Place a 5-quart pot over high heat and add the stock, Apple Syrup, and *remaining* seasoning mix, cover, and bring to a boil. Add the garlic and cook, covered, for 8 minutes. Drain the garlic, saving the liquid, and place the garlic in a large bowl.

Return the liquid to the pot, and repeat the covering, cooking, and draining process with the other vegetables as follows:

carrots and onion—4 minutes
mushrooms and bell pepper—4 minutes
cabbage—5 minutes
broccoli and cauliflower—4 minutes

Add the tamari and vinegar to the pot, bring to a boil, then add the cornstarch mixture and whisk continuously until the liquid comes to a full boil.

Turn off the heat.

Add the chicken to the cooked vegetables in the bowl and toss to mix, then add the liquid from the pot and gently stir to blend.

Note Tamari is a very rich, flavorful soy sauce, available in specialty markets and the international or ethnic food sections of many supermarkets. If you cannot find tamari where you shop, use any good quality soy sauce.

Per 1-cup serving: Calories 251   Protein 34g   Fat 3g
Carbohydrates 23g   11% calories from fat

Creamy Turkey Salad

Makes about 5 cups, enough for 5 main-dish servings

This creamy, delicious salad is different from traditional turkey or chicken salads, but I think you'll like it. It's very important not to overcook the turkey. The salad goes great with hot, crusty French bread, or homemade bread right out of the oven, or with almost any kind of toast or crackers.

Seasoning mix

  2 teaspoons salt
1½ teaspoons sweet paprika
1½ teaspoons garlic powder
  1 teaspoon dried savory leaves
  1 teaspoon onion powder
  1 teaspoon dillweed
  1 teaspoon dry mustard
  ¾ teaspoon black pepper
  ¾ teaspoon white pepper
  ¼ teaspoon cayenne

Creamy dressing

  5 ounces evaporated skim milk
  ½ cup nonfat whipped mayonnaise
  ½ cup nonfat cottage cheese
  ¼ cup nonfat cream cheese

  ¼ cup White Grape Syrup (page 45)
  1 tablespoon balsamic vinegar
  1 pound turkey, diced into ½-inch cubes
  ¼ cup defatted chicken stock (page 8)
  ¼ cup each finely chopped red, yellow, and green bell peppers
  ½ cup finely chopped onions
  ¼ cup finely chopped celery
  ¼ cup each finely chopped red and green cabbage
  1 cup finely chopped spinach
  1 cup finely chopped red leaf lettuce

Combine the seasoning mix ingredients in a small bowl.

Combine the dressing ingredients in a blender or food processor and purée until smooth. Set aside.

Sprinkle all surfaces of the diced turkey with 2 *tablespoons* of the seasoning mix and blend thoroughly.

Preheat a 10-inch skillet, preferably nonstick, over high heat to 350°, about 4 minutes. Brown the seasoned turkey on all sides, about 3 minutes, and add the stock. Cook about 2 minutes, turn off the heat, and cool to room temperature.

Once the turkey has cooled, combine it with all the remaining ingredients, and mix thoroughly.

Per 1-cup serving: Calories 279   Protein 33g   Fat 4g
Carbohydrates 28g   13% calories from fat

Chickpea Salad Evelyn

Makes 5 cups, enough for 8 to 10 side servings

 There are many different recipes for chickpeas in this book. Here, the little legumes form the base for a colorful and delicious salad.

½ pound dried chickpeas

Seasoning mix

2¼ teaspoons onion powder

1½ teaspoons salt

1½ teaspoons sweet paprika

1½ teaspoons garlic powder

1½ teaspoons dry mustard

¾ teaspoon white pepper

¼ teaspoon cayenne

Creamy dressing

½ cup nonfat cottage cheese

¼ cup nonfat sour cream

1 tablespoon tamari (see **Note**)

1 tablespoon Worcestershire sauce

½ cup evaporated skim milk

1 tablespoon brown mustard

2 (1-gram) packets artificial sweetener (page 4), optional

½ cup nonfat mayonnaise

4 cups defatted chicken stock (page 8)

2 tablespoons finely diced yellow bell peppers

2 tablespoons finely diced red bell peppers

2 tablespoons finely diced green bell peppers

½ cup finely chopped green cabbage

½ cup finely chopped iceberg lettuce

¼ cup finely diced onions

¼ cup finely diced celery

¼ cup finely diced zucchini

¼ cup finely diced cucumbers

¼ cup finely diced yellow squash

Day 1: Add enough water to the chickpeas to cover them by 3 or 4 inches, and soak overnight in the refrigerator. As the chickpeas absorb the water, they will more than double in volume.

Day 2: Combine the seasoning mix ingredients in a small bowl.

Place all of the dressing ingredients, except the mayonnaise, in a blender and add *1 tablespoon* of the seasoning mix. Purée until smooth and creamy. Add the mayonnaise, stir to blend thoroughly, and set aside.

Drain the chickpeas. Place a heavy 5-quart pot, preferably nonstick, over high heat and add the chicken stock, *remaining* seasoning mix, and drained chickpeas. Cook until the peas are tender and the liquid is thick and creamy-looking, about 50 minutes. If the level of the liquid seems low during the cooking time, add water 1 cup at a time. Once the peas are tender, drain (but do not rinse), and set them aside to cool.

When the peas are cool, place them in a large bowl, add all of the vegetables, and toss until evenly mixed. Add the dressing and fold gently until evenly distributed.

Note Tamari is a very rich, flavorful soy sauce, available in specialty markets and the international or ethnic food sections of many supermarkets. If you cannot find tamari where you shop, use any good quality soy sauce.

Per 1-cup serving: Calories 270   Protein 17g   Fat 4g
Carbohydrates 44g   12% calories from fat

White Bean Salad with Sweet and Creamy Mustard Dressing

Makes 6 cups, enough for 10 to 12 side or 6 main-dish servings

Bean salads are popular all over the country. They vary greatly in appearance and flavor, but what they all have in common is a lot of nutrition and appeal in one bowl. A bean salad makes a terrific light lunch or supper, accompanied by fresh-out-of-the oven bread.

½ pound dried white beans

Seasoning mix

2 teaspoons salt
2 teaspoons sweet paprika
2 teaspoons dry mustard
1 teaspoon onion powder
1 teaspoon garlic powder
1 teaspoon dried sweet basil
   leaves
1 teaspoon dried oregano leaves
1 teaspoon dried thyme leaves
½ teaspoon black pepper
¼ teaspoon white pepper
¼ teaspoon cayenne

Creamy dressing

½ cup nonfat cottage cheese
¾ cup nonfat sour cream
½ cup evaporated skim milk
1 tablespoon prepared yellow
   mustard
1 tablespoon balsamic vinegar

3 tablespoons brown mustard
4 (1-gram) packets artificial
   sweetener (page 4), optional
¼ cup nonfat mayonnaise

4 cups defatted chicken stock
   (page 8)
½ cup finely diced fresh
   tomatoes
¼ cup finely diced yellow bell
   peppers
¼ cup finely diced green bell
   peppers
½ cup finely diced celery
½ cup finely diced bok choy
   leaves and stalks
½ cup finely chopped fresh collard greens
½ cup finely chopped iceberg
   lettuce

1 cup finely chopped red leaf
   lettuce
1 cup finely chopped green leaf
   lettuce

¾ cup finely diced fresh
   mushrooms

Day 1: Add enough water to the beans to cover them by 3 or 4 inches, and soak overnight in the refrigerator. As the beans absorb the water, they will more than double in volume.

Day 2: Combine the seasoning mix ingredients in a small bowl.

Place all of the dressing ingredients, except the mayonnaise, in a blender and add *1 tablespoon* of the seasoning mix. Purée until smooth and creamy. Add the mayonnaise, stir to blend thoroughly, and set aside.

Drain the white beans. Place a heavy 5-quart pot, preferably nonstick, over high heat and add the chicken stock, the *remaining* seasoning mix, and the drained white beans. Cook until the beans are tender and the liquid is thick and creamy-looking, about 40 to 45 minutes. If the level of the liquid seems low during the cooking time, add water 1 cup at a time. Drain (but do not rinse), and set the beans aside to cool.

When the beans are cool, place them in a large bowl, add all the vegetables, and toss until evenly mixed. Add the dressing and fold gently until evenly distributed.

Per 1-cup serving: Calories 186   Protein 13g   Fat 3g
Carbohydrates 25g   12% calories from fat

Tijuana Pinto Bean Salad

Makes 6 cups, enough for 10 to 12 side or 6 main-dish servings

You've probably eaten pinto beans a dozen different ways, especially in Mexican or Tex-Mex dishes. Here's a recipe that definitely pays homage to its Hispanic ancestry, but with a twist—it's a salad! It can stand alone as a main dish or accompany any plain meat or chicken.

½ cup dried pinto beans

Seasoning mix
2 teaspoons onion powder
1¾ teaspoons garlic powder
1½ teaspoons salt
1 teaspoon sweet paprika
1 teaspoon dry mustard
1 teaspoon black pepper
1 teaspoon dried oregano leaves
1 teaspoon ground pasillo chile pepper (see **Note**)
1 teaspoon ground New Mexico chile pepper (see **Note**)
¾ teaspoon white pepper
¼ teaspoon cayenne

4 cups defatted chicken stock (page 8)
¾ cup finely diced onions, *in all*
½ cup finely chopped cabbage
½ cup finely diced bok choy leaves and stalks

1½ cups finely diced fresh mushrooms, *in all*
1 teaspoon ground pasillo chile pepper (see **Note**)
1 teaspoon ground New Mexico chile pepper (see **Note**)
1 teaspoon ground cumin
¼ cup balsamic vinegar
2 tablespoons Worcestershire sauce
2 tablespoons tamari (see **Note**)
1 cup apple juice
½ cup nonfat mayonnaise
½ cup finely diced carrots
¼ cup finely diced red bell peppers
¼ cup finely diced green bell peppers
¾ cup finely diced celery
1 cup finely diced peeled cucumbers
½ cup canned chopped mild green chiles

Day 1: Add enough water to the pinto beans to cover them by 3 or 4 inches, and soak overnight in the refrigerator. As the beans absorb the water, they will more than double in volume.

Day 2: Combine the seasoning mix ingredients in a bowl.

Drain the beans. Place a heavy 5-quart pot over high heat and add the chicken stock, *all but 1 tablespoon* of the seasoning mix, and the drained beans. Cook until the starches in the beans start to break down, the beans are tender, and the liquid is thick and starts to look creamy, about 50 minutes. If the level of the liquid seems low during the cooking time, add water 1 cup at a time. Once the beans are tender, drain (but do not rinse), and set them aside to cool.

Place ½ cup of the cooled beans in a blender with ¼ *cup* of the onions, the cabbage, bok choy, ½ *cup* of the mushrooms, the chile peppers, cumin, balsamic vinegar, Worcestershire sauce, tamari, apple juice, and the *remaining 1 tablespoon* of the seasoning mix, and purée until smooth. Add the mayonnaise and stir to blend thoroughly.

Place the *remaining* drained beans in a large bowl, add the *remaining* vegetables, and toss until evenly mixed. Add the mixture from the blender and fold gently until evenly distributed.

Note You can use any variety of chile peppers that are available, but do not use commercial ground chili powder. A combination of two or more kinds of chiles creates a well-balanced, or "round," flavor. Use fewer chiles if you prefer less heat. For more information on chile peppers, see page 5.

Tamari is a very rich, flavorful soy sauce, available in specialty markets and the international or ethnic food sections of many supermarkets. If you cannot find tamari where you shop, use any good quality soy sauce.

Per 1-cup serving: Calories 144   Protein 7g   Fat 0g
Carbohydrates 30g   2% calories from fat

color photograph 13

Shrimp and Artichoke Salad

Makes 8 cups, enough for 8 appetizer or 4 main-dish servings

Artichokes, the flowers of a thistlelike plant, are wonderfully versatile. This recipe uses just about all parts of the artichoke, and combines them for a dish you have probably never eaten before. The shrimp and sesame seeds add an extra dimension.

Serve this salad at room temperature or chilled, but refrigerate any leftovers.

Seasoning mix

1¾ teaspoons dry mustard
1½ teaspoons salt
1¼ teaspoons onion powder
1¼ teaspoons dried sweet basil
    leaves
1 teaspoon garlic powder
1 teaspoon dried oregano
    leaves
½ teaspoon sweet paprika
½ teaspoon black pepper
½ teaspoon white pepper

Creamy dressing

1 cup nonfat mayonnaise
5 ounces evaporated skim milk
½ cup nonfat cottage cheese
½ cup nonfat cream cheese
2 tablespoons White Grape
    Syrup (page 45), or 4
    (1-gram) packets artificial
    sweetener (page 4), optional

4 large artichokes
¼ cup sesame seeds
1 pound medium headless
    shrimp, peeled
¾ cup defatted seafood stock
    (page 8), *approximately*
½ cup thinly sliced green onions
½ cup finely diced onions
½ cup finely diced celery
½ cup finely chopped green
    cabbage
½ cup finely diced green bell
    peppers
½ cup finely diced red bell
    peppers
¼ cup finely diced yellow bell
    peppers

Combine the seasoning mix ingredients in a small bowl.

Combine the dressing ingredients in a blender and process until smooth and creamy. Refrigerate until needed.

Place an 8-quart pot of lightly salted water over high heat and add the artichokes. Cover and cook until the artichokes are tender, about 30 to 35 minutes. Drain the artichokes and let them cool.

Meanwhile, place a small skillet, preferably nonstick, over high heat and add the sesame seeds. Cook, shaking the skillet occasionally, until the seeds start to pop and turn brown, about 3 to 4 minutes. Remove from the heat and set aside.

Cut the shrimp into ½-inch pieces, and sprinkle them with *2 teaspoons* of the seasoning mix. Place a 10-inch skillet over high heat, and add *½ cup* of the seafood stock, bring it to a boil, and add the seasoned shrimp. Cover and cook until the shrimp start to turn pink and plump, about 3 to 5 minutes. Remove the skillet from the heat and let the shrimp steam for 3 minutes, then remove the cover and let them cool.

When the artichokes are cool, remove their leaves and, using a teaspoon, scrape the meat from all the leaves. Discard the leaves. Remove all the fiber, or the "choke," from the artichoke bottoms and dice the meat into bite-size pieces. Peel and dice the stems.

Drain the cooked shrimp, reserving the liquid, and place them in a large bowl along with the artichoke meat, diced artichoke bottoms and stems, toasted seeds, the other vegetables, and the *remaining* seasoning mix, and toss to mix. Measure the liquid in which the shrimp were cooked and add enough stock to equal *½ cup plus 1 tablespoon*. Stir the stock into the dressing, add the remaining seasoning mix, pour the dressing over the salad, and mix until completely blended.

Per 1-cup serving: Calories 187   Protein 17g   Fat 4g
Carbohydrates 24g   19% calories from fat

color photograph 18

Magic Brightening

Not a new way to cook (it's been enjoyed in the Orient for
generations) but a method that's new to many. In these
delicious broths, meat and vegetables brighten
to their peak of color and taste.

Since I'm a professional chef, I taste all kinds of dishes and investigate all kinds of cooking methods wherever I go, in the United States and abroad. And when I first encountered shabu-shabu, the traditional Oriental method of quickly cooking precut vegetables and thinly sliced beef, chicken, or seafood in simmering broth, I liked it so much, I mentally filed the technique away under "great ideas."

Years later, midway through developing the recipes for this book, the shabu-shabu file popped into my consciousness. "Try me!" it shrieked, but I was busy with other things, and more or less told it to leave me alone.

Then, when I was working on Bronzed Chicken Salad for the book, it dawned on me that the technique I was using was suspiciously like shabu-shabu. Sneaky idea! I tried to ignore it, but it didn't go away. And now I'm really glad, for I think that Magic Brightening Broths offer a wonderful way to prepare and serve food that is beautiful to look at and at the peak of flavor and nutrition.

The name Magic Brightening comes from what I observed when I tried shabu-shabu myself. It seemed magical how the vegetables, no matter which variety I used, actually brightened the moment they were cooked to perfect doneness. The color became intense, almost glowing. And the flavor was literally indescribable! It was an exciting discovery, and I could hardly wait to share it with you.

Nutritionists tell us that generally food is best for us when it's either raw or just barely cooked, so the Magic Brightening method has to be one of the most healthful ways to cook. And it's very easy. It takes some time and planning to make the stocks and dipping sauces, but it's certainly not difficult. Once that's done, then all you have to do is prepare the vegetables (and the meat, shrimp, chicken, or whatever), which doesn't take very long, and gather everyone around the table. Each person chooses his/her own favorite food, arranges it on an implement, cooks it in simmering broth, and perhaps adds a bit of sauce. As someone said, "It's a great way for people to visit and eat at the same time!"

For a party, you can offer several varieties of broth and sauces, but for just a few friends or your family, one or two of each should be sufficient. You can serve Magic Brightening Broth, along with the accompanying vegetables and meats, as an appetizer or as the main dish, or as a soup after the main dish. And although I've listed the foods that go well with each broth, don't hesitate to use any fresh, delicious local produce to develop your own specialties. Also, with this method of cooking, children may eat vegetables more readily, since the whole procedure's a lot of fun.

During testing, we simmered the broth in small cast-iron pots used on top of little tabletop burners equipped with cans of butane. An electric skillet, a portable wok, or a fondue pot would work just as well. I don't recommend using a crock pot because food takes too long to cook in it.

You can pierce the food with shish-kabob skewers, fondue forks, or even clean coathangers. We found little wire baskets with bamboo handles in which you can put the food before cooking it in the broth. Read through the procedure and look at the photographs, then scout kitchen supply sections of department stores, hardware stores, or restaurant supply companies for the few pieces of equipment you need.

In traditional shabu-shabu, which originated in China but was refined and popularized by the Japanese about 130 years ago, the stock is made with either fish or *konbu*, a seaweed. The stock isn't seasoned, not even with salt. Here I've used seafood, meat, poultry, and vegetables for the eleven different broths, and have seasoned them generously. Another departure from tradition is that our dipping sauces are somewhat spicier than their Chinese or Japanese counterparts.

Vegetables require a longer cooking time than meat, so cook the vegetables first, then add the meat, chicken, or seafood. Thinly sliced beef, in particular, tastes much better and has a better texture when it's cooked for just a minute or two rather than four or five minutes.

While the food is cooking, notice the rate of evaporation and add stock (preferably) or water as needed to maintain the same approximate level of liquid you started with, so that the seasoning remains balanced.

After everyone has cooked and eaten all the vegetables and meat (or seafood, chicken, etc.) they want, add rice or pasta to the broth. The result will be a light and tasty soup to finish off the meal. You've wasted nothing, there's very little to clean up, and you've enjoyed food at its absolute peak of perfection! Not a minor accomplishment.

So, round up your equipment and food—don't forget the sauces!—and gather your guests for a delicious meal (or many meals, I hope) that will look gorgeous, be good for you, and that is easy to prepare. Must be magic!

Preparing Vegetables, Poultry, and Meat

You can have great success cooking almost any fresh vegetable in Magic Brightening Broths. The vegetables should be just ripe, definitely not still green but not overripe. Very soft or pulpy vegetables, like tomatoes or okra, don't hold up well, and if you want to try green beans, you almost certainly will need a small wire basket.

Round vegetables work best if they are first peeled or scrubbed, then cut into wedges, while long, oval vegetables should be cut diagonally into ¼-inch to ½-inch slices. Hard vegetables, like potatoes or turnips, should be sliced ¼ inch thick, and the softer vegetables, such as zucchini, should be cut into ½-inch slices.

In case you're a little hesitant about trying something new, we've taken all the guesswork out of the vegetables in the following list. After you've been through the procedure once or twice, please use this list just as a guide and try any local fresh and delicious produce.

Cook the vegetables just until they reach their brightest color, almost always about 4 minutes, unless directed otherwise. Remember, the times are approximate, so watch the pot, not the clock.

Acorn squash: Peel, remove seeds, cut into 16 wedges. Cook 6 minutes.

Avocado: Peel, discard pit, cut into 16 wedges.

Banana squash: Peel, remove seeds, cut into 1½-inch cubes. Cook 3 minutes.

Beet: Trim end, peel, cut into 16 wedges.

Bell pepper (any color): Core, seed, and derib. Cut into strips or triangles.

Butternut squash: Peel, scoop out seeds and membrane, cut into 1½-inch cubes. Cook 6 minutes.

Carrots: Peel, trim each end, and cut into ½-inch slices.

Crookneck squash: Scrub (do not peel), cut off blossom and stem ends, cut in half lengthwise, and cut into 1½-inch slices.

Cucumber: Trim each end and cut into ½-inch diagonal slices.

Eggplant: Peel, cut in half, slice diagonally.

Japanese cucumber: Trim ends and slice diagonally.

Kabocha squash: Peel, remove seeds, cut into 16 wedges. Cook 5 minutes.

Mirliton: Peel, cut into 16 wedges.

Moqua squash: Peel, remove seeds, cut into 2¼-inch pieces.

Opo squash: Peel, remove seeds, cut into 16 wedges. Cook 4 to 5 minutes.

Parsnip: Trim each end, peel, and cut into ½-inch diagonal slices.

Potato: Peel, cut in half, slice diagonally.

Rutabaga: Peel, cut into 16 wedges.

Turnip: Trim each end, peel, and cut into bite-size pieces.

White summer squash (pattypan): Remove stem and blossom ends and cut into bite-size pieces.

Yellow summer squash: Scrub (do not peel), cut off stem and blossom ends, cut in half lengthwise, and cut into ½-inch slices.

Zucchini: Remove stem and blossom tips and cut into straight or diagonal ½-inch slices.

One thing to remember when preparing chicken or turkey breast, or beef flank or tenderloin, is the meat should be cut into strips or scalloped. See page 7 for a description of scalloping. Chicken and turkey, like the vegetables, need to be cooked the full 4 minutes. Some who've tested our Magic Brightening Broths prefer to cook the beef just a minute or two, so that it stays tender.

Broths

Just Veggies Broth

Makes 1½ quarts

This delicious broth isn't just for vegetarians, although they will certainly approve of it since it has no animal products. Use it with any of the foods suggested in the Magic Brightening Broth section. And it's wonderful to sip at the end of the meal.

1 gallon water
1 large unpeeled onion, quartered
1 large unpeeled carrot, cut into 2-inch pieces
1 rib celery, cut into 2-inch pieces
5 cloves unpeeled garlic, cut in half
1 medium unpeeled Idaho potato, quartered

1 stalk bok choy, cut into 2-inch pieces
2 teaspoons salt
2 teaspoons onion powder
2 teaspoons dry mustard
1 teaspoon garlic powder
½ teaspoon white pepper
¼ teaspoon black pepper
⅛ teaspoon cayenne

Place all the ingredients in a large pot over high heat. Bring to a boil, reduce the heat to medium, and simmer until the stock is reduced to 2 quarts, about 2 hours. Strain the stock and discard the cooked vegetables. Clean the pot and return the strained stock to it. Bring to a boil over high heat, reduce the heat to medium, and simmer until the stock is further reduced to 1½ quarts, about 30 minutes. Use immediately, or cool and refrigerate until needed.

Aunt Becky's Home-Style Chicken Broth

Makes 1½ quarts

Once you've tried this wonderful broth you'll want to keep some in the freezer for emergencies like the flu, a really sad movie, or a rainy weekend. Aunt Becky knows what's good for you!

And yes, it makes a really good Magic Brightening Broth! I can't think of anything that you couldn't cook in it, and the recipe is so basic that I'm sure you can come up with lots of your own ideas.

½ pound chicken backs	1½ teaspoons salt
½ pound chicken necks	1 teaspoon garlic powder
1 gallon water	1 teaspoon dry mustard
½ small unpeeled onion, quartered	1 teaspoon dried sweet basil leaves
1 cup chopped unpeeled carrots	1 teaspoon ground sage
½ cup chopped celery	¾ teaspoon onion powder
6 cloves unpeeled garlic, cut in half	¼ teaspoon black pepper
	¼ teaspoon white pepper
2 fresh basil leaves	⅛ teaspoon cayenne

Preheat the oven to 400°.

Place the chicken backs and necks on a cookie sheet or in a large roasting pan and roast, uncovered, for 25 minutes. Carefully drain off the fat, turn the backs and necks over, and roast for 25 minutes more.

Place the roasted backs and necks in a large pot, and add all the other ingredients. Bring to a boil over high heat, reduce the heat to medium, and simmer until the stock is reduced to 2 quarts, about 2 hours. Strain the stock and discard the cooked chicken and vegetables. Clean the pot and return the strained stock to it. Bring to a boil over high heat, reduce the heat to medium, and simmer until the stock is further reduced to 1½ quarts, about 30 minutes. Cool, then refrigerate until very cold and defat (page 8).

Fresh Herb Chicken Broth

Makes 1½ quarts

The herbal trio we've used here—basil, oregano, and sage—add a subtle but pleasant touch to this broth. If you grow your own herbs, or have a nearby market that offers them fresh, I'm sure you'll come up with some exciting combinations of your own.

½ pound chicken backs
½ pound chicken necks
1 gallon water
1 small unpeeled onion, quartered
1 small unpeeled carrot, cut into 2-inch pieces
1 celery rib, cut into 2-inch pieces
6 cloves unpeeled garlic, cut in half

3 fresh basil leaves
3 fresh oregano leaves
3 fresh sage leaves
1 teaspoon salt
¾ teaspoon garlic powder
½ teaspoon onion powder
½ teaspoon dry mustard
¼ teaspoon black pepper
¼ teaspoon white pepper

Preheat the oven to 400°.

Place the chicken backs and necks on a cookie sheet or in a large roasting pan and roast, uncovered, for 25 minutes. Carefully drain off the fat, turn the backs and necks over, and roast for 25 minutes more.

Place the roasted backs and necks in a large pot and add all the other ingredients. Bring to a boil over high heat, reduce the heat to medium, and simmer until the stock is reduced to 2 quarts, about 2 hours. Strain the stock and discard the cooked chicken and vegetables. Clean the pot and return the strained stock to it. Bring to a boil over high heat, reduce the heat to medium, and simmer until the stock is further reduced to 1½ quarts, about 30 minutes. Cool, then refrigerate until very cold and defat (page 8).

Hot-Hot-Hot Chicken Broth

Makes 1½ quarts

No need to call out the fire engines just yet. Although the broth itself gets a lot of its heat from the jalapeño and cayenne peppers, because of the rapid cooking the vegetables and chicken cooked in it won't absorb much of the heat. Fair warning, though: If you serve the broth after everyone has finished cooking, it will be a bit fiery.

½ pound chicken backs
½ pound chicken necks
1 gallon water
1 small unpeeled onion, quartered
1 small unpeeled carrot, cut into 2-inch pieces
1 celery rib, cut into 2-inch pieces
6 cloves unpeeled garlic, cut in half
2 jalapeño peppers, split open

1½ teaspoons garlic powder
1 teaspoon salt
1 teaspoon sweet paprika
1 teaspoon onion powder
1 teaspoon dried sweet basil leaves
1 teaspoon ground sage
1 teaspoon dried thyme leaves
½ teaspoon black pepper
½ teaspoon white pepper
½ teaspoon cayenne

Preheat the oven to 400°.

Place the chicken backs and necks on a cookie sheet or in a large roasting pan and roast, uncovered, for 25 minutes. Carefully drain off the fat, turn the backs and necks over, and roast for 25 minutes more.

Place the roasted backs and necks in a large pot and add all the other ingredients. Bring to a boil over high heat, reduce the heat to medium, and simmer until the stock is reduced to 2 quarts, about 2 hours. Strain the stock and discard the cooked chicken and vegetables. Clean the pot and return the strained stock to it. Bring to a boil over high heat, reduce the heat to medium, and simmer until the stock is further reduced to 1½ quarts, about 30 minutes. Cool, then refrigerate until very cold and defat (page 8).

Rich Turkey Broth

Makes 1½ quarts

This is a very versatile broth—perfect for cooking turkey, chicken, or vegetables—but delicious with beef or other meats, as well. It contains less fat than you might expect, even before being defatted. And the seasonings make it rich-tasting and satisfying. You could even serve it as a main dish, with just some cubed turkey breast or even dumplings.

½ pound turkey necks
1 gallon water
1 small unpeeled onion, quartered
1 small unpeeled carrot, cut into 2-inch pieces
1 rib celery, cut into 2-inch pieces
6 cloves unpeeled garlic, cut in half
3 tablespoons minced bay leaves

3 tablespoons minced fresh sage leaves
2 teaspoons salt
2 teaspoons onion powder
2 teaspoons dry mustard
1½ teaspoons garlic powder
1½ teaspoons dried sweet basil leaves
1 teaspoon sweet paprika
½ teaspoon white pepper
¼ teaspoon black pepper
¼ teaspoon cayenne

Preheat the oven to 400°.

Place the turkey necks on a cookie sheet or in a large roasting pan and roast, uncovered, for 25 minutes. Carefully drain off the fat, turn the necks over, and roast for 25 minutes more.

Place the roasted necks in a large pot and add all of the other ingredients. Bring to a boil over high heat, reduce the heat to medium, and simmer until the stock is reduced to 2 quarts, about 2 hours. Strain the stock and discard the cooked turkey and vegetables. Clean the pot and return the strained stock to it. Bring to a boil over high heat, reduce the heat to medium, and simmer until the stock is further reduced to 1½ quarts, about 30 minutes. Cool, then refrigerate until very cold and defat (page 8).

Sweet 'n Sour Turkey Broth

Makes 1½ quarts

Many cultures have some form of sweet and sour dish. The combination seems especially appropriate for Magic Brightening Broth, since its origins are decidedly Oriental. I think you'll agree our version captures the essence of the flavor contrasts. And it's low-fat besides!

½ pound turkey necks
1 gallon water
1 small unpeeled onion, quartered
1 small unpeeled carrot, cut into 2-inch pieces
1 celery rib, cut into 2-inch pieces
6 cloves unpeeled garlic, cut in half
2 tablespoons vinegar

2 tablespoons White Grape Syrup (page 45)
1½ teaspoons onion powder
1½ teaspoons dry mustard
1 teaspoon salt
1 teaspoon garlic powder
1 teaspoon dried sweet basil leaves
½ teaspoon dried thyme leaves
¼ teaspoon black pepper
¼ teaspoon white pepper

Preheat the oven to 400°.

Place the turkey necks on a cookie sheet or in a large roasting pan and roast, uncovered, for 25 minutes. Carefully drain off the fat, turn the necks over, and roast for 25 minutes more.

Place the roasted necks in a large pot and add all of the other ingredients. Bring to a boil over high heat, reduce the heat to medium, and simmer until the stock is reduced to 2 quarts, about 2 hours. Strain the stock and discard the cooked turkey and vegetables. Clean the pot and return the strained stock to it. Bring to a boil over high heat, reduce the heat to medium, and simmer until the stock is further reduced to 1½ quarts, about 30 minutes. Cool, then refrigerate until very cold and defat (page 8).

A-B-C Beef Broth

Makes 1½ quarts

This broth got its name from the fact that it's as basic as a recipe can be. It's fantastic as a Magic Brightening Broth, and can be used as the basis for a number of other wonderful soups and stews. Everyone who's tasted it so far has really liked its simplicity, and I hope you do too.

1 pound beef bones (ask your butcher to save them for you)	6 cloves unpeeled garlic, cut in half
1 gallon water	1 teaspoon salt
1 small unpeeled onion, quartered	1 teaspoon dry mustard
1 small unpeeled carrot, cut into 2-inch pieces	1 teaspoon dried thyme leaves
	¾ teaspoon onion powder
1 rib celery, cut into 2-inch pieces	¾ teaspoon garlic powder
	¼ teaspoon black pepper
	¼ teaspoon white pepper

Preheat the oven to 400°.

Place the beef bones on a cookie sheet or in a large roasting pan and roast, uncovered, for 20 minutes. Carefully drain off the fat, turn the bones over, and roast for 20 minutes more.

Place the roasted bones in a large pot and add all the other ingredients. Bring to a boil over high heat, reduce the heat to medium, and simmer until the stock is reduced to 2 quarts, about 2 hours. Strain the stock and discard the bones and vegetables. Clean the pot and return the strained stock to it. Bring to a boil over high heat, reduce the heat to medium, and simmer until the stock is further reduced to 1½ quarts, about 30 minutes.

Cool, then refrigerate until very cold and defat (page 8).

Rosemary Beef Broth

Makes 1½ quarts

In this broth, you'll want to use fresh rosemary, if you can find it. I think this wonderful herb jazzes up the Magic Brightening Broth and makes music in your mouth.

1 pound beef bones (ask your butcher to save them for you)	1¼ teaspoon onion powder
	1 teaspoon salt
1 gallon water	1 teaspoon dried summer savory
1 small unpeeled onion, quartered	3–4 fresh rosemary leaves or 1 teaspoon dried rosemary leaves
1 small unpeeled carrot, cut into 2-inch pieces	
1 rib celery, cut into 2-inch pieces	½ teaspoon garlic powder
	¼ teaspoon white pepper
6 cloves unpeeled garlic, cut in half	⅛ teaspoon black pepper
	⅛ teaspoon cayenne

Preheat the oven to 400°.

Place the beef bones on a cookie sheet or in a large roasting pan and roast, uncovered, for 20 minutes. Carefully drain off the fat, turn the bones over, and roast for 20 minutes more.

Place the roasted bones in a large pot and add all of the other ingredients. Bring to a boil over high heat, reduce the heat to medium, and simmer until the stock is reduced to 2 quarts, about 2 hours. Strain the stock and discard the bones and vegetables. Clean the pot and return the strained stock to it. Bring to a boil over high heat, reduce the heat to medium, and simmer until the stock is further reduced to 1½ quarts, about 30 minutes. Cool, then refrigerate until very cold and defat (page 8).

Very Hot Beef Broth

The heat in this broth is tempered by the other, more subtle seasonings, and helps produce its wonderful, rich flavor. What the broth does for vegetables cooked in it is pretty close to magic, and beef, quickly cooked in it, comes out tender and delicious.

1 pound beef bones (ask your butcher to save them for you)	6 whole cloves
	3 bay leaves
	1 teaspoon salt
1 gallon water	1 teaspoon garlic powder
1 small unpeeled onion, quartered	¾ teaspoon onion powder
	½ teaspoon dry mustard
1 small unpeeled carrot, cut into 2-inch pieces	½ teaspoon black pepper
	½ teaspoon white pepper
1 rib celery, cut into 2-inch pieces	½ teaspoon cayenne
6 cloves unpeeled garlic, cut in half	

Preheat the oven to 400°.

Place the beef bones on a cookie sheet or in a large roasting pan and roast, uncovered, for 20 minutes. Carefully drain off the fat, turn the bones over, and roast for 20 minutes more.

Place the roasted bones in a large pot and add all of the other ingredients. Bring to a boil over high heat, reduce the heat to medium, and simmer until the stock is reduced to 2 quarts, about 2 hours. Strain the stock and discard the bones and vegetables. Clean the pot and return the strained stock to it. Bring to a boil over high heat, reduce the heat to medium, and simmer until the stock is further reduced to 1½ quarts, about 30 minutes.

Cool, then refrigerate until very cold and defat (page 8).

Chef's Good Beef Stuff

This is one of my favorite Magic Brightening Broths. Allspice—whole berries or ground—isn't often used with beef, but I think you'll agree that it adds just the right touch.

1 pound beef bones (ask your butcher to save them for you)
1 gallon water
1 small unpeeled onion, quartered
1 small unpeeled carrot, cut into 2-inch pieces
1 rib celery, cut into 2-inch pieces
6 cloves unpeeled garlic, cut in half

4 allspice berries
1 teaspoon salt
1 teaspoon garlic powder
½ teaspoon onion powder
½ teaspoon dry mustard
½ teaspoon dried sweet basil leaves
½ teaspoon dried oregano leaves
½ teaspoon dried thyme leaves
¼ teaspoon black pepper
¼ teaspoon white pepper

Preheat the oven to 400°.

Place the beef bones on a cookie sheet or in a large roasting pan and roast, uncovered, for 20 minutes. Carefully drain off the fat, turn the bones over, and roast for 20 minutes more.

Place the roasted bones in a large pot and add all of the other ingredients. Bring to a boil over high heat, reduce the heat to medium, and simmer until the stock is reduced to 2 quarts, about 2 hours. Strain the stock and discard the bones and vegetables. Clean the pot and return the strained stock to it. Bring to a boil over high heat, reduce the heat to medium, and simmer until the stock is further reduced to 1½ quarts, about 30 minutes.

Cool, then refrigerate until very cold and defat (page 8).

Herbal Shrimp Broth

This delicious broth can be used for cooking potatoes and corn as well as shrimp and seafood. If you're serving several different Magic Brightening Broths, however, I recommend cooking shrimp only in shrimp broth.

1 pound headless shrimp (26/30 count)	1 teaspoon sweet paprika
1 gallon water	1 teaspoon onion powder
½ small unpeeled onion, quartered	1 teaspoon dry mustard
1 cup chopped carrots	¾ teaspoon dried sweet basil leaves
6 cloves unpeeled garlic, cut in half	½ teaspoon garlic powder
1 cup chopped potatoes	½ teaspoon black pepper
2 tablespoons minced fresh oregano leaves	½ teaspoon white pepper
1½ teaspoons salt	½ teaspoon dried oregano leaves
	½ teaspoon dried thyme leaves
	⅛ teaspoon cayenne

Peel the shrimp. Cover and refrigerate the peeled shrimp until time to serve.

Place the shrimp shells in a large pot and add all of the other ingredients. Bring to a boil over high heat, reduce the heat to medium, and simmer until the stock is reduced to 2 quarts, about 2 hours. Strain the stock and discard the shells and vegetables. Clean the pot and return the strained stock to it. Bring to a boil over high heat, reduce the heat to medium, and simmer until the stock is further reduced to 1½ quarts, about 30 minutes.

Cool, then refrigerate until very cold and defat (page 8).

Dipping Sauces for Magic Brightening Broth

We think cooking a vegetable in our Magic Brightening Broth brings out its natural flavor at its peak of perfection. As someone said when we were testing these recipes, "I've never known before how a vegetable really tastes!" Vegetables cooked this way are simple, but they are simply delicious.

But for those who want just a little extra flavor we developed these dipping sauces. When the vegetables—or the meat, seafood, or poultry—are cooked, you can dip them into the sauce or place one or more sauces on your plate for a variety of tastes.

Cayenne and Sweet Basil Dipping Sauce

Makes 2½ cups

This hot and spicy sauce won't overpower the meats and vegetables that have been freshly cooked in the Magic Brightening Broths. You can use it with any of the brightened foods, but it's particularly good with turnips and carrots.

4 (1-gram) packets artificial
    sweetener (page 4)
1 teaspoon salt
1 teaspoon cayenne
1 teaspoon dried sweet basil
    leaves
½ teaspoon onion powder

½ teaspoon garlic powder
2 cups defatted chicken stock
    (page 8)
¼ cup plus 1 tablespoon
    balsamic vinegar
3 tablespoons fresh lemon juice

Combine the 6 dry ingredients in a bowl. Add the chicken stock, balsamic vinegar, and lemon juice, and stir until thoroughly combined.

Per 1-ounce serving: Calories 4   Protein 0g   Fat 0g
Carbohydrates 1g   0% calories from fat

Garlic and Jalapeño Dipping Sauce

Makes 1 cup

Don't let the jalapeño peppers scare you away from making this exciting sauce; the other wonderful ingredients help deflect some of the heat. It goes well with all of the brightened foods, but especially so with cooked vegetables.

6 (1-gram) packets artificial sweetener (page 4)	3 tablespoons soy sauce
2 teaspoons garlic powder	3 tablespoons very dry sherry
1½ teaspoons dry mustard	¼ cup rice vinegar
1 teaspoon onion powder	¼ defatted chicken stock (page 8)
1 teaspoon ground coriander	
½ teaspoon salt	2 tablespoons minced fresh garlic
3 tablespoons tamari (see Note)	2 medium jalapeño peppers, thinly sliced

Combine the 6 dry ingredients in a bowl. Add the tamari, soy sauce, sherry, rice vinegar, and chicken stock, and stir until thoroughly combined. Add the fresh garlic and jalapeño peppers and mix well.

Note Tamari is a very rich, flavorful soy sauce, available in specialty markets and the international or ethnic food sections of many supermarkets. If you cannot find tamari where you shop, just double the amount of regular soy sauce.

Per 1-ounce serving: Calories 37   Protein 3g   Fat 0g
Carbohydrates 7g   6% calories from fat

Plum and Mustard Dipping Sauce

The name sounds more like a color scheme than a recipe, but this pretty pink sauce is a wonderful accompaniment to foods that have been brightened in Magic Broth seasoning, especially meats.

4 medium plums

1 cup Dijon mustard

2 tablespoons very dry sherry

¼ cup apple cider vinegar

8 (1-gram) packets artificial sweetener (page 4)

2 teaspoons cayenne

Quarter the unpeeled plums, discarding the pits; there should be about 2 cups. Liquefy the plums in a blender, to yield about 1 cup. Set aside.

Place the mustard, sherry, and vinegar in a bowl, and stir until blended. Add the artificial sweetener and cayenne, and stir again. Add the liquefied plums and stir until thoroughly combined.

Per 1-ounce serving: Calories 29   Protein 0g   Fat 0g
Carbohydrates 3g   0% calories from fat

Spicy Tomato Dipping Sauce

Makes 1½ cups

This is a beautiful red sauce that does beautiful things for all lightly cooked meats and vegetables. My absolute, number one preference for this sauce is seafood.

6 (1-gram) packets artificial
   sweetener (page 4)

1 teaspoon onion powder

1 teaspoon dried sweet basil
   leaves

½ teaspoon salt

½ teaspoon dry mustard

¼ teaspoon white pepper

¼ teaspoon cayenne

½ cup defatted chicken stock
   (page 8)

¾ cup tomato sauce

2 tablespoons rice vinegar

1 tablespoon tamari (see Note)

2 tablespoons minced fresh
   garlic

2 tablespoons minced fresh
   ginger

Combine the 7 dry ingredients in a bowl, add the chicken stock, and stir until well blended. Add the tomato sauce, rice vinegar, and tamari, and stir again. Add the minced garlic and ginger, and stir until thoroughly blended.

Note Tamari is a very rich, flavorful soy sauce, available in specialty markets and the international or ethnic food sections of many supermarkets. If tamari is unavailable, use any good quality soy sauce.

Per 1-ounce serving: Calories 15   Protein 1g   Fat 0g
Carbohydrates 4g   5% calories from fat

Black-eyed Pea Dipping Sauce

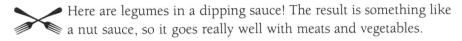

Makes 1¾ cups

Here are legumes in a dipping sauce! The result is something like a nut sauce, so it goes really well with meats and vegetables.

½ cup dried black-eyed peas, soaked overnight in refrigerator
1 medium onion
  Vegetable cooking oil
4 cloves garlic
1 teaspoon salt
1 teaspoon dry mustard
1 teaspoon dried sweet basil leaves

¾ teaspoon black pepper
½ teaspoon onion powder
½ teaspoon garlic powder
¼ teaspoon white pepper
½ cup defatted beef stock (page 8)
2 tablespoons very dry sherry
2 tablespoons balsamic vinegar
2 tablespoons red wine vinegar
2 tablespoons tamari (see **Note**)

Preheat a heavy 10-inch skillet, preferably nonstick, over high heat to 350°, about 4 minutes.

Add the black-eyed peas and roast them, stirring occasionally to keep them from burning, for 4 minutes. Remove from heat and set aside.

Preheat the oven to 350°.

Peel the onion and rub it with vegetable oil. Peel the garlic and place it with the onion on a sheet pan and oven-roast them for 30 minutes. When the onion and garlic are cool enough to handle, chop and set them aside.

Combine the 7 dry ingredients in a bowl, add the beef stock and stir. Add the sherry, balsamic vinegar, red wine vinegar and tamari, and blend. Add the roasted black-eyed peas, chopped roasted onion and garlic, and place in a blender and purée until smooth.

Note Tamari is a very rich, flavorful soy sauce, available in specialty markets and the international or ethnic food sections of many supermarkets. If you cannot find tamari where you shop, use any good quality soy sauce.

Per 1-ounce serving: Calories 25   Protein 2g   Fat 0g
Carbohydrates 4g   8% calories from fat

Five Little Peppers
Dipping Sauce

Makes 5 cups

This exciting sauce may remind you of gazpacho or fresh salsa, but when it meets brightened turkey or chicken, it may create a happy new memory.

1 teaspoon salt

1 teaspoon dry mustard

1 teaspoon dried sweet basil leaves

¾ teaspoon ground cinnamon

¼ teaspoon ground cloves

¼ cup balsamic vinegar

¼ cup tamari (see Note)

1¼ cups finely diced onions

1 tablespoon finely chopped fresh rosemary leaves

1 cup finely diced red bell peppers

¾ cup finely diced green bell peppers

¾ cup plus 2 tablespoons finely diced, seeded Anaheim peppers

¼ cup plus 2 tablespoons finely diced, seeded poblano peppers

1 tablespoon finely diced, seeded serrano peppers

Combine the 5 dry ingredients in a bowl, add the balsamic vinegar and tamari, and stir until well blended. Add the remaining ingredients and stir until thoroughly blended.

Note Tamari is a very rich, flavorful soy sauce, available in specialty markets and the international or ethnic food sections of many supermarkets. If you cannot find tamari where you shop, use any good quality soy sauce.

Per 1-ounce serving: Calories 9   Protein 1g   Fat 0g
Carbohydrates 2g   2% calories from fat

Hot and Sweet Dipping Sauce

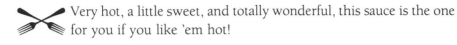

Makes 3½ cups

Very hot, a little sweet, and totally wonderful, this sauce is the one for you if you like 'em hot!

2 (1-gram) packets artificial sweetener (page 4)
1 teaspoon ground cinnamon
¼ teaspoon ground cloves
¼ teaspoon ground cumin
½ cup defatted chicken stock (page 8)
2 tablespoons balsamic vinegar
1½ tablespoons apple cider vinegar
1 cup medium diced fresh tomatoes
½ cup chopped onions
½ cup minced, unpeeled Red Delicious apple

½ cup medium diced roasted, seeded green bell peppers (page 5)
2 poblano peppers, roasted, seeded, and medium diced (page 5)
2 jalapeño peppers, roasted, seeded, and medium diced (page 5)
1½ tablespoons minced fresh cilantro leaves
1½ teaspoons minced fresh garlic

Combine the 4 dry ingredients in a bowl and add the chicken stock, balsamic vinegar, and cider vinegar. Stir to blend thoroughly, add the remaining ingredients, and stir until thoroughly combined.

Per 1-ounce serving: Calories 18   Protein 1g   Fat 0g
Carbohydrates 4g   6% calories from fat

Fresh Tomatillo Dipping Sauce

Makes 2 cups

This colorful sauce is sure to be a hit around your Magic Brightening table. Some of the ingredients are a little unusual, but the increasing popularity of exotic fruit, vegetables, and herbs means they are more widely available. Besides sparking brightened foods, this sauce works well as a dressing and adds pizzazz to salads and other cold dishes.

2 small unpeeled plums
¾ teaspoon onion powder
½ teaspoon salt
¼ teaspoon dry mustard
¼ teaspoon black pepper
¼ teaspoon white pepper
¼ teaspoon cayenne
¼ teaspoon ground cumin
½ cup defatted chicken stock (page 8)
½ tablespoon apple cider vinegar
5 fresh chopped tomatillos

3 Anaheim peppers, roasted, seeded, and medium diced (page 5)
1 poblano pepper, roasted, seeded, and medium diced (page 5)
½ cup minced fresh fennel
1 tablespoon minced fresh cilantro leaves
1 tablespoon minced fresh garlic

Quarter the unpeeled plums, discarding the pits, and liquefy them in a blender; set aside.

Combine the 7 dry ingredients in a bowl, add the chicken stock and cider vinegar, and stir until blended. Add the remaining ingredients and stir until thoroughly blended.

Per 1-ounce serving: Calories 16   Protein 1g   Fat 0g
Carbohydrates 3g   0% calories from fat

Jicama Dipping Sauce

Makes 2 cups

Sweet and crunchy jicama, a Latin American vegetable, is becoming more readily available in the United States. Although jicama can be cooked, here we're using it uncooked. Use this sauce as a delicious dressing on salads made of cooked or raw vegetables.

½ teaspoon salt
½ teaspoon dried sweet basil
   leaves
½ teaspoon ground cumin
½ teaspoon dried oregano
   leaves
¼ teaspoon black pepper
¼ teaspoon white pepper
½ cup defatted chicken stock
   (page 8)
2 tablespoons fresh lime juice
2 tablespoons red wine vinegar
1½ tablespoons fresh lemon
   juice

¼ cup minced fresh cilantro
   leaves
1½ cups finely diced fresh
   jicama
2 serrano peppers, roasted,
   seeded, and medium diced,
   (page 5)
1 Anaheim pepper, roasted,
   seeded, and medium diced,
   (page 5)
1 poblano pepper, roasted,
   seeded, and medium diced,
   (page 5)
½ cup finely diced leeks

Combine the 6 dry ingredients in a bowl, add the chicken stock, and stir. Add the lime juice, wine vinegar, and lemon juice, and stir again. Add the remaining ingredients and stir until thoroughly blended.

Per 1-ounce serving: Calories 16   Protein 1g   Fat 0g
Carbohydrates 3g   0% calories from fat

Terrific Tomato Dipping Sauce

Makes 4½ cups

This is another sauce that may make you think of salsa or gazpacho, and it's so good you may be tempted to eat it all by itself! But save it for the meats and vegetables that come out of your Magic Brightening Broth—you won't be disappointed. And try it cold with cold cooked meat.

4 (1-gram) packets artificial sweetener (page 4)
2 teaspoons dry mustard
1 teaspoon salt
1 teaspoon onion powder
1 teaspoon garlic powder
1 teaspoon dried sweet basil leaves
1 teaspoon dried oregano leaves
½ teaspoon black pepper
½ teaspoon white pepper
2 cups canned vegetable juice
1 cup tomato sauce
3 tablespoons fresh lime juice

3 tablespoons white vinegar
3 bay leaves
1¼ cups chopped onions
2 green bell peppers, roasted, seeded, and medium diced (page 5)
2 Anaheim peppers, roasted, seeded, and medium diced, (page 5)
¼ cup minced fresh cilantro leaves
1 tablespoon minced fresh garlic

Combine the 9 dry ingredients in a bowl. Add the vegetable juice, tomato sauce, lime juice, and vinegar, and stir until blended. Add the remaining ingredients and stir until thoroughly blended.

Per 1-ounce serving: Calories 11   Protein 0g   Fat 0g
Carbohydrates 2g   4% calories from fat

Fiesta Dipping Sauce

Makes 5 cups

This creamy dipping sauce is almost a party in itself, but wait till you try it with brightened vegetables and meat! It's tangy, very pretty, light, and fluffy. The sauce goes perfectly with potato salad, macaroni salad, and it's great with a raw vegetable salad.

4 (1-gram) packets artificial sweetener (page 4)
1½ teaspoons salt
1 teaspoon dry mustard
1 teaspoon ground cumin
1 teaspoon dried oregano leaves
½ teaspoon white pepper
¼ teaspoon black pepper
2 cups nonfat mayonnaise
½ cup defatted chicken stock (page 8)
¼ cup fresh lime juice

¼ cup rice vinegar
2 tablespoons fresh lemon juice
2 tablespoons Creole or brown mustard
6 poblano peppers, roasted, seeded, and medium diced (page 5)
1½ cups chopped onions
¼ cup minced fresh cilantro leaves
1 tablespoon minced fresh garlic

Combine all the dry ingredients in a bowl. Add the chicken stock, lime juice, vinegar, lemon juice, and brown mustard, and stir. Add the remaining ingredients and stir until thoroughly blended.

Per 1-ounce serving: Calories 20   Protein 0g   Fat 0g
Carbohydrates 5g   1% calories from fat

Fish and Seafood

*Louisiana waters are famous for the abundance and variety of
good things to eat swimming in them, but if you can't find
shrimp, crawfish, or catfish, use whatever fresh seafood
is available in your area.*

Oven-Fried Catfish

Makes 4 servings

This is such a wonderful way to prepare not only catfish but other varieties of fish as well that you won't miss skillet-frying one bit! The fresh parsley and green onions are very important to the end result, so don't leave them out. Catfish is a fatty fish, and to stay below the guideline of 30 percent of calories from fat, you'll need to serve it with low-fat or nonfat side dishes, like rice and steamed asparagus or broccoli.

Seasoning mix
1¼ teaspoons garlic powder
1 teaspoon salt
1 teaspoon onion powder
1 teaspoon dried sweet basil
   leaves
½ teaspoon sweet paprika
½ teaspoon black pepper
½ teaspoon white pepper
½ teaspoon dried oregano
   leaves
½ teaspoon ground cumin

⅛ teaspoon cayenne

4 (4 to 5 ounces each) fresh
   catfish fillets
½ cup toasted bread crumbs
2 tablespoons finely chopped
   fresh parsley
3 tablespoons finely sliced green
   onions
1 tablespoon olive oil

Combine the seasoning mix ingredients in a small bowl.

Sprinkle all surfaces of the fish evenly with *4 teaspoons* of the seasoning mixture.

Preheat the oven to 450°.

Combine the bread crumbs, parsley, green onions, and *remaining* seasoning mix in a bowl. Add the oil and mix it in with your fingers until the crumbs are moist.

Dredge the fish fillets, one at a time, in the bread-crumb mixture, pressing down gently on each side. Shake off any excess crumbs. Place the seasoned fish on a nonstick baking sheet, presentation side up, and cook 6 minutes. Turn the fish over and cook 6 minutes. Turn over one more time (presentation side up) and cook until done, about 4 minutes more. Serve immediately.

Per fillet: Calories 201   Protein 27g   Fat 9g
Carbohydrates 5g   38% calories from fat

Bronzed Catfish

Makes 4 servings

Catfish is a favorite south Louisiana treat, although you should know that it's naturally high in cholesterol. However, you can balance the meal by serving each person 4 ounces of steamed vegetables and a cup of rice.

Seasoning mix
  1 teaspoon salt
  ¾ teaspoon dried sweet basil
     leaves
  ½ teaspoon dry mustard
  ¼ teaspoon black pepper
  ¼ teaspoon white pepper
  ¼ teaspoon onion powder

  ¼ teaspoon garlic powder
  ¼ teaspoon dried oregano leaves
  ⅛ teaspoon cayenne

  4 (5 to 6 ounces each) fresh
     catfish fillets, about ¾ inch
     thick

Combine the seasoning mix ingredients, and sprinkle the entire mixture evenly over all sides of the catfish fillets.

Preheat a heavy 10-inch skillet, preferably nonstick, over high heat to 350°, about 4 minutes.

Place 2 fillets, curved side down, in the skillet and cook 1 minute. Turn and cook 1 minute, then turn over and cook 1 minute more. Turn one final time, and cook until fish is cooked throughout, about 1 minute more. Wipe the skillet clean, reheat it to 350°, and repeat the process for the remaining 2 fillets.

Per fillet: Calories 152   Protein 27g   Fat 5g
Carbohydrates 1g   27% calories from fat

Oven-Fried Talapia

Makes 4 servings

Although talapia doesn't come from Louisiana waters, its texture, flavor, and versatility have quickly endeared it to local cooks. If you can't find talapia, other varieties of fish work quite well. If you really want a treat, have the manager of the seafood department of your market order talapia.

Seasoning mix

1 teaspoon salt

¾ teaspoon sweet paprika

¾ teaspoon onion powder

¾ teaspoon dry mustard

½ teaspoon garlic powder

½ teaspoon white pepper

½ teaspoon ground cumin

½ teaspoon dried sweet basil leaves

½ teaspoon dried oregano leaves

¼ teaspoon black pepper

¼ teaspoon dried thyme leaves

4 (4 to 5 ounces each) fresh talapia fillets

½ cup toasted bread crumbs

2 tablespoons finely chopped fresh parsley

3 tablespoons finely sliced green onions

1 tablespoon olive oil

Combine the seasoning mix ingredients in a small bowl.

Sprinkle all surfaces of the fish evenly with *4 teaspoons* of the seasoning mix.

Preheat the oven to 450°.

Combine the bread crumbs, parsley, green onions, and *remaining* seasoning mix in a bowl. Add the oil and mix it in with your fingers until the crumbs are moist.

Place the fish fillets, one at a time, in the bowl of bread-crumb mixture and press down gently on each side. Shake off any excess crumbs. Place the seasoned fish on a nonstick baking sheet, presentation side up, and cook 6 minutes. Turn the fish over and cook 4 minutes. Turn the fillets again (presentation side up) and cook until done, about 4 minutes more. Serve immediately.

Per fillet: Calories 207   Protein 33g   Fat 6g
Carbohydrates 5g   25% calories from fat

Bronzed Talapia

Makes 6 servings

Talapia, while not native to Louisiana waters, has become extremely popular because it lends itself to different treatments. Bronzing is a versatile technique that works well on almost any firm fish. Experiment with seasonings and cooking times when you try other varieties of fish.

Seasoning mix

1 teaspoon salt

¾ teaspoon sweet paprika

¾ teaspoon onion powder

¾ teaspoon dry mustard

½ teaspoon garlic powder

½ teaspoon white pepper

½ teaspoon ground cumin

½ teaspoon dried sweet basil leaves

½ teaspoon dried oregano leaves

¼ teaspoon black pepper

¼ teaspoon dried thyme leaves

6 (4 to 5 ounces each) fresh talapia fillets

Vegetable-oil cooking spray

Combine the seasoning mix ingredients in a small bowl. Sprinkle each side of each fillet evenly with *½ teaspoon* of this mixture.

Preheat a 10-inch skillet, preferably nonstick, over high heat to 400°, about 5 minutes.

Spray the top side of each fillet evenly with vegetable-oil spray. Place the fillets, two at a time (sprayed side down), in the skillet, reduce the heat to medium, and cook 2 minutes. Turn the fillets over and cook until done, about 2 minutes more. Remove the cooked fillets, wipe the skillet clean, bring the heat back up to 400°, and repeat the process with the remaining fillets. Serve immediately.

Per fillet: Calories 159   Protein 32g   Fat 2g
Carbohydrates 1g   10% calories from fat

Shrimp Orleans

Makes about 5 cups, enough for 4 servings

Incredible, but true . . . this wonderfully fragrant and flavorful version of a traditional Creole shrimp dish is prepared without a drop of oil or butter.

Seasoning mix

1 tablespoon sweet paprika

2 teaspoons dried sweet basil leaves

1½ teaspoons onion powder

1½ teaspoons garlic powder

1 teaspoon salt

1 teaspoon dry mustard

½ teaspoon black pepper

½ teaspoon dried oregano leaves

½ teaspoon dried thyme leaves

¼ teaspoon white pepper

⅛ teaspoon cayenne

1 pound peeled medium shrimp

1½ cups chopped onions

1 cup chopped green bell peppers

½ cup chopped celery

3 bay leaves

1½ cups apple juice, *in all*

1 teaspoon minced fresh garlic

2 cups peeled, diced fresh tomatoes or 1 (14½-ounce) can diced tomatoes

½ cup tomato sauce

1 cup defatted seafood stock (page 8)

6 cups cooked long-grain white rice

Combine all the seasoning mix ingredients in a small bowl.

Sprinkle the shrimp evenly with *2 teaspoons* of the seasoning mix and set aside.

Preheat a heavy 10-inch skillet, preferably nonstick, over high heat to 350°, about 4 minutes.

Add the onions, bell peppers, celery, bay leaves, and *3 tablespoons* of the seasoning mix. Stir and cook until the vegetables start to brown, about 4 to 5 minutes. Add *1 cup* of the apple juice and the garlic, and stir to clear the bottom of the skillet of all brown bits. Cook until the apple juice evaporates completely and the bottom of the skillet dries out, about 12 to 13 minutes.

Stir the vegetables, spread them out, and cook 2 or 3 minutes until they are a rich-looking brown, to bring out their natural sweetness. Add the tomatoes and the *remaining* seasoning mix, scrape the bottom of the skillet completely, and cook 2 minutes. Stir in the tomato sauce, the stock, and *remaining* apple juice. Scrape the bottom of the skillet, bring to a boil, and cook about 7 to 8 minutes. Add the shrimp and cook just until they start to turn pink and plump, about 4 minutes. Turn off the heat and serve over the rice.

Per 1-cup serving: Calories 468   Protein 26g   Fat 3g
Carbohydrates 82g   6% calories from fat

color photograph 19

New Shrimp Remoulade

Makes 4 servings

What a perfect way to begin a meal! This classic New Orleans dish is popular with locals and visitors alike. We didn't want to mess too much with tradition, so our new version has all the goodness of the old—without all the fat.

Seasoning mix
- 1 teaspoon sweet paprika
- 1 teaspoon garlic powder
- ¾ teaspoon onion powder
- ½ teaspoon salt
- ½ teaspoon dry mustard
- ½ teaspoon dried sweet basil leaves
- ½ teaspoon dried thyme leaves
- ¼ teaspoon white pepper
- ¼ teaspoon black pepper
- ¼ teaspoon cayenne

- 1 pound unpeeled headless medium shrimp
- ½ cup nonfat mayonnaise
- 1 tablespoon catsup

- ½ cup chopped onions, _in all_
- ½ cup chopped green bell peppers, _in all_
- ½ cup chopped celery, _in all_
- ¼ cup chopped peeled cucumbers
- 1 tablespoon plus 1 teaspoon balsamic vinegar
- 1 teaspoon Creole or brown mustard
- 1 teaspoon Dijon mustard
- 1 tablespoon Worcestershire sauce
- 1 cup defatted seafood stock (page 8), _in all_
- 2 (1-gram) packets artificial sweetener (page 4)

Combine the seasoning mix ingredients in a small bowl. Sprinkle the shrimp with _1 tablespoon_ of this mixture, mix well, and set aside.

Place the mayonnaise, catsup, _¼ cup each_ of the onions, bell peppers, and celery, and the cucumbers, vinegar, Creole mustard, Dijon mustard, and Worcestershire sauce in a blender and purée. Set aside. Makes about 1⅔ cups.

Preheat a heavy 10-inch skillet, preferably nonstick, over high heat to 350°, about 4 minutes.

Add the *remaining* onions, bell peppers, celery, and seasoning mix, stir, and cook 1 minute. Add ½ *cup* of the stock, clear the bottom of the skillet, and cook until all the liquid evaporates, the vegetables begin to stick hard, and a good crust starts to form on the bottom of the skillet, about 6 to 7 minutes. Stir in the *remaining ½ cup* stock and the shrimp, and bring to a boil. Cover the skillet for 30 seconds, turn off the heat, and set aside for 5 minutes. Remove the shrimp to a container and place in the refrigerator to cool. Transfer all the vegetables and the liquid from the skillet to the blender and purée until smooth, then refrigerate until cool. When the shrimp are cool, peel and serve them with the sauce.

Per serving: Calories 177   Protein 25g   Fat 3g
Carbohydrates 13g   15% calories from fat

Shrimp Plaquemines

Makes about 1¼ quarts, enough for 3 to 4 servings

The combination of tomatoes and shrimp has been around for longer than I can remember. What makes this dish different is the variety of seasonings. If you use dried herbs, make sure they are still at the peak of their flavor—they won't stay fresh forever.

Seasoning mix

- 1 tablespoon sweet paprika
- 2 teaspoons salt
- 1½ teaspoons dried sweet basil leaves
- 1 teaspoon onion powder
- 1 teaspoon garlic powder
- 1 teaspoon dried oregano leaves
- ½ teaspoon black pepper
- ¾ teaspoon dried thyme leaves
- ½ teaspoon white pepper
- ½ teaspoon dry mustard
- ¼ teaspoon cayenne

- 1 pound peeled large shrimp
- 1 cup chopped onions

- ½ cup chopped red bell peppers
- ½ cup chopped yellow bell peppers
- ½ cup chopped green bell peppers
- ½ cup chopped celery
- 4 cups peeled, diced fresh tomatoes or 3 cups canned diced tomatoes, undrained
- 1 teaspoon minced fresh garlic
- ½ cup apple juice
- 1 cup defatted seafood stock (page 8)
- 2 (1-gram) packets artificial sweetener (page 4), optional
- 3 cups cooked long-grain white rice

Combine the seasoning mix ingredients in a small bowl.

Sprinkle the shrimp evenly with *1 tablespoon* of the seasoning mix, blend in thoroughly, and set aside.

Preheat a 12-inch skillet, preferably nonstick, over high heat to 350°, about 4 minutes.

Add the onions, bell peppers, celery, and the *remaining 3 tablespoons* of seasoning mix to the skillet and stir. Cook, scraping occasionally as vegetables stick and crusts form on the bottom of the skillet, for 5 minutes. Stir in the tomatoes and their liquid, and the garlic, and scrape the bottom of the skillet to clear it of any brown bits. Cook 3 to 4 minutes and add the apple juice. Cook 10 more minutes, stir in the stock, and cook 5 minutes. Add the shrimp and cook until they are just pink, 5 to 6 minutes. Turn off the heat and, if desired, add the artificial sweetener. Serve over the rice.

Per serving: Calories 543   Protein 32g   Fat 5g
Carbohydrates 97g   7% calories from fat

color photograph 20

Shrimp Bascom

━━ ━━ ━━ ━━ ━━ ━━ ━━ ━━ ━━ ━━ ━━ ━━ ━━ ━━ ━━ ━━ ━━ ━━ ━━

Makes 4 cups

✕ The extra-smooth tomato sauce sets this dish off from its near relatives. It's a good one to try when you want a familiar taste with a new twist.

Seasoning mix
- 2 teaspoons sweet paprika
- 1½ teaspoons garlic powder
- 1 teaspoon onion powder
- 1 teaspoon dry mustard
- 1 teaspoon salt
- 1 teaspoon dried thyme leaves
- ½ teaspoon black pepper
- ½ teaspoon white pepper
- ½ teaspoon cayenne

━━

- 1 pound medium peeled shrimp
- 1 cup chopped onions

- ¾ cup chopped green bell peppers
- ¼ cup chopped celery
- 2 teaspoons minced fresh garlic
- ½ cup apple juice
- 2 cups peeled, diced fresh tomatoes or 1 (14½-ounce) can diced tomatoes
- 1 tablespoon olive oil
- 1 cup defatted seafood stock (page 8)
- ¼ cup sliced green onions
- 4 cups cooked long-grain white rice

Combine the seasoning mix ingredients in a small bowl.

Sprinkle the shrimp evenly with *2 teaspoons* of the seasoning mix, combine thoroughly, and set aside.

Preheat a heavy 10-inch skillet, preferably nonstick, over high heat to 350°, about 4 minutes.

Add the onions, bell peppers, celery, garlic, and *1 tablespoon* of the seasoning mix. Stir and cook, scraping the bottom of the pan occasionally to clear it of all brown bits, for 4 minutes. Stir in the apple juice, clear the bottom of the pan, and continue to cook until all the liquid evaporates, about 4 to 5 minutes. Add the *remaining* seasoning mix and the tomatoes, clear the bottom of the skillet, mix well, and cook 6 to 7 minutes. Remove from the heat and transfer the contents of the skillet to a blender along with the oil and process until the vegetables are puréed, about 2 to 3 minutes. Return the puréed mixture to the skillet, add the stock, and whisk to blend. Turn the heat back to high, bring to a boil, and cook 3 minutes. Add the shrimp and green onions, and cook just until the shrimp turn pink and begin to plump, about 3 to 4 minutes. Serve over the rice.

Per 1-cup serving: Calories 456   Protein 29g   Fat 7g
Carbohydrates 68g   14% calories from fat

Sweet Pepper Cream Shrimp

─ ── ── ── ── ── ── ── ── ── ── ── ── ── ── ── ──

Makes 6 servings

This perfectly gorgeous shrimp dish—with colorful bell peppers in smooth, creamy sauce—is a good one to prepare for a very special occasion.

Seasoning mix

2 teaspoons salt

1 teaspoon sweet paprika

1 teaspoon onion powder

1 teaspoon garlic powder

1 teaspoon dried sweet basil
   leaves

½ teaspoon dry mustard

½ teaspoon white pepper

½ teaspoon dried thyme leaves

¼ teaspoon black pepper

¼ teaspoon ground nutmeg

¼ teaspoon cayenne

1 pound medium peeled shrimp

Creamy mixture

1 (12-ounce) can evaporated
   skim milk

½ cup nonfat cream cheese

¾ cup chopped onions

¾ cup chopped red bell
   peppers, *in all*

¾ cup chopped yellow bell
   peppers, *in all*

¾ cup chopped green bell
   peppers, *in all*

½ cup defatted seafood stock
   (page 8)

1½ cups apple juice, *in all*

½ teaspoon minced fresh garlic

6 tablespoons nonfat dry milk

¼ cup nonfat mayonnaise

3 cups cooked rice or 6 cups
   cooked pasta shells

Combine the seasoning mix ingredients in a small bowl and set aside.

Peel the shrimp and set them aside.

Place the creamy mixture ingredients in a blender and purée until smooth and creamy.

Preheat a heavy 10-inch skillet, preferably nonstick, over high heat to 350°, about 4 minutes.

Add the onions, *¼ cup each* of the red, yellow, and green bell peppers, and *1 tablespoon plus 1 teaspoon* of the seasoning mix. Stir, and cook 3 minutes. Add the stock, *½ cup* of the apple juice, and the garlic, scrape the bottom of the skillet to clear it of all brown bits, and cook until most of the liquid evaporates, about 12 minutes. Add *½ cup* apple juice, scrape the bottom to clear it, and cook 2 minutes. Transfer the mixture from the skillet to a blender, add the dry milk, and purée until smooth.

Return the puréed mixture to the skillet over high heat, and stir in the *remaining* bell peppers and the *remaining ½ cup* apple juice. Cook, scraping the bottom occasionally to keep the mixture from sticking, for 7 minutes. Add the *remaining* seasoning mix and shrimp, stir, and cook 3 minutes. Stir in the creamy mixture.

Caution: Dishes using these creamy mixtures can "break" or curdle easily if they are brought to a full boil. Therefore, bring the liquid just to a gentle boil, about 3 minutes, and stir immediately. Reduce the heat to medium and cook, stirring continuously, until the shrimp are plump and firm, about 2 minutes.

Turn off the heat. Remove 1 cup of the liquid, strain it, and purée it with the nonfat mayonnaise. Stir this mixture back into the mixture in the skillet.

Serve over the rice or pasta.

Per serving: Calories 332   Protein 25g   Fat 2g
Carbohydrates 53g   6% calories from fat

Shrimp-Stuffed Acorn Squash

Makes 4 generous servings

This dish is glamorous-looking enough to impress company, yet hearty and satisfying. You could balance the tongue-tingling spiciness with a cool salad and creamy nonfat dressing.

2 medium acorn squash

2½ cups defatted chicken stock
(page 8), *in all*

Seasoning mix
 1 tablespoon sweet paprika
 2 teaspoons salt
1½ teaspoons onion powder
1½ teaspoons dried sweet basil
  leaves
 1 teaspoon garlic powder
 1 teaspoon dry mustard
 1 teaspoon white pepper
 1 teaspoon dried thyme leaves
 ½ teaspoon dried oregano
  leaves

½ teaspoon black pepper
½ teaspoon cayenne

1 pound medium peeled shrimp
1 whole plain bagel
2 cups chopped onions
1 cup chopped green bell
  peppers
1 cup chopped celery
2 cups peeled, finely diced
  apple (1 large)
1 teaspoon minced fresh garlic
½ cup apple juice
4 ounces grated nonfat Cheddar
  or Muenster cheese

Preheat the oven to 350°.

Cut the unpeeled squash in half crosswise and scrape out the seeds and membranes. Cut a thin slice off the stem and blossom ends so all the halves can stand without tipping. Place the squash halves in a 9 × 9 × 2-inch baking pan, with *1 cup* of the stock. Cover with foil and bake until tender, about 45 to 50 minutes. When the squash is cool enough to handle, scoop out the meat from the shells, leaving just a thin layer with the skin. Set the squash shells aside. Transfer the meat to a large bowl, mash it with the side of a large spoon to break it up, and set it aside.

Meanwhile, combine the seasoning mix ingredients in a small bowl.

Select 12 of the most perfect shrimp and set them aside for garnish. Cut the remaining shrimp into ½-inch pieces and sprinkle them with *2 teaspoons* of the seasoning mix; blend in well and set aside.

Stand the bagel on its side, cut it into 3 even rings, then toast and cut the rings into ¼-inch cubes.

Preheat a heavy 12-inch skillet, preferably nonstick, over high heat to 350°, about 4 minutes.

Add the onions, bell peppers, celery, apple, and *remaining* seasoning mix to the skillet. Cook 10 minutes, scraping the bottom of the skillet to clear it of all brown bits. Add *½ cup* stock and the garlic, scrape the bottom of the skillet, and cook 5 minutes. Stir in the apple juice and another *½ cup* stock, clear the bottom and sides of the skillet, and add the shrimp. Stir together and cook 3 minutes. Turn off the heat, add the bagel cubes and mix thoroughly.

To make the stuffing, transfer the mixture from the skillet to the bowl with the reserved squash, and fold in until ingredients are thoroughly combined.

Preheat the oven to 450°.

Place 1 cup of the stuffing in each squash shell, and garnish each with 1 ounce of the grated cheese and 3 of the reserved whole shrimp. Place the stuffed squash in a baking pan, add *½ cup* stock, and bake until the cheese is melted and brown on top, about 14 to 15 minutes.

To serve, place ¼ of the remaining stuffing on each plate, form a shallow nest with the back of a spoon, and place a stuffed squash half in each nest.

Per serving: Calories 470   Protein 37g   Fat 10g
Carbohydrates 52g   19% calories from fat

Crawfish-Stuffed Artichokes with Lagniappe

Makes 6 stuffed artichokes

"Lagniappe" is an old New Orleans word that means "a little some-thing extra." In years past, when life seemed a little slower and a lot more gentle, the baker often would give a cookie or two—lagniappe—to children whose mothers ordered dinner rolls or bread. At the end of this recipe, you'll find a little something extra—a delicious salad dressing that uses the leftover stuffing from the artichokes.

Seasoning mix

2 teaspoons dried sweet basil
  leaves
1 teaspoon salt
1 teaspoon sweet paprika
1 teaspoon onion powder
1 teaspoon garlic powder
1 teaspoon dry mustard
1 teaspoon crushed red pepper
½ teaspoon black pepper
¼ teaspoon white pepper
⅛ teaspoon cayenne

1½ pounds cooked crawfish tail
  meat, *in all*
6 artichokes
2 medium cucumbers, peeled
  and chopped (save ½ of the
  skins)
1½ cups nonfat mayonnaise
1 (5-ounce) can evaporated
  skim milk
2 tablespoons freshly grated
  Parmesan cheese, optional

Combine the seasoning mix ingredients in a small bowl.

Sprinkle the crawfish tail meat evenly with *1 tablespoon* of the seasoning mix, combine thoroughly, and set aside.

Place a large pot half-filled with water over high heat. Add the artichokes, cover, and cook just until the artichokes are tender, about 25 minutes. Remove the artichokes and let them cool.

Place the cucumbers, reserved cucumber skins, *remaining* seasoning mix, mayonnaise, skim milk, and *½ pound* of the crawfish tail meat in a blender and purée until smooth and creamy. Set aside.

When the artichokes are cool, cut about ½ inch off the top of each and snip the sharp points off all the leaves. Slice off the stems (do not discard them) to flatten the bottoms, but be careful not to cut too close to the artichokes, as you want to keep them intact. Remove all the leaves that have started to fall off, until the artichoke has a nice round appearance. Using your fingers, grab the center leaves around the fuzzy choke, and remove but do not discard them. Carefully remove the choke, and remove and discard all the fibers. With a teaspoon scrape the artichoke leaves and reserve the pulpy meat. Peel the stems and dice them into small pieces.

In a large bowl combine the *remaining 1 pound* of crawfish tail meat, the diced artichoke, the scrapings from the leaves, and *2½ cups* of the mixture from the blender.

Place ¾ cup of this mixture in the center of each artichoke. If you wish, you can at this point serve the artichokes cold. Or, if you prefer them hot, place the filled artichokes in a baking pan and add enough water to come 1 inch up the sides of the pan. Sprinkle about 1 teaspoon Parmesan cheese, if desired, over each artichoke, and bake, uncovered, in a 350° oven until the stuffing is hot and the cheese is brown, about 25 to 30 minutes.

Per serving: Calories 450   Protein 51g   Fat 16g
Carbohydrates 79g   22% calories from fat

Lagniappe
(Artichoke and Cucumber Salad Dressing)

Makes about 2½ cups of cool, wonderful salad dressing

Remaining dressing from
  stuffed artichokes
  (about 2 cups)

1 (5-ounce) can evaporated
  skim milk
2 tablespoons balsamic vinegar

Place all ingredients in a blender and process until well mixed.

Crawfish in Cream Sauce with Pasta

* * * * * * * * * * * * * * * * * * * *

Makes 4 servings

 Crawfish are low in fat yet high in cholesterol, so eat them sparingly if you're on a low-cholesterol diet.

Creamy mixture

1 cup nonfat cottage cheese
½ cup nonfat cream cheese
12 ounces evaporated skim milk
¼ cup nonfat mayonnaise

Seasoning mix

1¼ teaspoons sweet paprika
1¼ teaspoons salt
1 teaspoon onion powder
1 teaspoon garlic powder
¾ teaspoon dried sweet basil
   leaves
¾ teaspoon dry mustard
¾ teaspoon dried thyme leaves
½ teaspoon black pepper
¼ teaspoon white pepper
¼ teaspoon dillweed
⅛ teaspoon cayenne
⅛ teaspoon ground nutmeg

1 pound fresh crawfish tails
   (about 4 pounds whole
   crawfish, or buy the tails
   already shelled and cleaned)
1 cup chopped onions, *in all*
¾ cup chopped green bell
   peppers, *in all*
1¼ cups defatted seafood stock
   (page 8), *in all*
2 tablespoons all-purpose flour
1 cup sliced fresh mushrooms
½ teaspoon minced fresh garlic
4 cups cooked pasta

Place the creamy mixture ingredients in a blender or food processor and purée until smooth and creamy. Set aside.

Combine the seasoning mix ingredients in a small bowl. Sprinkle the crawfish evenly with *1 tablespoon* of the seasoning mix and blend in thoroughly.

Preheat a heavy 10-inch skillet, preferably nonstick, over high heat to 350°, about 4 minutes.

Add *½ cup* of the onions, *¼ cup* of the bell peppers, and cook, scraping the bottom of the skillet once or twice, about 3 minutes. Add *¼ cup* of the stock, scrape the bottom of the skillet to clear it of all brown bits, and cook until the liquid evaporates, about 2 minutes (the bottom of the skillet will be brown). Add *¼ cup* stock, *2 teaspoons* of the seasoning mix, and the *remaining* onions and bell peppers, stir, and cook until the liquid evaporates and the vegetables start to stick, about 3 to 4 minutes. Add *½ cup stock* plus the flour, and stir until the flour is completely absorbed, a paste forms, and no flour is visible. Add the mushrooms and garlic, stir, and spread evenly in the skillet. Cook, scraping the bottom of the skillet as crusts form, for 5 minutes. If the mixture looks as though it might burn, add the *final ¼ cup* of stock, clear the bottom of the skillet, and let the liquid evaporate. Add the seasoned crawfish and *remaining* seasoning mix, clear the bottom of the skillet, and cook 2 minutes. Stir in the creamy mixture and cook, stirring continuously, until the mixture starts to boil. Caution: Creamy mixtures can "break" or curdle easily if they are brought to a full boil. Therefore, bring the liquid just to a gentle boil and stir immediately. Add the cooked, drained pasta to the skillet, stir until the pasta is hot, being careful not to let it boil, toss and serve.

Per serving: Calories 479   Protein 42g   Fat 3g
Carbohydrates 70g   5% calories from fat

New Crawfish Etouffée

Makes 4 servings

Every family in southwest Louisiana has a different version of this dish, and they're all wonderful! Crawfish etouffée is probably the most often-ordered item in Cajun country restaurants, and now you can prepare it at home—and make it healthful!

Seasoning mix
1 teaspoon salt
1 teaspoon sweet paprika
¾ teaspoon onion powder
½ teaspoon garlic powder
½ teaspoon dry mustard
¼ teaspoon black pepper
¼ teaspoon white pepper
⅛ teaspoon cayenne

1 cup chopped onions
½ cup chopped green bell peppers

¼ cup chopped celery
½ cup apple juice
5 tablespoons all-purpose flour, browned (page 7)
2 cups defatted seafood stock (page 8)
1 pound (cooked) fresh crawfish tails (about 4 pounds whole crawfish, or buy the tails already shelled, cooked, and cleaned)
2 cups cooked long-grain white rice

Combine the seasoning mix ingredients in a small bowl.

Preheat a 10-inch skillet, preferably nonstick, over high heat to 350°, about 4 minutes.

Add the onions, bell peppers, celery, and *two teaspoons* of the seasoning mix. Stir and cook, scraping the bottom of the skillet to clear all the brown bits, about 2 minutes. Stir in the apple juice, scrape to clear the bottom of the skillet, and cook until all the liquid evaporates and a glaze forms on the bottom of the skillet, about 7 to 8 minutes. Add the browned flour and *remaining* seasoning mix, and stir until the flour is completely absorbed, a paste forms, and no flour is visible. If necessary, add small amounts of stock to moisten the flour. Spread the mixture across the bottom of the skillet, and cook until the mixture sticks very hard, about 1 to 3 minutes. Stir in the stock and bring to a boil, stirring constantly. Cook for 2 minutes, add the crawfish tails, mix well, and return to a full boil. Turn off the heat and serve over the rice.

Per serving: Calories 594   Protein 65g   Fat 6g
Carbohydrates 41g   8% calories from fat

Company Crawfish

The touch of sherry in this dish adds a nice flavor and makes it a little bit special, like for Saturday night. All the mushrooms are nice too, and the little bit of butter, if you decide to use it, finishes the dish in a very exciting way.

Seasoning mix

1½ teaspoons salt
¾ teaspoon sweet paprika
¾ teaspoon white pepper
¾ teaspoon dried thyme leaves
¾ teaspoon ground turmeric
½ teaspoon onion powder
½ teaspoon garlic powder
½ teaspoon ground cumin
¼ teaspoon black pepper
⅛ teaspoon cayenne

Creamy mixture

¾ cup nonfat cottage cheese
1 (5-ounce) can evaporated skim milk

1 cup chopped onions
½ cup defatted seafood stock (page 8)
½ cup plus 2 tablespoons dry sherry, *in all*
¼ cup tomato sauce
2 cups sliced fresh mushrooms
1 pound cooked crawfish tail meat
1 tablespoon butter, optional
3 cups cooked long-grain white rice

Combine the seasoning mix ingredients in a bowl.

Place the creamy mixture ingredients in a blender and process until smooth and creamy; set aside.

Preheat a heavy 10-inch skillet, preferably nonstick, over high heat to 350°, about 4 minutes.

Add the onions and *1 tablespoon* of the seasoning mix and cook, scraping the bottom occasionally, until the onions start to brown, about 2 to 3 minutes. Add the stock and cook until the liquid evaporates, about 3 minutes. Stir in ¼ *cup* of the sherry and the tomato sauce and cook until most of the liquid evaporates and the tomato sauce starts to look dry, about 3 minutes.

Add *another 1/4 cup* sherry, the mushrooms, crawfish tails, and the *remaining* seasoning mix. Stir and cook, scraping the bottom, for 4 to 5 minutes; the mixture will thicken. Add the puréed creamy mixture, stir, and cook just until the liquid begins to boil at the sides of the skillet. **Caution:** Do not let the liquid come to a full boil, as it will "break," or curdle. Once the liquid has started to boil, turn off the heat, stir in the *remaining 2 tablespoons* of sherry and add the butter for an even richer taste. Serve over the rice.

Per 1-cup serving (without butter): Calories 844   Protein 30g   Fat 3g
Carbohydrates 171g   3% calories from fat

Mustard Crawfish

Makes 3⅓ cups, enough for 4 main-dish servings

In Louisiana we have so many crawfish we've developed what seems like a hundred ways to prepare them. The combination of flavors here is a little different—notice we've used two kinds of mustard, which makes this one of the best cold crawfish dishes I've ever had.

Seasoning mix

2 teaspoons dry mustard

1½ teaspoons salt

1½ teaspoons dried sweet basil leaves

1 teaspoon garlic powder

¾ teaspoon sweet paprika

¾ teaspoon onion powder

¼ teaspoon black pepper

¼ teaspoon white pepper

3 ounces evaporated skim milk

2 tablespoons Creole or brown mustard

1½ tablespoons lemon juice

1½ pounds cooked crawfish tail meat

½ cup thinly sliced green onions

Creamy dressing

1 cup nonfat cottage cheese

Combine the seasoning mix ingredients in a small bowl. Sprinkle *2 teaspoons* of this mixture over the crawfish and mix it in.

Combine the dressing ingredients in a blender and purée until smooth and creamy.

Place the crawfish, *remaining* seasoning mix, and green onions in a large bowl, add the dressing, and gently fold together until completely blended. Chill until ready to serve.

Per serving: Calories 487   Protein 91g   Fat 6g
Carbohydrates 12g   10% calories from fat

Chicken and Turkey

*A boon to low-fat cooking, these recipes demonstrate
how versatile and thrifty poultry can be.*

Chicken Brassica

─ ─ ─ ─ ─ ─ ─ ─ ─ ─ ─ ─ ─ ─ ─ ─ ─ ─ ─

Makes 4 servings

The name of this dish refers to the fact that it contains leafy green vegetables—we all know they're good for us, and this is an interesting, new way to enjoy them. Serve over fluffy, long-grain rice for smiles all around the table!

Seasoning mix
1 tablespoon sweet paprika
1 tablespoon dried sweet basil
   leaves
2 teaspoons salt
2 teaspoons onion powder
2 teaspoons dried oregano
   leaves
1 teaspoon garlic powder
1 teaspoon dry mustard
1 teaspoon white pepper
¾ teaspoon dried thyme leaves
½ teaspoon black pepper
½ teaspoon ground coriander

─

1 (3-pound) chicken, all skin
   and visible fat removed
   (don't worry about the
   wings), cut into 8 pieces

4 cups chopped onions, *in all*
2 cups chopped green bell
   peppers, *in all*
2 cups sliced fresh
   mushrooms, *in all*
3 cups chopped fresh collard
   greens, *in all*
3 bay leaves
2½ cups defatted chicken stock
   (page 8), *in all*
¼ cup all-purpose flour
2 (14½-ounce) cans diced
   tomatoes
3 cups cooked long-grain
   white rice

Combine the seasoning mix ingredients in a small bowl.

Preheat a heavy 5-quart pot, preferably nonstick, over high heat to 350°, about 4 minutes.

Sprinkle all surfaces of the chicken evenly with 5 *teaspoons* of the seasoning mix and rub it in well. Place the chicken in the pot and cook, turning twice, until browned on all sides, about 10 minutes in all. You may have to cook the chicken in batches. When the chicken is brown, remove it from the pot and set it aside.

To the pot add *2 cups* of the onions, *1 cup* of the bell peppers, *1 cup* of the mushrooms, *1 cup* of the greens, the bay leaves, and the *remaining* seasoning mix. Cook, scraping the bottom of the pot frequently, until the vegetables begin to stick, turn brown, and seem in danger of burning, about 5 minutes. Add *½ cup* of the stock, scrape the bottom of the pot clear, and cook, scraping occasionally, until the stock is almost absorbed, about 6 minutes. Blend in the flour and cook until it starts to brown, about 3 minutes. Add the tomatoes with their liquid and the *remaining* ingredients and bring to a boil. Add the chicken and any juices that have accumulated. Reduce the heat to a fast simmer and cook, covered, until done, approximately 20 minutes. Serve over the rice.

Per serving: Calories 668   Protein 58g   Fat 12g
Carbohydrates 75g   15% calories from fat

Chicken and Black-eyed Peas

Makes 4 servings

Combining black-eyed peas, spinach, and chicken in one recipe may seem unusual, but give it a try. I think you'll find it's an exciting flavor medley. The peas contribute a rich creaminess to the gravy, as well as the nutrients for which legumes are famous.

1¼ cups dried black-eyed peas

Seasoning mix
- 1 tablespoon salt
- 1 tablespoon sweet paprika
- 2 teaspoons black pepper
- 1½ teaspoons dried sweet basil leaves
- 1 teaspoon onion powder
- 1 teaspoon garlic powder
- 1 teaspoon dry mustard
- 1 teaspoon ground cumin
- ¾ teaspoon white pepper
- ¾ teaspoon dried thyme leaves
- ¼ teaspoon cayenne

- 1 (3-pound) chicken, all skin and visible fat removed (don't worry about the wings), cut into 8 pieces
- 1½ cups chopped onions
- 1 cup chopped green bell peppers
- 1 cup chopped celery
- 2 cups apple juice
- 1 teaspoon minced fresh garlic
- 3½ cups defatted chicken stock (page 8), *in all*
- 4 cups sliced fresh mushrooms
- 4 cups chopped fresh spinach

Day 1: Add enough water to the black-eyed peas to cover them by 3 or 4 inches, and soak overnight in the refrigerator. As the peas absorb the water, they will more than double in volume.

Day 2: Combine the seasoning mix ingredients in a small bowl.

Sprinkle all surfaces of the chicken evenly with *4 teaspoons* of the seasoning mix and rub it in well.

Preheat a heavy 5-quart pot, preferably nonstick, over high heat to 350°, about 4 minutes.

Drain the peas and set them aside.

Brown the seasoned chicken in the pot about 1½ to 2 minutes on each side; this may have to be done in two batches. Remove the chicken and set it aside. Place the onions, bell peppers, celery, and apple juice in the pot, and scrape the bottom to clear it of brown bits. Add the garlic, drained black-eyed peas, and *remaining* seasoning mix, and cook for 3 minutes. Stir in 2½ *cups* of the stock, cover and cook, stirring occasionally, for 1 hour and 20 minutes. Add the chicken and any juices that have accumulated, plus the *remaining* stock, and bring to a boil. Reduce the heat to medium, and cook, covered, until the peas are tender, and the liquid is thick and starts to look creamy, about 20 minutes. Add the mushrooms and spinach, stir, and simmer uncovered for 10 minutes.

Per serving: Calories 602   Protein 61g   Fat 14g
Carbohydrates 59g   21% calories from fat

Chicken with Mushrooms and Chickpeas

Makes 4 servings

> This dish is great served over rice or couscous, with a tomato salad and fresh green beans cooked tender-crisp. A friend, who tested this recipe with friends and family, used a Moroccan dressing on the tomatoes. Her verdict: "a meal fit for a sheikh!"

1½ cups dried chickpeas

Seasoning mix
 1 tablespoon dried sweet basil
    leaves
 2 teaspoons salt
 2 teaspoons sweet paprika
1½ teaspoons onion powder
1½ teaspoons garlic powder
 1 teaspoon dried thyme leaves
 ¾ teaspoon dry mustard
 ¾ teaspoon white pepper
 ½ teaspoon black pepper
 ½ teaspoon ground nutmeg
 ½ teaspoon cayenne

 ½ teaspoon ground coriander
 ¼ teaspoon ground cardamom

 1 (3- to 4-pound) chicken, all
    skin and visible fat removed
    (don't worry about the
    wings), cut into 8 pieces
 3 cups diced onions, *in all*
 5 cups sliced fresh mushrooms,
    in all
3½ cups defatted chicken stock
    (page 8), *in all*
 1 tablespoon minced fresh garlic

Day 1: Soak the chickpeas in 1½ cups of water, covered, in the refrigerator overnight. As the peas absorb the water, they will more than double in volume.

Day 2: Combine the seasoning mix ingredients in a small bowl.

Preheat a heavy 5-quart pot, preferably nonstick, over high heat to 350°, about 4 minutes.

Sprinkle all surfaces of the chicken with *2 tablespoons* of the seasoning mix and rub it in well. Place the large pieces of chicken in the pot and cook until they are brown on all sides, about 6 minutes. Remove the chicken and set it aside. Reduce the heat to medium and add the smaller pieces of chicken to the pot, placing them around the perimeter of the pot, leaving the center open. Add *1 cup* of the onions and all the chickpeas to the center of the pot, letting them start to cook while you brown the smaller pieces of chicken on both sides. When the smaller pieces are brown, remove them and set aside.

Return the heat to high and add *2 cups* of the mushrooms and *½ cup* stock, scrape the bottom clear, and cook 10 to 12 minutes. Add the *remaining* seasoning mix, onions, stock, and mushrooms, the garlic and the chicken, and cook until the chicken is completely done, about 20 minutes.

Per serving: Calories 834   Protein 66g   Fat 17g
Carbohydrates 102g   18% calories from fat

Citrus Tomato Chicken

Makes 4 servings

This dish has a very appealing tropical taste. It may take time to prepare the vegetables, but I'm sure you'll agree that the result is well worth the effort! This is definitely a dish to serve to your favorite family members and company.

Seasoning mix

1½ teaspoons garlic powder
1½ teaspoons sweet paprika
1½ teaspoons dry mustard
 1 teaspoon salt
 1 teaspoon onion powder
 1 teaspoon dried dillweed
 ½ teaspoon black pepper
 ½ teaspoon white pepper
 ½ teaspoon ground ginger
 ½ teaspoon dried sweet basil
   leaves
 ½ teaspoon ground cumin
 ¼ teaspoon ground cardamom
 ¼ teaspoon cayenne

Marinade

 2 tablespoons apple juice
 2 tablespoons orange juice
1½ tablespoons Seasoning mix
 1 tablespoon lemon juice

 1 tablespoon balsamic vinegar

 1 (3- to 4-pound) chicken, all
   skin and visible fat removed
   (don't worry about the
   wings), cut into 8 pieces
 2 cups apple juice
1½ cups chopped onions
 1 cup chopped green bell
   peppers
 ½ cup grated carrots
 1 teaspoon minced fresh garlic
 1 (8-ounce) can tomato sauce
 1 cup peeled, diced fresh
   tomatoes or 7 ounces
   canned diced tomatoes
 1 cup defatted chicken stock
   (page 8)
 4 cups cooked long-grain
   white rice

Combine the seasoning mix ingredients in a small bowl.

Blend the marinade ingredients. Place the chicken in a large bowl, pour the marinade over the chicken, cover, and refrigerate at least 4 hours, but preferably overnight.

Preheat the broiler. Remove the chicken from the marinade and reserve the marinade. Place the chicken in a baking pan and broil until brown on both sides, about 7 minutes in all. Remove the chicken and set aside.

While the chicken is broiling, place the apple juice in a saucepan, bring to a boil, reduce to 1 cup, and set aside.

Preheat a heavy 5-quart pot, preferably nonstick, over high heat to 350°, about 4 minutes.

Add the onions, bell peppers, carrots, and *1 tablespoon* of the seasoning mix, cover, and cook 3 minutes. At this point, the vegetables will start to stick and turn light brown.

Add the garlic, mix in well, and scrape the bottom of the pot to clear it of all brown bits. Re-cover and cook 3 more minutes. Add the reduced apple juice and *remaining* seasoning mix, and scrape the bottom clear. By now the mixture will have turned medium brown. Cook 4 minutes. Stir in the tomato sauce, diced tomatoes, stock, and reserved marinade. Add the chicken to the pot, bring to a boil, reduce the heat to medium, and cook until the meat is tender, about 20 minutes. Serve over the rice.

Per serving: Calories 661   Protein 77g   Fat 13g
Carbohydrates 83g   17% calories from fat

Chicken Carter

Makes 4 servings

This very flavorful and satisfying dish is not nearly as hot and spicy as some of my other recipes, so you can serve it to those who prefer things a little on the mild side.

Seasoning mix

- 1 teaspoon salt
- 1 teaspoon sweet paprika
- ½ teaspoon onion powder
- ½ teaspoon dry mustard
- ½ teaspoon ground sage
- ½ teaspoon ground cumin
- ½ teaspoon dried marjoram leaves
- ¼ teaspoon garlic powder
- ¼ teaspoon black pepper
- ¼ teaspoon white pepper
- ¼ teaspoon ground allspice

- 1 (3-pound) chicken, all skin and visible fat removed (don't worry about the wings), cut into 8 pieces
- 2 cups defatted chicken stock (page 8), *in all*
- 1 cup chopped onions, *in all*
- ½ cup chopped celery
- ½ teaspoon minced fresh garlic
- 2 tablespoons all-purpose flour, browned (page 7)
- 2 cups chopped fresh tomatoes
- 1½ cups sliced fresh mushrooms
- 3 cups cooked long-grain white rice

Combine the seasoning mix ingredients in a small bowl.

Sprinkle all surfaces of the chicken evenly with *4 teaspoons* of the seasoning mix and rub it in well.

Preheat a heavy 5-quart pot, preferably nonstick, over high heat to 350°, about 4 minutes.

Place the chicken in the pot and cook, turning once, just until it starts to turn a golden brown, about 5 minutes. Remove the chicken and set it aside.

Add ½ *cup* of the stock to the pot and scrape the bottom and sides of the pot to clear it of all brown bits. Add ½ *cup* of the onions, the celery, garlic, and the *remaining* seasoning mix. Cook about 8 minutes, stirring occasionally, until the liquid evaporates and the vegetables begin to stick to the pot.

Add ½ cup stock and return to a full boil, about 2 minutes. Add the browned flour, and stir until it is completely absorbed, no more of the brown flour is visible, and a paste forms. Cook 2 minutes, scraping once, then stir in ½ cup stock and clear the bottom of the pot. At this point, the vegetables should be a rich red-brown. Stir in the tomatoes, the *remaining* onions, the mushrooms, and the *remaining* stock. Return the chicken to the pot, cover, bring to a boil, and cook about 4 minutes. Reduce the heat to low and simmer until the chicken and vegetables are tender, about 15 minutes. Serve over the rice.

Per serving: Calories 384   Protein 28g   Fat 5g
Carbohydrates 54g   11% calories from fat

Chicken Jean Marie

Makes 4 servings

I have to be honest with you. You can't whip up this dish in 30 minutes after you get home from the office. But if you appreciate old-fashioned, down-home taste, you'll look forward to making it when you have some time. Two people can make it together: one to wash and chop the greens while the other takes care of the onions, peppers, and garlic. If you're doing it by yourself, that's OK too. Just put on some good music and pretend you picked the greens from your own garden.

Seasoning mix

2½ teaspoons sweet paprika
1½ teaspoons salt
1½ teaspoons onion powder
1½ teaspoons garlic powder
1½ teaspoons dried tarragon
leaves
½ teaspoon black pepper
½ teaspoon dry mustard
¾ teaspoon white pepper
½ teaspoon dried sweet basil
leaves
¼ teaspoon ground sage

1 (3- to 4-pound chicken, all
skin and visible fat removed
(don't worry about the
wings), cut into 8 pieces
2½ cups chopped onions, *in all*
1 cup chopped green bell
peppers
3 tablespoons all-purpose
flour, browned (page 7)
2½ cups defatted chicken stock
(page 8), *in all*
4 cups chopped fresh greens,
in all (see Note)
1 tablespoon minced fresh
garlic

Preheat a heavy 5-quart pot, preferably nonstick, over high heat to 350°, about 4 minutes.

Combine the seasoning mix ingredients in a small bowl. Sprinkle all surfaces of the chicken with *4 teaspoons* of the seasoning mix and rub it in well.

Place the large pieces of chicken in the pot and cook them, turning once, just until brown, about 6 minutes. Remove the browned chicken and set it aside. Reduce the heat to medium and add the smaller pieces of chicken to the pot, placing them around the outer rim of the pot, leaving the center open. Add *1½ cups* of the onions and the bell peppers to the center of the pot, to start them cooking while you brown the smaller pieces of chicken on both sides. When the smaller pieces are brown, remove and set them aside.

Add *½ cup* of the stock to the pot and scrape the bottom thoroughly to remove all brown bits. Add the browned flour and the *remaining* seasoning mix, and cook 2 minutes, scraping the bottom clear occasionally. This mixture will look slightly pasty and be a rich, reddish-brown color. Add the *remaining* onions, *2 cups* of the greens, and the garlic, and cook 2 minutes. Stir in the *remaining 2 cups* of the stock and cook 3 minutes. Return the chicken and any accumulated juices to the pot, turn the heat to high, and bring to a boil. Reduce the heat to a simmer and cook until the chicken is tender, about 20 minutes. Stir in the *remaining* greens.

Serve this chicken with rice that has cooked in chicken stock, and a big plate of sliced fresh tomatoes.

Note Use any combination of three kinds of greens except bitter ones like iceberg lettuce, radicchio, or poke salad greens. We often combine spinach, collards, and mustard greens, but use what is fresh and available and enjoy!

Per serving: Calories 287   Protein 50g   Fat 15g
Carbohydrates 18g   29% calories from fat

Lemon Dill Chicken

Makes 4 servings

This is an elegant dish with a combination of unusual and wonderful flavors. Not only does it taste marvelous, but it makes a very attractive main dish you'll be really proud to serve.

Seasoning mix

1 teaspoon salt

1 teaspoon dillweed

1 teaspoon dried sweet basil
   leaves

¼ teaspoon black pepper

¼ teaspoon white pepper

8 (2 to 3 ounces each) boneless,
   skinless chicken breasts

1 tablespoon plus 2 teaspoons
   cornstarch

1 cup apple juice, *in all*

1½ cups defatted chicken stock
   (page 8), *in all*

2 cups julienned onions

½ cup fresh lemon juice, *in all*

2 (1-gram) packets artificial
   sweetener (page 4), optional

Combine the seasoning mix ingredients in a small bowl.

Sprinkle all surfaces of the chicken evenly with *2 teaspoons* of the seasoning mix and rub it in well.

Dissolve the cornstarch in ¼ *cup* of apple juice and set aside.

Preheat a heavy 10-inch skillet, preferably nonstick, over high heat to 350°, about 4 minutes.

Place 4 of the chicken breasts in the skillet, lower the heat to medium, and brown them for at least 1 minute per side. Remove these 4 breasts, brown the other 4, and set all the chicken aside.

Return to heat to high and stir in ½ *cup* of the stock, scraping the bottom of the skillet to clear it of all the browned bits. Add the onions and the *remaining* seasoning mix, stir and cook until all the liquid evaporates, about 3 to 4 minutes. Stir in ¼ *cup* of the lemon juice, scrape the bottom of the skillet again to clear it, and cook until liquid evaporates, about 3 to 4 minutes.

Add ½ *cup* of the apple juice, clear the bottom and sides of the skillet, and cook until about half the liquid evaporates, about 2 to 3 minutes. Stir in the *remaining 1 cup* of stock, the ¼ *cup* lemon juice, and the ¼ *cup* apple juice. Bring to a boil (will take 2 to 3 minutes), whisk in the cornstarch/apple juice mixture, and return to a boil. Return the chicken to the skillet, lower the heat to medium, and cook until the chicken is done all the way through, about 4 to 5 miuntes. Turn off the heat, remove the chicken, and, if desired, whisk in the artificial sweetener.

Per serving: Calories 274   Protein 38g   Fat 5g
Carbohydrates 19g   16% calories from fat

Slow-Roasted Hen

Serves 6

Most of us grew up feasting on baked or roasted chicken; it's a staple of traditional cooking in the United States. Our version is seasoned in a very untraditional way, but it's likely to become a family favorite.

Seasoning mix
- 2 teaspoons salt
- 2 teaspoons sweet paprika
- 1½ teaspoons onion powder
- 1 teaspoon garlic powder
- 1 teaspoon dried thyme leaves
- 1 teaspoon ground sage
- 1 teaspoon dried savory leaves
- ½ teaspoon dry mustard
- ½ teaspoon black pepper
- ½ teaspoon white pepper
- ¼ teaspoon cayenne

- 1 (6- to 8-pound) roasting hen
- 3 tablespoons thinly sliced fresh ginger
- ½ medium onion, peeled and quartered
- 1 celery rib, cut in half crosswise
- ½ green bell pepper, cored, seeded, and cut into 2-inch strips
- 2 carrots, peeled and sliced in half lengthwise

Combine the seasoning mix ingredients in a small bowl.

Remove, but do not discard, the large, fatty deposits found inside the breast and tail cavities of the hen.

Place a 10-inch skillet over high heat and render the chicken fat until only about 1 tablespoon remains. Add the ginger and ¼ *teaspoon* of the seasoning mix, and sauté until the ginger just begins to turn brown and soft, about 2 to 3 minutes. Remove from the heat, drain, remove any fat that may still remain, and set aside to cool.

Preheat the oven to 225°.

Work your fingers between the breast meat and the skin to form pockets, and place the cooled sautéed ginger evenly inside these pockets. Sprinkle *1 tablespoon* seasoning mix evenly inside the breast cavity, then place all the vegetables inside the cavity. Position the carrots last because they're the easiest to put in.

Sprinkle the *remaining* seasoning mix evenly over the outside of the hen. Place the hen into a large roasting pan and roast uncovered until tender and golden brown, about 4 to 4½ hours. To test for doneness, after about 4 hours, remove the hen from the oven and run a skewer into the thickest part of the thigh along the bone. Remove the skewer and press down on the hole. If the liquid runs clear, the hen is done. If not, place the hen back into the oven and continue checking for doneness until the liquid runs clear.

Per serving: Calories 285   Protein 43g   Fat 7g
Carbohydrates 9g   23% calories from fat

Slow-Roasted Turkey

Serves 10 to 12

The aroma of roasting turkey is one of the most pleasant memories of many of us who grew up in this country. Both large and small families would pull out all the stops and present a beautiful bird for holiday meals. This version, with garlic placed between the skin and the meat, is a little different from traditional recipes.

Seasoning mix

- 2 teaspoons salt
- 2 teaspoons sweet paprika
- 2 teaspoons onion powder
- 1¾ teaspoons garlic powder
- 1 teaspoon dry mustard
- 1 teaspoon dried sweet basil leaves
- 1 teaspoon dried thyme leaves
- ¾ teaspoon white pepper
- ½ teaspoon black pepper
- ½ teaspoon cayenne

- 1 (10- to 12-pound) turkey
- 36 garlic cloves, peeled and cut in half
- 1 medium onion, peeled, quartered, and separated
- 2 celery ribs, cut in half crosswise
- ½ large green bell pepper, cored, seeded, and cut into 2-inch strips
- 2 large carrots, peeled and cut in half lengthwise

Combine the seasoning mix ingredients in a small bowl.

Remove, but do not discard, the large, fatty deposits found inside the flaps by the breast and tail cavities of the turkey.

Place a 10-inch skillet over high heat and render the turkey fat. Discard all but 1 tablespoon and return this to the skillet. Add the garlic and ½ *teaspoon* of the seasoning mix, and sauté until the garlic just begins to turn brown and soft, about 2 to 3 minutes. Remove from the heat and drain. Blot with paper towels to remove any fat that may still remain, and set aside to cool.

Preheat the oven to 225°.

Work your fingers between the breast meat and the skin to form pockets, and place the cooled sautéed garlic evenly inside these pockets. Sprinkle 2 *tablespoons* of the seasoning mix inside the breast cavity, then place the vegetables inside the cavity. Position the carrots last because they're the easiest to put in.

Sprinkle the *remaining* seasoning mix evenly over the outside of the turkey. Place the turkey in a large roasting pan and roast uncovered until tender and golden brown, about 6 to 6½ hours. To test for doneness, after about 6 hours, remove the turkey from the oven and run a skewer into the thickest part of the thigh along the bone. Remove the skewer and press down on the hole. If the liquid runs clear, the turkey is done. If not, place the turkey back into the oven, and continue to check periodically until the liquid runs clear.

Per serving: Calories 302   Protein 76g   Fat 10g
Carbohydrates 15g   15% calories from fat

Stuffed Turkey Roast

Makes 8 servings

When we were working on this recipe, everyone who tasted it raved about how tender and delicious it is. It's also incredibly easy to prepare, and it makes a very nice presentation.

Seasoning mix

- 2 teaspoons sweet paprika
- 1 teaspoon salt
- 1 teaspoon dried sweet basil leaves
- 1 teaspoon dried summer savory
- ¾ teaspoon garlic powder
- ½ teaspoon onion powder
- ½ teaspoon black pepper
- ¼ teaspoon white pepper

- 1 (2-pound) turkey roast, all skin, visible fat, and the pop-up timer (if your roast has one) removed
- 1 cup chopped onions
- ½ cup chopped green bell peppers
- ½ cup chopped celery
- 1 cup apple juice
- 1½ cups defatted chicken stock (page 8), *in all*
- ¼ cup nonfat mayonnaise

Combine the seasoning mix ingredients in a small bowl.

In the top of the roast, cut 8 to 10 slits, 1 inch wide and about ¾ of the way through. Sprinkle all the surfaces of the roast with *1 tablespoon* of the seasoning mix and rub it in well. Preheat the oven to 225°.

Preheat a 12-inch skillet, preferably nonstick, over high heat to 350°, about 4 minutes.

Add the onions, bell peppers, celery, and the *remaining* seasoning mix. Cook, scraping the bottom of the skillet occasionally, until the vegetables start to brown, about 5 to 6 minutes. Add the apple juice and cook until most of the liquid evaporates, about 10 minutes. Transfer the ingredients from the skillet to a blender or food processor and purée until smooth, remove the puréed mixture to a plate, and cool about 2 to 3 minutes.

Put *1 tablespoon* of the puréed mixture into each of the slits in the roast. Spread *1 tablespoon* of the mixture evenly on top of the roast, and place the *remaining* mixture in the center of a 9 × 12-inch roasting pan. Place the roast directly on top of the purée, and roast for 1 hour. Add *1 cup* of the stock to the pan and roast until tender and golden brown, about 30 minutes more.

To make a rich-tasting, healthful gravy, remove the roast to a platter and add the *remaining* stock to the pan. Place the pan over high heat and scrape the bottom to clear it of all brown bits. Bring to a boil and transfer 1 cup of the liquid to a blender. Add the mayonnaise and blend completely. Turn off the heat and whisk the blended mixture into the liquid in the pan. To serve, carve the roast and drizzle some of the gravy over each portion. Pass the rest of the gravy—it's great with potatoes, rice, or biscuits.

Per serving: Calories 221   Protein 35g   Fat 4g
Carbohydrates 8g   18% calories from fat

Stuffed Turkey Chops

Makes 4 servings

Here's an imaginative way to serve food that has the look and taste of the eighties, but reflects the health and nutrition concerns of the nineties. The preparation method and seasonings turn plain turkey into an exciting new dish that's wonderful to look at and even better to eat.

Seasoning mix

2 teaspoons salt

2 teaspoons sweet paprika

1 teaspoon onion powder

1 teaspoon garlic powder

1 teaspoon dry mustard

1 teaspoon black pepper

1 teaspoon dried sweet basil
  leaves

1 teaspoon ground sage

½ teaspoon white pepper

½ teaspoon dried thyme leaves

¼ teaspoon cayenne

1 pound turkey roast (see
  Note)

8 ounces medium peeled
  shrimp

2 cups chopped onions

1½ cups chopped green bell
  peppers

¾ cup chopped celery

1½ cups defatted seafood stock
  (page 8), *in all*

1¼ cups apple juice, *in all*

¼ cup toasted unseasoned
  bread crumbs

Combine the seasoning mix ingredients in a small bowl.

Lay the turkey roast on a flat surface and slice it evenly into four 4-ounce chops, each about 1½ inches thick. Place a chop on its edge and, using a small paring knife, cut a slit about 1½ inches long into its side. Then carefully work the blade through the chop to form a pocket, without cutting all the way through. Repeat the process with the remaining chops. Sprinkle the outside surfaces of the chops with *a total of 1 tablespoon* seasoning mix and set them aside.

Select 8 of the most uniform shrimp, sprinkle them evenly with *1 teaspoon* of the seasoning mix, and set them aside. Dice the *remaining* shrimp into small pieces.

Preheat the oven to 250°.

Preheat a 12-inch skillet, preferably nonstick, over high heat to 350°, about 4 minutes.

Add the onions, bell peppers, and celery, and cook, stirring occasionally, just until the vegetables start to brown, about 5 to 6 minutes. Remove *2 cups* of the cooked vegetables from the skillet and set them aside. To the vegetables in the skillet add the *remaining* seasoning mix, ½ *cup* of the stock, and ½ *cup* of the apple juice. Scrape the bottom of the skillet to clear it of all the brown bits and cook until the liquid has almost completely evaporated, about 10 minutes. Add the diced shrimp and ¼ cup apple juice, and cook just until the shrimp are plump and firm, about 2 to 3 minutes. Turn off the heat and add the bread crumbs. Mix well and set aside to cool slightly.

Spread the reserved *2 cups* vegetables in a 10-inch round pan. Fill each chop with ¼ of the vegetable/shrimp mixture, and place the stuffed chops, slit side up, in the pan on the vegetables. Place 2 seasoned shrimp on each chop. Add the *remaining 1 cup* stock and ½ *cup* apple juice to the pan, cover loosely with foil, and bake for 1 hour, or until the chops are done.

Note Turkey roast is a turkey breast especially cut and packaged for roasting. Very likely you will find it in the refrigerated poultry section of your market; if not ask your butcher.

Per serving: Calories 353   Protein 48g   Fat 7g
Carbohydrates 22g   18% calories from fat

Spicy Turkey Loaf

Makes 10 to 12 servings

I give you fair warning: This is not some mild, flavorless little meat loaf. In fact, you might want to cut down on the amount of peppers. Mashed or baked potatoes go very well with this and are a good foil for the spiciness of the turkey.

Seasoning mix
- 1 tablespoon salt
- 1 tablespoon sweet paprika
- 1½ teaspoons dried sweet basil
- 1 teaspoon onion powder
- 1 teaspoon dry mustard
- 1 teaspoon ground cumin
- ¾ teaspoon garlic powder
- ¾ teaspoon black pepper
- ½ teaspoon white pepper
- ¼ teaspoon cayenne
- ¼ teaspoon ground allspice

- 1½ cups chopped onions
- ¾ cup chopped green bell peppers
- ½ cup chopped celery
- 1 tablespoon minced fresh garlic
- 2 tablespoons balsamic vinegar
- 2 tablespoons Worcestershire sauce
- 1½ cups evaporated skim milk
- 1¼ cups unseasoned bread crumbs
- 4 ounces egg substitute
- 1¾ pounds freshly ground turkey

Combine seasoning mix ingredients in a small bowl.

Preheat a heavy 10-inch skillet, preferably nonstick, over high heat to 350°, about 4 minutes.

Add the onions, bell peppers, celery, and *3 tablespoons* of the seasoning mix. Cook just until the vegetables start to soften, about 2 to 3 minutes. Add the garlic, vinegar, and Worcestershire sauce, and cook, stirring two or three times to keep the vegetables from sticking too hard, until all the liquid evaporates, about 5 minutes. Stir in the evaporated milk and continue to cook until the liquid comes to a full boil. Turn off the heat and let the mixture cool to room temperature.

Preheat the oven to 300°.

When the vegetables and liquid reach room temperature, place them in a large bowl, add the *remaining* seasoning mix and combine thoroughly. Stir in the bread crumbs and eggs. Add the ground turkey and gently stir just until combined—do not overmix. Press the mixture into a 12 × 9 × 3-inch loaf pan and bake until done, about 40 to 45 minutes.

Per serving: Calories 198   Protein 29g   Fat 3g
Carbohydrates 12g   15% calories from fat

Turkey Boiled Dinner

Makes 4 servings

✕ I think you'll enjoy this healthful new twist on a favorite old standard—it looks beautiful on the plate, tastes wonderful, and is easy to make.

Seasoning mix I

1 tablespoon garlic powder

2 teaspoons salt

1 teaspoon onion powder

1 teaspoon white pepper

¼ teaspoon ground nutmeg

▬

2 (1 pound each) turkey breasts, all skin, bones, and visible fat removed

Seasoning mix II

24 black peppercorns

12 allspice berries

9 whole cloves

6 cardamom seeds

4 bay leaves

1 tablespoon black mustard seeds

1 tablespoon yellow mustard seeds

1 teaspoon dillweed

▬

8 cups defatted chicken stock (page 8)

1 large potato, peeled and cut into 8 wedges

1 large turnip, peeled and cut into 8 wedges

3 large carrots, peeled and cut into 1-inch diagonal slices

1 large onion, peeled and cut into 8 wedges

2 cups bok choy, cut into 1-inch diagonal slices

Day 1: Combine the ingredients for seasoning mix I in a small bowl and sprinkle it evenly over the turkey breasts. Refrigerate overnight in a covered bowl.

Day 2: Combine the ingredients for seasoning mix II in a heavy 5-quart pot. Stir in the stock, turn the heat to high, and bring the mixture to a boil. Put in the turkey breasts and cook for 10 minutes. Add the potato, turnip, and carrots, and cook for 5 minutes. Add the onion and bok choy, and cook until the turkey is done, about 15 minutes more. Cut the turkey into serving pieces, and serve the portions with some of each vegetable.

Per serving: Calories 520   Protein 76g   Fat 10g
Carbohydrates 28g   18% calories from fat

Steam-Stirred Turkey

Makes 4 to 6 servings

This is an exciting dish because it's easy to make, pretty to look at, and so delicious to eat. Just maybe this is a whole new way to cook! The color and flavor of spinach are marvelous in this dish. Great tossed with pasta and terrific over rice.

Seasoning mix

- 1 tablespoon sweet paprika
- 2 teaspoons salt
- 2 teaspoons ground ginger
- 1 teaspoon garlic powder
- 1 teaspoon dried summer savory
- 1 teaspoon ground sage
- ½ teaspoon onion powder
- ½ teaspoon dry mustard
- ½ teaspoon black pepper
- ½ teaspoon cayenne
- ¼ teaspoon ground nutmeg

- 1 pound julienned turkey breast
- 2½ cups defatted chicken stock (page 8), *in all*
- 2 tablespoons cornstarch
- 2 tablespoons poppy seeds
- 3 tablespoons sesame seeds
- 1 cup julienned red bell peppers
- 1 cup julienned yellow bell peppers
- 1 cup julienned green bell peppers
- 1 cup diagonally sliced bok choy stalks
- ¾ cup diagonally sliced celery
- 2 cups sliced fresh mushrooms
- 2 cups chopped fresh spinach
- 1½ cups julienned onion
- 5 tablespoons tamari (see **Note**)
- 1 tablespoon minced fresh ginger
- 1 to 3 (1-gram) packets artificial sweetener (page 4), optional

Combine the seasoning mix ingredients in a small bowl.

Sprinkle all surfaces of the turkey with *1 tablespoon* of the seasoning mix, rub it in well, and set the seasoned turkey aside.

Dissolve the cornstarch in *4 tablespoons* of the stock, and set aside.

Preheat a 12-inch skillet, preferably nonstick, over high heat to 450°, about 4 minutes.

Add the poppy and sesame seeds, and when they start to pop and jump around in the pan, add the vegetables. Cover and cook 3 minutes. If you don't have a 12-inch lid, use aluminum foil, another skillet the same size turned upside down, or even a pizza pan! Add the tamari, the *remaining* seasoning mix, and the fresh ginger, cover, and cook 2 more minutes. Stir in the stock/cornstarch mixture and the *remaining* stock, and bring to a boil. Add the turkey, cover, and cook until the turkey is tender, about 5 to 6 minutes. Turn off the heat and, if desired, add up to 3 packets of artificial sweetener.

Note Tamari is a very rich, flavorful soy sauce, available in specialty markets and the international or ethnic food sections of many supermarkets. If you cannot find it where you shop, use any good quality soy sauce.

Per serving: Calories 367   Protein 43g   Fat 10g
Carbohydrates 25g   25% calories from fat

Hot and Sweet Turkey

This wonderful dish has just a hint of the exotic, which may make you think of faraway places. But it couldn't be easier to prepare, so you can enjoy it at home anytime.

Seasoning mix

2 teaspoons salt

1½ teaspoons dry mustard

1 teaspoon sweet paprika

1 teaspoon onion powder

¾ teaspoon garlic powder

½ teaspoon black pepper

½ teaspoon white pepper

½ teaspoon ground ginger

¼ teaspoon cayenne

¼ teaspoon ground nutmeg

¼ teaspoon ground coriander

---

1 pound turkey breast, cut into 2 × ¼-inch julienne strips

3 tablespoons cornstarch

2½ cups defatted chicken stock (page 8)

¼ cup thinly sliced fresh ginger

1 small onion, peeled and cut into julienne strips

¾ cup carrots, peeled and sliced diagonally ¼ inch thick

¾ cup julienned red bell peppers

¾ cup julienned yellow bell peppers

¾ cup julienned green bell peppers

2 teaspoons thinly sliced fresh garlic

¼ cup tamari (see **Note**)

¼ cup balsamic vinegar

1 (8-ounce) can tomato sauce

6 (1-gram) packets artificial sweetener (page 4), optional

4 cups cooked long-grain white rice

Combine the seasoning mix ingredients in a small bowl.

Sprinkle all surfaces of the turkey evenly with *1 tablespoon* of the seasoning mix and rub it in well.

Dissolve the cornstarch in *4 tablespoons* of the stock, set aside.

Preheat a heavy 12-inch skillet, preferably nonstick, over high heat to 350°, about 4 minutes.

Add the turkey, stir, and cook until it starts to brown, about 2 minutes. Add the fresh ginger and onions, stir and cook for 2 minutes. Add the *remaining* vegetables and seasoning mix, and cook for 3 minutes. Stir in the tamari and vinegar, and cook for 2 minutes. Stir in the tomato sauce and *remaining* stock, bring to a boil, and cook 2 minutes. Add the cornstarch mixture, cook for 2 minutes, remove from the heat, and, if desired, add artificial sweetener. Serve over the rice.

Note Tamari is a very flavorful kind of soy sauce, available in specialty markets and the international or ethnic food sections of many supermarkets. If you cannot find it where you shop, substitute the best soy sauce available.

Per serving: Calories 530   Protein 44g   Fat 5g
Carbohydrates 76g   8% calories from fat

New Turkey Etouffée

Makes 4 servings

Crawfish etouffée, or smothered crawfish, is famous throughout south Louisiana, and with good reason—it's incredibly good. There's a recipe for it in the Fish and Seafood section of this book. Since you can't always find crawfish, we've come up with this turkey alternative. Try it—you'll like it!

Seasoning mix

2 teaspoons salt

2 teaspoons sweet paprika

1 teaspoon garlic powder

1 teaspoon dry mustard

¾ teaspoon onion powder

¾ teaspoon black pepper

½ teaspoon white pepper

¼ teaspoon cayenne

1 pound large-diced turkey breast

½ cup finely diced red bell peppers

½ cup finely diced yellow bell peppers

½ cup finely diced green bell peppers

1 cup finely diced onions

¾ cup finely diced celery

1 teaspoon minced fresh garlic

3 cups defatted chicken stock (page 8), *in all*

7 tablespoons all-purpose flour, browned (page 7)

3 cups cooked long-grain white rice

Combine the seasoning mix ingredients in a small bowl.

Sprinkle all surfaces of the diced turkey evenly with *1 tablespoon plus 2 teaspoons* of the seasoning mix and set aside.

Preheat a heavy 5-quart pot, preferably nonstick, over high heat to 350°, about 4 minutes.

Add the bell peppers, onions, celery, garlic, and *remaining* seasoning mix to the pot, and cook just until the vegetables soften and start to brown, about 2 minutes. Push the vegetables to one side of the pot and add the seasoned turkey to the other. Cook, turning once, until the turkey starts to brown, about 2 minutes. Stir the ingredients together and cook 2 more minutes. Stir in ½ *cup* of the stock and scrape the bottom of the pot to clear it of any brown bits. Cook 1 minute, add the browned flour, and mix thoroughly until the flour is completely absorbed, the browned flour is no longer visible, and a paste forms. Stir in the *remaining* stock and cook until the turkey is tender, and the sauce is a rich brown color and creamy-textured, about 8 to 10 minutes. Serve over the rice.

Per serving: Calories 454   Protein 67g   Fat 5g
Carbohydrates 56g   10% calories from fat

Tchoupitoulas Hash

Makes 4 servings

This delicious dish is hearty enough to make a complete meal, with a simple salad or a side vegetable. Or play with it. For instance, put eggs on top for a great breakfast. Chill it, add nonfat mayonnaise, and you have a fabulous salad. At room temperature, toss with chopped greens and add a little mustard—wonderful! Let your imagination ride a mustang!

Seasoning mix

1 tablespoon sweet paprika
2 teaspoons salt
1½ teaspoons dried thyme leaves
1 teaspoon garlic powder
1 teaspoon dried sweet basil leaves
½ teaspoon onion powder
½ teaspoon black pepper
½ teaspoon dried rosemary leaves
¼ teaspoon white pepper
¼ teaspoon cayenne

1 pound turkey breast, medium diced
4 cups (about 2 medium to large) medium-diced potatoes
2 cups chopped onions, *in all*
1½ cups defatted chicken stock (page 8), *in all*
4 ounces turkey tasso (see **Note**), finely diced
3 cups chopped fresh mushrooms

Combine the seasoning mix ingredients in a small bowl.

Place the diced turkey in a 9 × 13-inch baking pan. Sprinkle all surfaces of the turkey evenly with *1 tablespoon plus 1½ teaspoons* of the seasoning mix, rub it in well, and set aside.

Preheat a heavy 5-quart pot, preferably nonstick, over high heat to 350°, about 4 minutes.

Add the potatoes, *1 cup* of the onions, ½ *cup* of the stock, and the *remaining* seasoning mix. Cook, scraping occasionally, until browned and sticking hard, about 10 minutes.

Preheat the oven to 450°.

Add the *remaining* onions, the tasso, and the mushrooms to the pot. Stir and cook until the mixture sticks again, about 5 minutes. Stir in the *remaining 1 cup* of stock, and pour over the turkey in the baking pan. Stir to distribute the ingredients evenly and bake for 50 minutes.

Note If you cannot find turkey tasso, you can substitute smoked turkey thighs or wings.

Per serving: Calories 337   Protein 43g   Fat 6g
Carbohydrates 23g   17% calories from fat

color photograph 31

Turkey Rex

Makes 8 cups, enough for 4 generous servings

This dish is festive enough for a special occasion (Rex is the New Orleans King of Carnival), but easy enough to serve often! Our version of an old favorite is so smooth and creamy, and the flavor is so traditional, that no one is going to believe it's a reduced-fat dish.

Seasoning mix

2 teaspoons salt
2 teaspoons onion powder
1 teaspoon sweet paprika
1 teaspoon garlic powder
1 teaspoon dry mustard
½ teaspoon white pepper
¼ teaspoon ground nutmeg
⅛ teaspoon cayenne

---

1 pound turkey breast, diced into ¾-inch cubes
1 cup chopped onions

¾ cup chopped red bell peppers
¾ cup chopped yellow bell peppers
¾ cup chopped green bell peppers
3 cups sliced fresh mushrooms
2½ cups defatted chicken stock (page 8), *in all*
10 tablespoons nonfat dry milk
3 tablespoons all-purpose flour
½ cup nonfat cream cheese
6 cups cooked long-grain white rice

Combine the seasoning mix ingredients in a small bowl.

Preheat a heavy 5-quart pot, preferably nonstick, over high heat to 350°, about 4 minutes.

Sprinkle all surfaces of the diced turkey evenly with *1 tablespoon* of the seasoning mix and rub it in well. Spread the seasoned turkey cubes evenly over the bottom of the pot and cook, turning as necessary, until they are brown on all sides, about 3 to 5 minutes. Add the onions, peppers, mushrooms, and the *remaining* seasoning mix. Cook, stirring occasionally, for 4 minutes.

While the mixture is cooking, place *1 cup* of the stock, the dry milk, and the flour in a blender, and process until smooth and creamy. Transfer this mixture to the pot and add the *remaining* stock. Cook just until it comes to a gentle boil, about 3 minutes. Lower the heat and simmer 4 to 6 minutes. Turn off the heat. Remove 1 cup of the liquid from the pot and place it in the blender, add the cream cheese, and blend. Stir this mixture back into the pot and serve immediately over the rice.

Per serving: Calories 647   Protein 47g   Fat 5g
Carbohydrates 99g   7% calories from fat

Turkey Cutlets in Onion Custard

Makes 8 servings

The custard in the recipe title refers to the creamy, rich-tasting sauce. It's kind of an old-fashioned name, but we've given the recipe a contemporary twist with low-fat ingredients and revved-up seasonings.

½ cup dried chickpeas

Seasoning mix

2½ teaspoons salt
2 teaspoons sweet paprika
2 teaspoons dried sweet basil
   leaves
1 teaspoon onion powder
1 teaspoon garlic powder
½ teaspoon dry mustard
½ teaspoon black pepper
½ teaspoon white pepper
½ teaspoon ground allspice
½ teaspoon ground cayenne
¼ teaspoon ground cardamom
¼ teaspoon ground nutmeg

8 (3-ounce) skinless turkey
   breast cutlets, pounded thin

Creamy mixture

1 cup evaporated skim milk
1 cup fresh skim milk
4 ounces nonfat cream cheese
4 tablespoons nonfat dry milk

1½ cups defatted chicken stock
   (page 8), *in all*
1½ cups apple juice, *in all*
1½ cups sliced onions, separated
   into rings
1 medium onion, peeled and
   thinly sliced

Day 1: Add enough water to the chickpeas to cover them by 3 or 4 inches, and soak overnight in the refrigerator. As the peas absorb the water, they will more than double in volume.

Day 2: Combine the seasoning mix ingredients in a small bowl.

Sprinkle all surfaces of the cutlets evenly with *4 teaspoons* of the seasoning mixture and set aside.

Drain the chickpeas and place them in a blender. Add the canned and fresh skim milks a little at a time, and process until the peas are completely puréed. Add the remaining creamy mixture ingredients and process until smooth and creamy. Set aside.

Preheat a heavy 12-inch skillet, preferably nonstick, over high heat to 350°, about 4½ minutes.

Place the seasoned turkey, 3 or 4 cutlets at a time, in the skillet and sear them quickly, about 30 seconds on each side. Watch the cutlets closely as they cook and be careful not to burn them. After the first batch is done, reduce the heat to medium. As the cutlets are browned, remove them from the skillet and set aside.

Add *1 cup* of the stock, *½ cup* of the apple juice, the onion rings, and the *remaining* seasoning mix to the skillet, and scrape the bottom to clear it of all the brown bits. Cook until the liquid evaporates, about 15 minutes.

Turn off the heat, and add *½ cup* apple juice and *1 cup* of the creamy mixture. Transfer to a blender and purée. Return to the skillet, and add the *remaining ½ cup* stock and *½ cup* apple juice. Bring to a boil, add the thinly sliced onion, and cook until the onion starts to brown and the apple juice evaporates, about 10 minutes. Whisk in the *remaining* creamy mixture. **Caution:** Dishes using creamy mixtures can "break" or curdle easily if they are brought to a full boil. Therefore, bring the liquid just to a bubble, and stir immediately. Reduce the heat to low and add the cutlets. Simmer (be careful not to boil the liquid) until the meat is done, about 8 to 10 minutes. Allow 1 cutlet and ½ cup sauce per serving.

Per serving: Calories 305   Protein 35g   Fat 4g
Carbohydrates 29g   13% calories from fat

Bobby's Curry

Makes 9 cups, enough for 4 to 5 servings

Don't let the unusual ingredients scare you away from this wonderful dish! Chickpeas, also known as garbanzos, are readily available in most supermarkets. The mirliton, a pear-shaped member of the squash family, is grown in many New Orleans home gardens. Mirlitons are also known as chayotes in other parts of the country. If mirlitons or chayotes are unavailable just omit them. Condiments that go well with curry are plump raisins, flaked coconut, sunflower seeds, very thinly sliced green onions, or chutney.

1 cup dried chickpeas

Seasoning mix
- 2 tablespoons curry powder (see **Note**)
- 3 teaspoons salt
- 2 teaspoons turmeric
- 1½ teaspoons dried sweet basil leaves
- 1 teaspoon garlic powder
- 1 teaspoon onion powder
- 1 teaspoon dry mustard
- 1 teaspoon black pepper
- 1 teaspoon white pepper
- 1 teaspoon ground cinnamon
- 1 teaspoon ground cumin
- ½ teaspoon ground cardamom
- ½ teaspoon ground nutmeg
- ½ teaspoon ground coriander
- ½ teaspoon cayenne, optional
- ¼ teaspoon ground allspice

1 pound medium-diced turkey breast

3 cups chopped onions

1 medium mirliton, halved, parboiled until tender, seeded, peeled, and finely diced

2 cups chopped very ripe bananas (approximately 2 large)

3½ cups defatted chicken stock (page 8), *in all*

1 cup apple juice

3 cups sliced fresh mushrooms

1 (12-ounce) can evaporated skim milk

1 cup finely diced unpeeled red apples

1 cup finely diced unpeeled green apples

¼ cup White Grape Syrup (page 45)

3½ cups cooked long-grain rice, white or brown

Day 1: Add enough water to the chickpeas to cover them by 3 or 4 inches, and soak overnight in the refrigerator.

Day 2: Combine the seasoning mix ingredients in a small bowl.

Drain the chickpeas, saving the soaking liquid, and set both aside.

Preheat the oven to 400°.

Sprinkle all surfaces of the turkey evenly with 2 *tablespoons* of the seasoning mix and rub it in well. Place the seasoned turkey in a baking pan, bake for 15 minutes, remove it from the oven, and set aside.

Meanwhile, preheat a heavy 5-quart pot, preferably nonstick, over high heat to 350°, about 4 minutes.

Add the onions, the mirliton, the drained chickpeas, and the bananas, and cook, stirring occasionally, until the mixture starts to brown, about 10 minutes. Stir in *1 cup* of the stock and 3 *tablespoons* of the seasoning mix, and cook about 15 minutes. Add the apple juice, mushrooms, and *4 cups* of the liquid in which the chickpeas were soaked (adjust the amount by adding or pouring off water), and cook 25 minutes more. Stir in the *remaining* seasoning mix and *2 cups* stock, and cook 15 minutes.

Now purée the entire mixture. We used a hand-held appliance to purée the mixture right in the pot, but if you use a food processor or blender, just pour the mixture into the appliance, purée it, and pour it back into the pot. Don't worry if you have to pour it back and forth—just be sure to scrape out all the mixture each time.

Continue to cook the mixture in the pot over high heat. Stir in the evaporated milk and the *remaining* stock. Remove ½ cup of the mixture from the pot and use it to deglaze the baking pan in which the turkey was cooked, then add the turkey and all the liquid from the pan to the pot. Add the apples and turn the heat to low. Simmer for 2 to 3 minutes, turn off the heat, and stir in the White Grape Syrup. Serve over the rice.

Note Use the very best-quality curry powder you can find. Check the expiration date for freshness, and discard any that isn't used up by that date.

Per serving: Calories 885   Protein 59g   Fat 9g
Carbohydrates 143g   9% calories from fat

color photograph 33

Turkey Tacos

─ ─ ─ ─ ─ ─ ─ ─ ─ ─ ─ ─ ─ ─ ─ ─

Makes 20 small tacos

You may think it's strange to put the lettuce and tomatoes in the tacos before baking them, that they wouldn't be good that way. But try it—you'll be surprised!

Seasoning mix

1 tablespoon salt
1 tablespoon ground New Mexico chile pepper (see **Note**)
2 teaspoons dry mustard
2 teaspoons dried cilantro leaves
1½ teaspoons garlic powder
1½ teaspoons ground cumin
1¼ teaspoons white pepper
1 teaspoon onion powder
1 teaspoon crushed dried guajillo chile (see **Note**)
¾ teaspoon black pepper
½ teaspoon crushed dried, dark-roasted ancho chile (see **Note**)
½ teaspoon dried thyme leaves
¼ teaspoon ground nutmeg

Taco mixture

1½ pounds freshly ground turkey breast

2 cups chopped onions
2 cups chopped green bell peppers
1 cup chopped canned mild green chiles
1 cup defatted chicken stock (page 8)
1 cup apple juice
1 tablespoon minced fresh garlic
Vegetable-oil cooking spray

Garnishes

20 6-inch corn tortillas
2½ cups shredded lettuce
2½ cups peeled, chopped fresh tomatoes
2½ cups grated skim-milk cheese

Combine the seasoning mix ingredients in a large bowl. Add the taco mixture ingredients to the bowl and mix thoroughly.

Preheat a heavy 14-inch skillet, preferably nonstick, over high heat to 350°, about 4 minutes. If your skillet is smaller than 14 inches, cook the taco mixture in two batches.

After the skillet is heated, spray the surface with a light coating of vegetable-oil spray. Place the taco mixture evenly across the entire bottom of the skillet and cook it for 20 minutes, turning occasionally to brown the meat evenly. The meat will not begin to brown until most of the liquid evaporates, about 13 to 15 minutes. After 20 minutes, turn off the heat.

Preheat the oven to 400°.

In a 10-inch skillet, bring about ½ inch of water to a boil. Using tongs, dredge 1 tortilla at a time through the boiling water to soften them. Do not leave the tortillas in the water more than 2 or 3 seconds, as they become soft and fragile very quickly and will tear. Place the softened tortillas on a flat surface, and on the edge of each, place ¼ cup of the taco mixture, 2 tablespoons each of the lettuce, tomato, and grated cheese, and roll up the tortillas. Repeat the process until the desired number are filled.

Place the filled tortillas, seam side down, on a nonstick baking sheet and put them in the oven. Bake for 15 minutes, or until the tacos are crunchy. Serve immediately.

Note Use whatever chile peppers are available—not commercial ground chili powder. A variety of chiles creates a "round" flavor. Also, use a smaller amount of chiles if you prefer less heat.

Per serving (2 tacos): Calories 360   Protein 28g   Fat 8g
Carbohydrates 38g   22% calories from fat

Turkey Jambalaya

Makes 16 appetizer or 8 to 9 main-dish servings, about 4½ quarts

Jambalaya, an ever-popular dish, was immortalized back in the fifties by a song heard all over the country by people who had no idea what it was. Now, with the popularizing of Louisiana and other regional cuisines, Jambalaya has made friends far and wide. This recipe is easy to prepare at home, and very satisfying. Serve it with plenty of hot crusty French bread and something good and cold to drink.

Seasoning mix

1 tablespoon sweet paprika
1 tablespoon onion powder
1 tablespoon salt
2 teaspoons garlic powder
1 teaspoon white pepper
1 teaspoon black pepper
1 teaspoon dry mustard
1 teaspoon dried thyme leaves
½ teaspoon ground cumin
½ teaspoon cayenne

3 cups chopped onions, *in all*
3 cups chopped green bell peppers, *in all*

1 cup chopped celery
1 cup julienne turkey tasso (see **Note**)
2 cups turkey andouille sausage, cut into ¼-inch rounds (see **Note**), *in all*
3 bay leaves
6 cups defatted chicken stock (page 8), *in all*
2 cups peeled, chopped fresh tomatoes
8 ounces julienne turkey breast
3 cups uncooked long-grain white rice

Combine seasoning mix ingredients in a small bowl.

Preheat a heavy 5-quart pot, preferably nonstick, over high heat to 350°, about 4 minutes.

Add *2 cups* of the onions, *2 cups* of the bell peppers, the celery, tasso, *1 cup* of the andouille, the bay leaves, and *3 tablespoons* of the seasoning mix. Cook, scraping the bottom of the pot frequently, until the crust seems in danger of burning, about 12 minutes. Stir in *1 cup* of the stock, scrape the bottom of the pot to clear it of all brown bits, and cook for 10 minutes more. Add the tomatoes, turkey, and *remaining* seasoning mix, and cook for 5 minutes. Add the *remaining* onions, peppers, andouille, and stock, and bring to a boil. Stir in the rice and return to a boil. Reduce the heat to a slow simmer, cover, and cook until the liquid is completely absorbed, about 15 minutes.

Note If you cannot find turkey tasso, use smoked turkey thighs or wings. If turkey andouille (a low-fat version of a Cajun favorite) is unavailable, substitute any flavorful smoked turkey sausage.

Per main dish serving: Calories 415   Protein 23g   Fat 5g
Carbohydrates 68g   10% calories from fat

Turkey Meatballs

Makes about 24 to 30 1½-inch meatballs

These delicious meatballs, with just a hint of Oriental seasoning, are a great cocktail party appetizer, but don't wait for a party to serve them!

Seasoning mix

- 1 teaspoon salt
- 1 teaspoon onion powder
- 1 teaspoon garlic powder
- 1 teaspoon dry mustard
- ½ teaspoon sweet paprika
- ½ teaspoon black pepper
- ½ teaspoon ground cinnamon
- ½ teaspoon ground nutmeg
- ¼ teaspoon white pepper
- ¼ teaspoon cayenne
- ⅛ teaspoon ground star anise
- ⅛ teaspoon ground cloves

- 1 tablespoon olive oil
- ½ cup finely diced onions
- 1 tablespoon grated fresh ginger
- 1 pound freshly ground turkey breast
- 1½ tablespoons tamari (see **Note**)
- ¼ cup defatted chicken stock (page 8)
- ¾ cup toasted unseasoned bread crumbs
- ¼ cup evaporated skim milk
  Vegetable-oil cooking spray

Day 1: Combine the seasoning mix ingredients in a small bowl.

Pour the oil into a nonstick 10-inch skillet and heat to 400° over high heat, about 4 minutes. Add the onions and ginger, sprinkle with *1 tablespoon* of the seasoning mix, and stir. Sauté until the onions become translucent and tender; let cool.

Combine the onions and ginger with the remaining ingredients, including the *remaining* seasoning mix, in a large bowl and mix thoroughly. Refrigerate overnight.

Day 2: Preheat a nonstick 10-inch skillet over high heat to 400°, about 4 minutes.

Preheat the oven to 350°.

With a teaspoon form the turkey mixture into small balls. Brown the meatballs, a few at a time, in the skillet, then reshape any that fall apart.

Coat a baking pan large enough to hold all the meatballs with vegetable-oil·spray, and place the meatballs in it. Bake until done, about 30 minutes.

Note Tamari is a very rich, flavorful soy sauce, available in specialty markets and the international or ethnic food sections of many supermarkets. If you cannot find tamari where you shop, use any good quality soy sauce.

Per serving (4 meatballs): Calories 183   Protein 25g   Fat 6g
Carbohydrates 7g   28% calories from fat

Chicken Pieces Jessica

Makes 4 servings

This is an exciting but messy little appetizer! Offer a tray of moistened, rolled-up towels—or damp paper towels if you're entertaining very informally.

Seasoning mix

½ teaspoon salt
½ teaspoon onion powder
½ teaspoon garlic powder
½ teaspoon dried sweet basil
  leaves
½ teaspoon ground sage
¼ teaspoon sweet paprika
¼ teaspoon dry mustard
¼ teaspoon dried thyme leaves
¼ teaspoon dried summer
  savory   •

⅛ teaspoon black pepper
⅛ teaspoon white pepper
⅛ teaspoon cayenne

4 boneless chicken breast
  halves, skin and visible fat
  removed
Vegetable-oil cooking spray
¼ cup White Grape Syrup
  (page 45)

(continued)

Combine the seasoning mix ingredients in a small bowl.

Sprinkle all surfaces of the chicken evenly with *4 teaspoons* of the seasoning mix.

Preheat a heavy 10-inch skillet, preferably nonstick, over high heat to 400°, about 4 minutes.

Lightly coat each side of both breast halves with the vegetable-oil spray and place them in the skillet. Turn the heat to medium, cook 1½ to 2 minutes, turn the chicken over, and cook the other sides. Repeat the process with the other 2 pieces of chicken. Set chicken aside to cool.

Preheat the broiler.

When the chicken is cool enough to handle, slice it into ½-inch wide strips. Place in a container and toss with the grape syrup. Arrange on a baking sheet and broil until the chicken is brown and a sticky glaze forms, about 4 minutes. Then get out of the way!

Per serving: Calories 140   Protein 19g   Fat 3g
Carbohydrates 10g   18% calories from fat

Meats

Most of these are one-dish meals complete with vegetables and a starch, so you don't have to prepare anything else except a simple salad.

color photograph 36

Round Steak in Onion Gravy

Makes 4 servings

This is truly southern comfort food—hearty, delicious, and good for you! In this recipe the sweeter the onions, the better the dish. The best onions to use are Vidalia, Walla-Walla, or Maui-Maui.

½ cup dried black-eyed peas

Seasoning mix
- 2 teaspoons salt
- 2 teaspoons sweet paprika
- 2 teaspoons dry mustard
- 1½ teaspoons garlic powder
- 1½ teaspoons onion powder
- 1 teaspoon white pepper
- 1 teaspoon thyme
- 1 teaspoon ground cumin
- ¾ teaspoon black pepper
- ½ teaspoon cayenne

- 3 tablespoons balsamic vinegar
- 1½ pounds top round steak, about ½ inch thick, all visible fat removed
- 7 cups defatted beef stock (page 8), *in all*
- 3 medium onions, peeled and cut into julienne slices, *in all*
- 4 cups cooked long-grain white rice

Day 1: Add enough water to the black-eyed peas to cover them by 3 or 4 inches, and soak overnight in the refrigerator. As the peas absorb the water, they will more than double in volume.

Combine the seasoning mix ingredients in a small bowl. Add the vinegar and mix to form a paste.

Cut the steak into 4 equal pieces. Rub *3 tablespoons* of the paste on both sides of each piece of meat. Refrigerate the seasoned steaks in a covered container overnight, and store the remaining paste in a covered container.

Day 2: Drain the black-eyed peas and set aside.

Preheat a heavy 5-quart pot, preferably nonstick, over high heat to 350°, about 4 minutes.

Brown each steak on both sides, about 1 minute per side; do this in two batches so the steaks don't overlap in the pot. Remove the steaks and set them aside.

Add *2 cups* of the stock to the pot and scrape to clear all the browned bits. Add ¾ *cup* of the onions, soaked, drained peas, and the *remaining* seasoning paste, and cook 15 minutes. Transfer all the ingredients from the pot to a blender or food processor, add *1 cup* stock, and purée until smooth. Pour this puréed mixture back into the pot, and add *3 cups* stock, the *remaining* onions and peas, and the steaks and their accumulated juices. Bring to a boil, cook 5 minutes, then reduce the heat to medium, and simmer for 40 minutes. Stir in the *remaining 1 cup* stock and simmer until the peas are tender and the liquid is thick and starts to look creamy, about 20 minutes. Some peas have more starch than others, so if the liquid in this dish seems too thick, add a little more stock. Serve over the rice.

Per serving: Calories 683   Protein 66g   Fat 14g
Carbohydrates 74g   18% calories from fat

Creamy Beef and Mushrooms

Makes 4 servings

 This recipe produces some of the tenderest beef you've ever eaten, and some of the tastiest, too.

Sour cream mixture

12 ounces low-fat cottage cheese

2 ounces nonfat cream cheese

3 tablespoons vinegar

Seasoning mix

2 teaspoons salt

2 teaspoons sweet paprika

2 teaspoons pink peppercorns (see Note)

1½ teaspoons onion powder

1½ teaspoons garlic powder

1 teaspoon dry mustard

1 teaspoon white peppercorns (see Note)

1 teaspoon green peppercorns (see Note)

½ teaspoon black pepper

½ teaspoon white pepper

¼ teaspoon cayenne

1 pound top round steak, all visible fat removed, scalloped (page 7)

2 cups chopped onions

4 cups defatted beef stock (page 8), *in all*

6 tablespoons flour, sifted

8 cups sliced fresh mushrooms

6 cups cooked wide noodles

Day 1: Combine the sour cream mixture ingredients in a blender or food processor and purée until smooth and creamy. If the mixture is very thick, push it down toward the blades a few times. Cover and refrigerate overnight.

Day 2: Combine the seasoning mix ingredients in a bowl.

Sprinkle all surfaces of the meat evenly with *2 tablespoons* of the seasoning mix, rub it in well, and set aside.

Preheat a heavy 5-quart pot, preferably nonstick, over high heat to 350°, about 4 minutes.

Add the onions and cook just until they start to brown, about 2 to 3 minutes. Move the onions to one side of the pot and add the seasoned meat to the other side, along with the *remaining* seasoning mix. Cook, stirring the meat once or twice, for 5 minutes. Add ½ *cup* of the stock, mix the meat and onions together, and scrape the bottom of the pot to clear it of all brown bits. Cook until most of the liquid evaporates and the mixture starts to stick, about 5 minutes. Add ½ *cup* stock and clear the bottom of the pot again. Stir in the sifted flour and mix until it is completely absorbed, so that none of the flour is visible, a paste forms, and the beef is moist and sticky. Add the mushrooms, stir, and cook, scraping the bottom of the pot occasionally to prevent sticking, for 5 minutes. Add the *remaining* stock, stir to clear the bottom and sides of the pot, and cook 10 minutes. Add the sour cream mixture and, with a wire whisk, whip until the mixture is completely blended into the sauce. Serve over the wide noodles.

Note If you cannot find separate containers of colored peppercorns where you shop, some stores sell jars with a mixture of pink, white, green, and black peppercorns.

Per serving: Calories 428   Protein 47g   Fat 9g
Carbohydrates 38g   19% calories from fat

Beef in Gumbo Sauce

Makes 4 servings

Your family (or guests) will never guess there are apple and prune juices in this dish. All they'll taste will be the wonderful meat and the vegetables, plus a touch of sweetness. They'll also get extra vitamins from the juices.

Seasoning mix

2½ teaspoons dried thyme leaves

2 teaspoons onion powder

2 teaspoons garlic powder

1½ teaspoons salt

1½ teaspoons dry mustard

1½ teaspoons ground cumin

1 teaspoon sweet paprika

½ teaspoon black pepper

½ teaspoon cayenne

----

1 pound flank steak, all visible fat removed, and the beef scalloped (page 7)

3 cups chopped onions, *in all*

2 cups chopped green bell peppers

3 cups sliced fresh mushrooms, *in all*

2 cups sliced okra, *in all*

½ cup apple juice

½ cup prune juice

3 cups defatted beef stock (page 8)

3 cups cooked long-grain white rice

Combine the seasoning mix ingredients in a small bowl.

Sprinkle all surfaces of the beef scallops evenly with 2 *teaspoons* of the seasoning mix and rub it in.

Preheat a heavy 5-quart pot, preferably nonstick, over high heat to 350°, about 4 minutes.

Add 2 *cups* of the onions, all of the bell peppers, *1 cup* of the mushrooms, *1 cup* of the okra, and 2 *tablespoons* of the seasoning mix. Stir and cook 7 minutes, scraping the pot 2 or 3 times as sticking occurs.

Once a light brown crust forms over the bottom of the pot, add the apple and prune juices and the *remaining* seasoning mix. Scrape the bottom of the pot to clear it of any brown bits, and cook until most of the liquid evaporates, about 7 to 8 minutes.

Transfer the mixture from the pot to a blender and purée. Place the seasoned beef in the pot and, with the heat still on high, cook 1 minute on each, side. Then add the *remaining* onions, mushrooms, okra, and the stock. Clear the bottom of the pot, stir in the puréed mixture, and cook until the meat is tender, about 15 to 17 minutes. **Caution:** Check the bottom of the pot often, as sticking will occur while the mixture cooks. Serve over the rice.

Per serving: Calories 476   Protein 31g   Fat 15g
Carbohydrates 54g   28% calories from fat

Beef Livingston

Makes 4 servings

Once you get the hang of scalloping your steak, this recipe is a breeze to make. One of our testers said it was her number one favorite dish.

¾ cup dried black-eyed peas

Seasoning mix

2 teaspoons salt
2 teaspoons sweet paprika
1½ teaspoons dry mustard
1½ teaspoons dried oregano leaves
1 teaspoon onion powder
1 teaspoon garlic powder
1 teaspoon dried sweet basil leaves
¾ teaspoon white pepper
½ teaspoon dried thyme leaves
¼ teaspoon black pepper
¼ teaspoon cayenne

1 pound flank steak, all visible fat removed, and the beef scalloped (page 7)
2 cups chopped onions
1 cup chopped celery
2 cups defatted beef stock (page 8), *in all*
4 cups peeled, diced fresh tomatoes or 2 (14½-ounce) cans diced tomatoes
¼ cup thinly sliced fresh garlic
3 cups sliced fresh mushrooms
2 cups cooked long-grain white rice

Day 1: Add enough water to the black-eyed peas to cover them by 3 or 4 inches, and soak overnight in the refrigerator. As the peas absorb the water, they will more than double in volume.

Day 2: Combine the seasoning mix ingredients in a small bowl.

Sprinkle all surfaces of the meat evenly with *2 teaspoons* of the seasoning mix, rub it in, and set the meat aside.

Drain the black-eyed peas and purée them with *1 cup* of the stock; set aside.

Preheat a heavy 5-quart pot, preferably nonstick, over high heat to 350°, about 4 minutes.

In the pot combine the onions, celery, meat, and *2 tablespoons* of the seasoning mix, stir and cook 5 minutes, scraping the bottom of the pot to clear all the brown bits. Add *1 cup* stock, clear the bottom of the pot, and cook until all the liquid evaporates, about 10 minutes; there should be a nice, even brown crust on the bottom of the pot. Add the pea purée, diced tomatoes, garlic, and *remaining* seasoning mix. Scrape the bottom of the pot to clear, and cook 10 minutes. Add the mushrooms and cook another 10 minutes, scraping the bottom of the pot occasionally. Reduce the heat to medium and simmer 10 minutes. Serve over the rice.

Per serving: Calories 642   Protein 44g   Fat 22g
Carbohydrates 58g   30% calories from fat

Scalloped Beef with Tomatoes

Makes 6 servings

This wonderful recipe has everything you need right in one dish—meat, green vegetables, and tomatoes for Vitamin C. Add some thick slices of dark bread, and you'll have a meal to satisfy even the hungriest person at your table.

Seasoning mix

2 teaspoons sweet paprika

1½ teaspoons salt

1½ teaspoons onion powder

1½ teaspoons garlic powder

1½ teaspoons dry mustard

1½ teaspoons dried thyme leaves

¾ teaspoon black pepper

¾ teaspoon white pepper

⅛ teaspoon cayenne

1 pound flank steak, all visible fat removed, and the beef scalloped (page 7)

2 cups chopped onions

2 cups chopped green bell peppers

1 cup chopped celery

1 cup apple juice

4 cups peeled, diced fresh tomatoes or 2 (14½-ounce) cans diced tomatoes

1 teaspoon minced fresh garlic

9 cups mixed, washed, and chopped fresh greens (see **Note**)

2 cups defatted chicken stock (page 8)

Combine the seasoning mix ingredients in a small bowl.

Sprinkle all surfaces of the scalloped flank steak evenly with *1 tablespoon* of the seasoning mix and rub it in well.

Preheat a heavy 5-quart pot, preferably nonstick, over high heat to 350°, about 4 minutes.

Add the onions, bell peppers, celery and *remaining* seasoning mix, and stir. Cook, occasionally scraping the bottom of the pot to clear all the browned bits, for 5 minutes. Add the apple juice, clear the bottom of the pot, and cook until all the liquid evaporates and a glaze forms on the bottom of the pot, about 14 minutes.

Push the vegetables to one side of the pot and add the seasoned meat to the other side. Cook, turning once or twice to brown evenly, about 3 minutes. Add the tomatoes and garlic, stir to clear the bottom of the pot, and add the greens and the stock. Stir again, and cook until the meat and greens are tender, about 10 minutes.

Note Use any combination of three kinds of greens, except for bitter ones like iceberg lettuce and radicchio. Spinach, collards, and mustard greens make a fine medley, but experiment and enjoy!

Per serving: Calories 419   Protein 28g   Fat 13g
Carbohydrates 48g   28% calories from fat

Flank and Greens

Makes 6 servings

If you've never cooked greens right in the pot with meat, you're in for a pleasant surprise. You don't lose all those vitamins since you don't throw out the liquid the greens were cooked in, and the flavor is indescribable.

Seasoning mix

1 tablespoon sweet paprika
2 teaspoons salt
2 teaspoons dry mustard
1½ teaspoons onion powder
1 teaspoon garlic powder
1 teaspoon dried thyme leaves
1 teaspoon ground ginger
¾ teaspoon white pepper
½ teaspoon black pepper
½ teaspoon ground cumin
¼ teaspoon cayenne

1½ pounds flank steak, all visible fat removed, and the beef scalloped (page 7)
2 cups chopped onions
12 cups mixed, washed, and chopped greens (see Note), *in all*
6 cups defatted beef stock (page 8), *in all*
5 tablespoons all-purpose flour, browned (page 7)
6 cups cooked long-grain white rice

Combine the seasoning mix ingredients in a small bowl.

Sprinkle all surfaces of the scalloped steak evenly with *2 tablespoons* of the seasoning mix and rub in well.

Preheat a heavy 5-quart pot, preferably nonstick, over high heat to 350°, about 4 minutes.

Add the seasoned meat and brown it on all sides, about 2 to 3 minutes. Add the onions, the *remaining* seasoning mix, and ½ *cup* of each type of greens. Cover and cook, scraping the bottom of the pot to clear all the brown bits, for 8 minutes. Add *1 cup* of the stock and cook, covered, for 15 minutes, checking occasionally for sticking. Add the browned flour and mix until it is completely absorbed, the brown flour is no longer visible, and the meat looks moist and very pasty. Add the *remaining* stock and greens, bring to a boil, reduce the heat to medium, and, occasionally checking the bottom of the pot for sticking, cook until the meat and greens are tender, about 20 minutes. Serve over the rice.

Note Any combination of greens is fine as long as the greens aren't bitter ones like iceberg lettuce and radicchio. We often combine spinach, collards, and mustard greens, but experiment and enjoy! Three kinds are best for a rounded taste.

Per serving: Calories 626   Protein 48g   Fat 20g
Carbohydrates 66g   29% calories from fat

Flank and Black-eyed Peas

This recipe works well with other cuts of meat; we use flank steak often because it's low in fat but you can substitute a less costly cut.

1½ cups dried black-eyed peas

Seasoning mix
- 1 tablespoon plus ½ teaspoon black pepper
- 2 teaspoons sweet paprika
- 1½ teaspoons dry mustard
- 1 teaspoon salt
- 1 teaspoon onion powder
- 1 teaspoon garlic powder
- 1 teaspoon dried sweet basil leaves
- 1 teaspoon dried thyme leaves
- ½ teaspoon white pepper
- ⅛ teaspoon cayenne

1 pound flank steak, all visible fat removed, and the beef scalloped (page 7)
2 cups chopped onions
1 cup chopped green bell peppers
½ cup chopped celery
4 bay leaves
1 cup apple juice
8 cups water
4 cups defatted beef stock (page 8), *in all*
3 cups cooked long-grain white rice

Day 1: Add enough water to the black-eyed peas to cover them by 3 or 4 inches, and soak overnight in the refrigerator.

Day 2: Drain and rinse the black-eyed peas and set aside.

Combine the seasoning mix ingredients in a small bowl and sprinkle the beef scallops evenly with *2 teaspoons* of the mixture.

Preheat a heavy 5-quart pot, preferably nonstick, over high heat to 350°, about 4 minutes.

Add the onions, bell peppers, celery, bay leaves, and the *remaining* seasoning mix. Stir and cook until the vegetables start to turn brown and stick to the bottom of the pot, about 4 minutes. Add the apple juice and black-eyed peas, and scrape the bottom of the pot to clear all the brown bits. Cook until the apple juice evaporates and a glaze forms on the bottom of the pot, about 10 to 12 minutes. Add the water and again clear the bottom of the pot of all brown bits. Bring to a boil and cook until the peas are tender and most of the liquid evaporates, about 1 hour and 20 minutes. The remaining liquid in the pot should be thick and creamy-looking.

While the peas are cooking, preheat a 10-inch skillet, preferably nonstick, over high heat to 350°, about 4 minutes. Add half the scalloped beef to the skillet and cook 1 minute, then turn it over and cook 1 minute more. Remove the cooked meat from the skillet and repeat the process with the other half of the meat.

Once the water has evaporated from the pot, stir in *3 cups* of the beef stock, and cook 10 minutes. Add the cooked meat and the *remaining cup* of stock, and cook until the peas are tender, about 10 minutes. Serve over the rice.

Per serving: Calories 454   Protein 31g   Fat 13g
Carbohydrates 54g   25% calories from fat

Smothered Flank Steak

This dish is great served over rice, or with wide noodles or plenty of mashed potatoes. And save some gravy for some of the low-fat breads in this book. Flank steak is low in fat, but you can use other, less expensive cuts if you prefer.

Seasoning mix

- 2 teaspoons salt
- 1½ teaspoons onion powder
- 1½ teaspoons garlic powder
- 1¼ teaspoons sweet paprika
- 1 teaspoon dried chervil
- ¾ teaspoon dry mustard
- ½ teaspoon black pepper
- ½ teaspoon white pepper
- ½ teaspoon cayenne
- ½ teaspoon ground cumin

- 1 pound flank steak, all visible fat removed, and the beef scalloped (page 7)
- 2 cups chopped onions
- 1½ cups chopped green bell peppers
- 1 cup chopped celery
- 5 cups defatted chicken stock (page 8), *in all*
- 6 tablespoons all-purpose flour, browned (page 7)
- 3 cups cooked long-grain white rice

Combine the seasoning mix ingredients in a small bowl.

Preheat a heavy 5-quart pot, preferably nonstick, over high heat to 350°, about 4 minutes.

While the pot is heating, sprinkle all surfaces of the steak with *2 tablespoons* of the seasoning mix and rub it in well. Place the seasoned steak in the pot and brown it on all sides, about 4 to 5 minutes. Remove the steak from the pot and set it aside. Add the onions, bell peppers, celery, and *remaining* seasoning mix to the pot, stir, and cook 2 minutes. Stir in *1 cup* of the stock, scrape the bottom of the pot to clear it of all brown bits, and cook until the vegetables start to brown, about 10 to 12 minutes. Add the browned flour and mix it in until all the flour is absorbed, the brown flour is no longer visible, and a paste forms. Add *3 cups* of stock, and return the steak and all

212   *Chef Paul Prudhomme's Fork in the Road*

its juices to the pot. Stir well, and bring to a boil. Turn the heat down to medium, and simmer, stirring occasionally, until the sauce is thick, about 30 minutes. Add the *remaining cup* of stock and continue to cook, stirring occasionally to keep the mixture from sticking on the bottom, until the steak is tender, about 30 minutes. Serve over the rice (or pasta or potatoes).

Per serving: Calories 571   Protein 46g   Fat 19g
Carbohydrates 81g   25% calories from fat

Wonderful Beef and Vegetables

Makes 6 servings

If you want to change the mix of vegetables—add a few more carrots, or substitute rutabaga for the turnip—that's OK, because then it will be *your* dish.

Seasoning mix

1 tablespoon sweet paprika

2 teaspoons salt

1½ teaspoons dried thyme leaves

1 teaspoon onion powder

1 teaspoon garlic powder

1 teaspoon dry mustard

1 teaspoon black pepper

1 teaspoon ground cumin

½ teaspoon white pepper

¼ teaspoon cayenne

----

1 pound flank steak, all visible fat removed, and the beef scalloped (page 7)

2 large carrots, peeled, cut in half lengthwise, and cut into 1-inch pieces, *in all*

1 large turnip, peeled and cut into 10 wedges, *in all*

½ small green cabbage, cut into 6 wedges, *in all*

1 cup fresh green beans (about 5 ounces), cut into 1-inch pieces, *in all*

1 large green bell pepper, cored, seeded, and cut into pieces about 1 inch square, *in all*

1 large onion, peeled and cut into 10 wedges, *in all*

2 ribs celery, cut into 1-inch pieces, *in all*

6 cups defatted beef stock (page 8), *in all*

4 tablespoons all-purpose flour, browned (page 7)

2 medium potatoes, peeled, cut into 1-inch slices, and quartered

4 cups cooked long-grain brown rice

Combine the seasoning mix ingredients in a small bowl.

Sprinkle the scalloped steak evenly with *2 tablespoons* of the seasoning mix and rub it in well.

Preheat a heavy 5-quart pot, preferably nonstick, over high heat to 350°, about 4 minutes.

Add the seasoned steak and cook, turning as necessary, until it is brown on all sides, about 4 minutes. Remove the steak and set it aside.

Place ⅓ of all the vegetables, except the potatoes, in the pot along with *1 cup* of the stock and the *remaining* seasoning mix. Cook, stirring two or three times, until the liquid is almost evaporated and a crust has formed on the bottom of the pot, about 10 to 12 minutes. Add *1 cup* stock, scrape the bottom of the pot clear, and transfer the ingredients from the pot to a food processor or blender. Add the browned flour, and purée. Place the puréed mixture back into the pot, add the *remaining* stock, bring to a boil, and cook 10 minutes. Add the potatoes, the steak, and the juices that have accumulated, and bring to a boil again. Add the remaining vegetables, reduce the heat to medium and cook, stirring the bottom occasionally to keep from sticking, until the vegetables are fork tender, about 20 minutes. Serve over brown rice.

Per serving: Calories 471   Protein 29g   Fat 13g
Carbohydrates 59g   26% calories from fat

color photograph 38

Garlic Roast

▬▬ ▬▬ ▬▬ ▬▬ ▬▬ ▬▬ ▬▬ ▬▬ ▬▬ ▬▬ ▬▬ ▬▬ ▬▬ ▬▬ ▬▬ ▬▬ ▬▬ ▬▬

Makes 4 servings

✕ As the name suggests, this is a well-seasoned roast. In addition to garlic, the peppercorns add a wonderful lively flavor. This is not a quickie recipe, but I think you'll prepare it over and over again.

Seasoning mix
- 2 teaspoons onion powder
- 2 teaspoons garlic powder
- 1½ teaspoons salt
- 1 teaspoon sweet paprika

Sour cream mixture
- 1 cup nonfat cottage cheese
- ½ cup nonfat sour cream
- 2 tablespoons white vinegar

▬

- 1 (2-pound) eye of round roast, all visible fat removed

- 80 fresh green peppercorns (see **Note**)
- 80 fresh pink peppercorns (see **Note**)
- 20 medium fresh garlic cloves, peeled
- 2½ cups defatted beef stock (page 8)
- 4 tablespoons all-purpose flour, browned (page 7)
- ½ medium carrot, peeled and cut into ¼-inch rounds
- 1 cup chopped fresh spinach
- ½ cup sliced fresh mushrooms

Combine the seasoning mix ingredients in a small bowl.

Place the sour cream mixture ingredients in a blender and purée until smooth and creamy. Refrigerate until needed.

Preheat the oven to 250°.

Cut about 20 slits, evenly spaced and approximately ¾ inch long and ¾ of the way through, in the top of the roast. Into each slit place 4 green and 4 pink peppercorns, then ⅛ *teaspoon* of the seasoning mix, then 1 clove of garlic, pressing in as far as they will go. Sprinkle the *remaining* seasoning mix over the entire roast and gently rub it in. Place the roast, along with ½ *cup* of the stock, into a 10-inch diameter × 2-inch high pan. Roast for 1 hour, then cover with foil, and continue to roast until done, about 40 minutes.

Remove the roast from the pan and set it aside. Add ½ *cup* stock to the pan and scrape the bottom to clear it of all brown bits. Add the browned flour to the *remaining 1½ cups* stock, mix completely, and set aside.

Transfer the mixture from the pan to a 2-quart pot and bring to a boil. Whisk in the flour/stock mixture, and add the carrots, spinach, and mushrooms. Return to a boil and cook 10 minutes. Transfer the ingredients from the pot to a food processor and purée until smooth, then place the puréed mixture back into the pot and bring it to a boil. Reduce the heat to low and simmer for 5 minutes. Whisk in the sour cream mixture, return to a boil, and serve over the roast.

Note If separate containers of colored peppercorns are unavailable where you shop, some stores carry jars with a mixture of pink, white, green, and black peppercorns.

Per serving: Calories 585   Protein 86g   Fat 19g
Carbohydrates 18g   28% calories from fat

color photograph 39

Roast Leg of Lamb

━━ ━━ ━━ ━━ ━━ ━━ ━━ ━━ ━━ ━━ ━━ ━━ ━━ ━━ ━━ ━━ ━━

Makes 8 to 10 servings

This variation on a traditional spring favorite is terrific with roasted potatoes and a green salad with a tart nonfat dressing. This is one of the few recipes in which the number of calories from fat exceeds 30 percent of the total—in this case 37 percent. Seven percent isn't much; still, to stick to the guidelines, just serve the lamb with side dishes that are very low in fat.

Seasoning mix
- 1 tablespoon sweet paprika
- 2 teaspoons salt
- 1½ teaspoons onion powder
- 1 teaspoon garlic powder
- 1 teaspoon dry mustard
- 1 teaspoon dried cilantro leaves
- 1 teaspoon rubbed sage
- ½ teaspoon black pepper
- ½ teaspoon white pepper
- ½ teaspoon ground coriander
- ½ teaspoon ground ginger
- ¼ teaspoon cayenne

━━

- 1 cup chopped onions
- ½ cup chopped green bell peppers
- ½ cup chopped celery
- ½ cup defatted chicken stock (page 8)
- 1 (4-pound) boneless leg of lamb
- Mint Sauce

Combine the seasoning mix ingredients in a small bowl.

Preheat the oven to 225°.

Preheat an 8-inch skillet, preferably nonstick, over high heat to 350°, about 2 to 3 minutes.

Add the onions, bell peppers, celery, and 2 *tablespoons* of the seasoning mix. Stir and cook for 3 minutes. Add the stock, scrape the bottom of the skillet to clear it of all brown bits, and continue to cook until most of the liquid evaporates but the mixture is still moist, about 5 minutes. Turn off the heat and set aside to cool to room temperature.

While the vegetables are cooling, unroll the leg of lamb and with a sharp knife remove as much fat as possible, being careful not to cut through the seams. Take your time to do this right—the process will take about 15 minutes. Next, sprinkle the inside of the leg evenly with *1 tablespoon* of the seasoning mix, then spread the cooled vegetables evenly around the entire inner surface of the leg. Carefully roll the leg back into shape, and sprinkle the *remaining* seasoning mix evenly over the entire roast. Place the leg, seam side down, in a 9 × 12-inch roasting pan, cover with foil, and roast until done, about 2½ to 3 hours. Keep roast warm while you make the Mint Sauce. To serve, drizzle each serving of the roast with a little sauce and pass the rest.

Per serving: Calories 304   Protein 42g   Fat 13g
Carbohydrates 3g   37% calories from fat

Mint Sauce

Makes 2½ cups

¼ cup plus 2 tablespoons
  all-purpose flour, browned
  (page 7)
  Liquid from roast
2 cups defatted beef stock
  (page 8)

5 fresh mint leaves
3 (1-gram) packets artificial
  sweetener (page 4)

Combine the browned flour with ½ cup of the liquid from the roast and set aside.

Place the remaining liquid from the roast, the beef stock, and the mint leaves into a heavy 3-quart pot over high heat. Bring to a full boil, whisk in the flour/stock mixture, reduce the heat to medium, and simmer for 5 minutes. Remove from the heat and add the artificial sweetener.

Per serving: Calories 24   Protein 1g   Fat 1g
Carbohydrates 4g   38% calories from fat

Lamb Stew

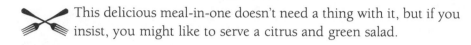

Makes 4 servings

This delicious meal-in-one doesn't need a thing with it, but if you insist, you might like to serve a citrus and green salad.

1½ cups dried chickpeas

Seasoning mix
 1 tablespoon curry powder
2½ teaspoons salt
 2 teaspoons sweet paprika
 2 teaspoons garlic powder
1½ teaspoons dry mustard
1½ teaspoons dried sweet basil
    leaves
1¼ teaspoons black pepper
 1 teaspoon onion powder
 1 teaspoon white pepper
 1 teaspoon ground cardamom
 1 teaspoon chili powder
 ¾ teaspoon cayenne
 ¾ teaspoon ground allspice
 ½ teaspoon ground cumin
 ½ teaspoon ground nutmeg

 1 pound lamb shank or loin,
    all visible fat removed, diced
    into 1-inch cubes

5½ cups defatted chicken stock
    (page 8), *in all*
 1 large onion, peeled and cut
    into 8 wedges, *in all*
 ½ small head green cabbage,
    cut into 4 wedges, *in all*
 1 medium turnip, peeled and
    cut into 10 wedges, *in all*
 2 ribs celery, cut into 2-inch
    pieces, *in all*
 2 large carrots, peeled and cut
    in half lengthwise, then into
    2-inch chunks, *in all*
 1 large green bell pepper,
    cored, seeded, and cut into
    2-inch squares, *in all*
 1 large potato, peeled, cut into
    2-inch rounds, and
    quartered, *in all*
2½ cups apple juice
 4 cups cooked long-grain
    brown rice

Day 1: Add enough water to the chick-peas to cover them by 3 or 4 inches, and soak overnight in the refrigerator. As the peas absorb the water, they will more than double in volume.

Day 2: Combine the seasoning mix ingredients in a small bowl.

Preheat a heavy 8-quart pot, preferably nonstick, over high heat to 350°, about 4 minutes. Sprinkle 2 *teaspoons* of the seasoning mix evenly over the lamb and rub it in well. Place the seasoned lamb in the pot and brown it on all sides, about 5 minutes. Remove the lamb and set it aside.

Add *1 cup* of the stock to the pot and scrape the bottom to clear it of all brown bits.

Drain the chick-peas and add them to the pot, along with *half* of the vegetables and the *remaining* seasoning mix. Cover and cook until the vegetables are fork tender, about 15 minutes. Transfer the ingredients from the pot in batches to a blender or food processor, along with *1 cup* stock, and purée until smooth.

Return the puréed mixture to the pot, and stir in the *remaining* stock and apple juice. Add the remaining vegetables, and the lamb and its juices. Bring to a boil, reduce the heat to medium, cover, and simmer, scraping the bottom of the pot two or three times, until the vegetables are tender, about 20 minutes.

Serve over the brown rice.

Per serving: Calories 904   Protein 55g   Fat 16g
Carbohydrates 136g   16% calories from fat

color photograph 40
Bronzed Veal Chops

Makes 4 servings

These chops have more than 30 percent of their calories from fat. To stay within the nutritional guidelines, serve nonfat or low-fat side dishes such as vegetables and rice or potatoes. You can even garnish potatoes with nonfat sour cream, and you won't feel the slightest bit underprivileged!

Seasoning mix

1½ teaspoons salt

1½ teaspoons garlic powder

1¼ teaspoons onion powder

1 teaspoon dried thyme leaves

1 teaspoon ground cumin

¾ teaspoon dry mustard

½ teaspoon sweet paprika

½ teaspoon black pepper

½ teaspoon white pepper

¼ teaspoon cayenne

6 (10 to 12 ounces each) veal chops, all visible fat removed

Vegetable-oil cooking spray

Combine the seasoning mix ingredients in a small bowl.

Lay the veal chops on a cutting board, take the point of a boning knife and, following the curve of the bone, cut through the meat a little less than half the thickness of the bone; do this on both sides. This step helps reduce the thickness of the meat while keeping it still attached to the bone, so the chops will cook very quickly over high heat and retain maximum moisture.

Pound the entire meaty part of the chop with a meat mallet, reducing the thickness of the chops to no more than ½ inch. Sprinkle all surfaces of the chops evenly with the seasoning mix.

Preheat a 12-inch skillet, preferably nonstick, over high heat to 400°, about 5 minutes.

While the skillet is heating, spray each chop lightly with the vegetable-oil spray. Place the chops in the skillet two at a time, and cook 1 minute. Turn the chops over and cook 2 minutes, then turn back to the other side and cook 1 minute more. Remove the cooked chops, wipe the skillet clean, place back over high heat, and repeat the process with the remaining chops.

Per serving: Calories 791   Protein 127g   Fat 29g

Carbohydrates 2g   33% calories from fat

Side Dishes

Vegetables, rice, beans, and pasta in numerous combinations can accompany a plain dish, but if you make the portions a little more generous, the side dishes can suddenly blossom into your principal course.

Candied Butternut Squash

Makes 6 cups, enough for 6 side servings

 This is an excellent side dish, especially with roasted meat; you can serve it in place of sweet potatoes or yams.

Seasoning mix
½ teaspoon ground nutmeg
½ teaspoon ground cinnamon
¼ teaspoon salt
⅛ teaspoon ground cloves

1½ pounds butternut squash

1 medium navel orange
3 tablespoons cornstarch
3 cups plus 5 tablespoons water
8 (1-gram) packets artificial sweetener (page 4), optional
1 teaspoon vanilla extract

Combine the seasoning mix ingredients in a small bowl.

Peel the squash, split it in half, and remove the seeds and pulp. Cut the squash meat into chunks measuring approximately 2 × 1½ × ¾ inch, and set aside.

Cut the orange into quarters. Slice one orange quarter very thin, squeeze the juice from the other three quarters, and set aside.

Dissolve the cornstarch in 5 tablespoons of cool water, and set aside.

Preheat a heavy 5-quart pot, preferably nonstick, over high heat to 350°, about 4 minutes.

Place the squash in the pot and cook until light brown on one side, about 4 to 6 minutes, then turn and cook on the other side, about 3 minutes. Sprinkle the seasoning mix over the squash, add 3 cups of water and the orange juice. Stir gently and cook for 5 minutes. Add the cornstarch mixture and the orange slices. Cook for 5 to 7 minutes, or until the squash is tender. Turn off the heat and add the vanilla, and, if desired, the artificial sweetener.

Per serving: Calories 76   Protein 1g   Fat 1g
Carbohydrates 18g   8% calories from fat

Smothered Okra, Eggplant, and Tomato

■ ■ ■ ■ ■ ■ ■ ■ ■ ■ ■ ■ ■ ■ ■ ■ ■ ■ ■

Makes 5 cups

✕ This is the kind of dish that brings back happy memories for a lot of Louisianans. Traditional, economical, and wonderful-tasting too, it's absolutely fantastic served with cornbread.

Seasoning mix

1½ teaspoons onion powder

1 teaspoon salt

1 teaspoon dry mustard

1 teaspoon dried thyme leaves

½ teaspoon garlic powder

½ teaspoon black pepper

½ teaspoon white pepper

½ teaspoon dillweed

⅛ teaspoon cayenne

■

2 cups chopped onions, *in all*

1 cup chopped green bell peppers

2 cups chopped okra, *in all*

1 cup peeled, finely diced eggplant

2½ cups apple juice, *in all*

3 cups peeled, diced fresh tomatoes or 2 cups canned diced tomatoes, *in all*

1 cup peeled, medium-diced eggplant

½ cup tomato sauce

5 cups cooked long-grain white rice

Combine the seasoning mix ingredients in a small bowl.

Preheat a heavy 10-inch skillet, preferably nonstick, over high heat to 350°, about 4 minutes.

Add *1 cup* of the onions, the bell peppers, *1 cup* of the okra, the finely diced eggplant, and the seasoning mix. Stir and cook until the vegetables start to brown and stick to the bottom of the skillet. This step, when done just right, caramelizes the vegetables and brings out their natural sweetness.

Stir in *1 cup* of apple juice and *1 cup* of the tomatoes, and scrape the bottom

(continued)

of the skillet to clear it of all brown bits. Cook, occasionally checking the bottom of the skillet for sticking, until all the liquid evaporates and the vegetables begin to dry and look pasty, about 20 minutes. Add the *remaining* onions, okra, apple juice and tomatoes, and the medium diced eggplant and tomato sauce. Scrape the bottom of the skillet clear, and continue to cook, checking the bottom of the skillet for sticking, about 10 minutes. Serve over the rice.

Per 1-cup serving: Calories 373   Protein 7g   Fat 1g
Carbohydrates 83g   2% calories from fat

color photograph 41
Maque Choux Thibodaux

Makes 4 cups or 4 side servings

Pronounced "mock shoe," this sweet and highly seasoned corn dish has always been a favorite in my family. We have several versions and hope you like this newest addition to the family collection.

Caramelizing the puréed vegetables is crucial to the final taste of the dish, so don't rush this step. And use the freshest corn you can find. Not only does it taste better, but the fresher the corn, the more starch it contains; it's the browned starch that builds up the crust to form the wonderful flavor of the finished dish. Different types of corn have different amounts of starch, which will affect the thickness of this dish. It should have the consistency of rich, thick bisque.

Seasoning mix

1½ teaspoons onion powder
  1 teaspoon salt
  1 teaspoon sweet paprika
  1 teaspoon garlic powder
  ¾ teaspoon dry mustard
  ¼ teaspoon black pepper
  ¼ teaspoon white pepper

2 cups chopped onions, *in all*
1 cup chopped celery, *in all*
4 cups fresh corn kernels, *in all*
2 cups defatted chicken stock
   (page 8), *in all*
½ cup apple juice
½ cup prune juice
½ cup evaporated skim milk
¼ cup nonfat dry milk

Combine the seasoning mix ingredients in a small bowl.

Combine *1 cup* of the onions, ½ *cup* of the celery, and *2 cups* of the corn in a blender with ½ *cup* of the stock. Purée until completely smooth.

Preheat a heavy 10-inch skillet, preferably nonstick, over high heat to 350°, about 4 minutes.

This next step—caramelizing the puréed vegetables—is the most important stage in developing the flavor of the finished dish. Place the puréed mixture in the hot skillet and cook, scraping periodically, about 12 to 13 minutes in all. To do this successfully, cook a few minutes, and after a very thin brown crust develops and starts sticking to the bottom of the skillet, stir and scrape up this crust and blend it in with the rest of the purée. Cook a little longer until another crust forms, scrape it up and blend it in, and repeat this process until the mixture is very thick and a dark golden brown. Taste one of the bits of crust that separate from the skillet; you'll find it still has a real corn flavor but is incredibly sweet with just a hint of caramel.

At the end of the 12 or 13 minutes, add the apple and prune juices, the *remaining* vegetables and seasoning mix, and the *remaining 1½ cups* stock. Scrape the bottom of the skillet to clear it of all brown bits, stir, and cook until the liquid comes to a full boil, about 8 to 10 minutes. Reduce the heat to medium and cook for 35 minutes, checking the bottom of the skillet for sticking.

Combine the skim milk and dry milk in a blender, and process until the dry milk is completely dissolved. Add the blended milk mixture to the skillet, scrape the bottom and sides clear, bring to a simmer, and cook for 5 minutes.

Per 1-cup serving: Calories 264   Protein 12g   Fat 1g
Carbohydrates 55g   5% calories from fat

French Market Vegetable Casserole

Makes 6 cups

For a long time, the freshest vegetables in New Orleans were found at the famous French Market on Decatur Street. Now, thank goodness, most supermarkets and neighborhood grocery stores can offer their customers really fresh produce. Nevertheless, some of us still remember the old market when we cook with vegetables.

½ cup dried white beans

Seasoning mix
2¼ teaspoons onion powder
1½ teaspoons salt
1½ teaspoons sweet paprika
1½ teaspoons garlic powder
1½ teaspoons ground cumin
1½ teaspoons dried thyme leaves
1¼ teaspoons dry mustard
½ teaspoon black pepper
¼ teaspoon white pepper
¼ teaspoon cayenne

1 cup chopped onions
1 cup chopped green bell peppers
1 cup chopped celery
2 bay leaves

1 teaspoon minced fresh garlic
2 cups apple juice, *in all*
1½ cups vegetable stock (page 8)
1 large carrot, scrubbed and sliced diagonally, exposing as much of the inside as possible, into medium bite-size pieces
1 large yellow squash, scrubbed and sliced diagonally, exposing as much of the inside as possible, into medium bite-size pieces
1 large zucchini, scrubbed and sliced diagonally, exposing as much of the inside as possible, into medium bite-size pieces

3 parsnips, scrubbed and sliced
   diagonally, exposing as
   much of the inside as
   possible, into medium
   bite-size pieces

12 asparagus spears, cut into
   1-inch pieces
½ medium onion, peeled and
   cut into medium-to-large
   bite-size pieces

Day 1: Add enough water to the white beans to cover them by 3 or 4 inches, and soak them overnight in the refrigerator. As the beans absorb the water, they will more than double in volume.

Day 2: Drain the white beans.

Combine the seasoning mix ingredients in a small bowl.

Preheat a heavy 10-inch skillet, preferably nonstick, over high heat to 350°, about 4 minutes.

Combine the chopped onions, bell peppers, celery, drained white beans, bay leaves, garlic, and the seasoning mix in the skillet. Stir and cook, scraping the bottom of the skillet to clear it of all brown bits, for 4 to 6 minutes. Add *1 cup* of the apple juice, scrape the bottom of the skillet, and cook until all the liquid evaporates and the vegetables start to stick and turn brown, about 20 minutes. Stir in the stock, clear the bottom of the skillet, bring to a full boil, and turn off the heat.

Preheat the oven to 350°.

Remove and discard the bay leaves. Transfer the ingredients from the skillet to a blender, add the *remaining* apple juice, and purée until completely smooth. Place the puréed mixture in a large bowl and add all the cut vegetables. Mix thoroughly and transfer the mixture to a 17 × 11 × 2½-inch casserole, cover with foil, and bake until done, about 40 minutes.

Per 1-cup serving: Calories 171   Protein 6g   Fat 1g
Carbohydrates 37g   5% calories from fat

White Beans Orleans

Makes about 9 cups, enough for 9 side servings

To make this a completely vegetarian dish, just use vegetable stock instead of chicken stock. The flavor is a little different, but still wonderful. This dish should be the consistency of a rich, thick bisque.

1 pound white beans

Seasoning mix

2 teaspoons salt
2 teaspoons sweet paprika
2 teaspoons dried thyme leaves
1½ teaspoons garlic powder
1 teaspoon onion powder
1 teaspoon white pepper
1 teaspoon dried oregano leaves
½ teaspoon black pepper
¼ teaspoon cayenne

3 cups chopped onions, *in all*
2 cups chopped green bell peppers, *in all*
½ cup chopped celery
4½ cups defatted chicken stock (page 8), *in all*
4 cups peeled, chopped fresh tomatoes or 2 (14½-ounce) cans chopped tomatoes
2 teaspoons minced fresh garlic
1 cup apple juice

Day 1: Add enough water to the beans to cover them by 3 or 4 inches, and soak overnight in the refrigerator. As the beans absorb the water, they will more than double in volume.

Day 2: Combine the seasoning mix ingredients in a small bowl.

Drain the beans and set aside.

Preheat a heavy 5-quart pot, preferably nonstick, over high heat to 350°, about 4 minutes.

Add *2 cups* of the onions, *1 cup* bell peppers, the celery, and *2 tablespoons* of the seasoning mix. Stir and cook until the vegetables start to turn brown, about 5 minutes. Add ½ *cup* of the stock, scrape the bottom of the pot to clear it of all the browned bits, and cook until the liquid evaporates, about

5 minutes. Add the *remaining* onions, stir and scrape the bottom of the pot, and cook 5 minutes. Add the tomatoes and the *remaining* seasoning mix and bell peppers. Clear the bottom of the pot and cook 5 minutes. Add the drained beans, *3 cups* of stock, and the garlic, and cook 10 to 12 minutes. Reduce the heat to medium and cook 50 minutes. Stir in the *remaining 1 cup* of stock and the apple juice, and cook until the beans are tender, and the liquid is thick and starts to look creamy, about 50 minutes more.

Per 1-cup serving: Calories 222   Protein 13g   Fat 2g
Carbohydrates 40g   8% calories from fat

Not Yo' Mama's Red Beans

Makes about 7 cups, enough for 6 main-dish servings

Red beans with rice is an old traditional New Orleans Monday supper dish. Monday used to be wash day, and the story goes that the beans could simmer while the laundry was being done. When the wash was finished, so were the beans. In the past, in order to make the beans really good, the cook started off with a lot of oil. While this recipe eliminates the oil, it still is mouth-watering.

1 pound red beans

Seasoning mix
2 teaspoons salt
1½ teaspoons onion powder
1½ teaspoons dried sweet basil
　　leaves
1 teaspoon garlic powder
1 teaspoon dry mustard
½ teaspoon black pepper
½ teaspoon white pepper
½ teaspoon dried oregano
　　leaves

½ teaspoon cayenne

3 cups chopped onions, *in all*
1 cup chopped green bell
　　peppers
½ cup chopped celery
8½ cups defatted chicken stock
　　(page 8), *in all*
2 cups grape juice, *in all*
4 cups cooked long-grain
　　white rice

Day 1: Add enough water to the red beans to cover them by 3 or 4 inches, and soak overnight in the refrigerator. As the beans absorb the water, they will more than double in volume.

Day 2: Combine the seasoning mix ingredients in a small bowl.

Drain the beans and set them aside.

Preheat a heavy 5-quart pot, preferably nonstick, over high heat to 350°, about 4 minutes.

Add *2 cups* of the onions, the bell peppers, the celery, and *1 tablespoon* of the seasoning mix. Stir and cook until the vegetables start to turn brown, about 5 minutes. Add ½ *cup* of the stock, scrape the bottom of the pot to clear all the browned bits, and cook 3 minutes. Add the *remaining* 1 cup of onions, stir, and cook 5 minutes. Add the drained beans, *5 cups* of the stock, and the *remaining* seasoning mix. Stir and cook for 45 minutes, scraping the bottom of the pot occasionally to check for sticking. Add *1 cup* grape juice and continue to cook for 25 minutes. **Caution:** At this point, the starches in the beans start to break down and sticking will occur more often. It is therefore important to check and clear the bottom of the pot frequently. Add the *remaining* stock and grape juice, turn the heat to medium, and cook until the beans are tender, and the liquid is thick and begins to look creamy, about 30 to 35 minutes. Serve over the rice.

Per serving: Calories 409   Protein 17g   Fat 3g
Carbohydrates 81g   5% calories from fat

color photograph 42
Chickpeas Warren

Makes about 11 cups, enough for 11 side servings

Here's another recipe using versatile chickpeas (or garbanzos). They have a nice nutty taste served just plain, but we've spiced them up to make them even more delicious.

1 pound dried chickpeas

Seasoning mix
2 teaspoons salt
2 teaspoons onion powder
2 teaspoons dry mustard
2 teaspoons ground cumin
1 teaspoon garlic powder
1 teaspoon white pepper
½ teaspoon black pepper
¼ teaspoon cayenne

2 cups chopped onions
2½ cups chopped green bell peppers, *in all*
½ cup chopped celery
6½ cups defatted chicken stock (page 8), *in all*
1 teaspoon minced fresh garlic
1 cup apple juice
2 cups finely diced carrots
1 cup finely diced onions

Day 1: Add enough water to the chickpeas to cover them by 3 or 4 inches, and soak overnight in the refrigerator. As the peas absorb the water, they will increase in volume.

Day 2: Combine the seasoning mix ingredients in a small bowl.

Drain the chickpeas and set aside.

Preheat a heavy 5-quart pot, preferably nonstick, over high heat to 350°, about 4 minutes.

Add the chopped onions, *1 cup* of the bell peppers, the celery, and *2 tablespoons* of the seasoning mix. Stir and cook until the vegetables start to brown, about 5 minutes. Add *½ cup* of the stock, scrape the bottom of the pot to clear all the brown bits, and cook until the liquid evaporates, about 5 minutes. Stir in *4 cups* stock, the drained chickpeas, and *remaining* seasoning mix. Clear the bottom of the pot and cook 5 minutes, then add the garlic and *remaining* bell peppers. Cook 10 to 12 minutes, then reduce the heat to medium, and continue to cook for 45 minutes, clearing the bottom of the pot occasionally as sticking occurs. Add the apple juice, carrots, finely diced onions, and *remaining* stock, and cook until the peas are tender, and the liquid is thick and begins to look creamy, about 1 hour. With this recipe, it is more important to trust your eyes and taste buds than to watch the clock. Taste a couple of chickpeas; if the flavor is good and they are tender and creamy, they're done. Serve warm.

Per 1-cup serving: Calories 197   Protein 10g   Fat 3g
Carbohydrates 34g   13% calories from fat

Sweet and Creamy
Black-eyed Peas

Makes 8 cups, enough for 8 side servings

In Louisiana we eat black-eyed peas on New Year's Day for good luck (and cabbage or other greens for wealth). You'll have good luck anytime you eat a plate of these, and they taste great with greens and cornbread.

1 pound dried black-eyed peas

Seasoning mix

2 teaspoons salt
2 teaspoons sweet paprika
2 teaspoons garlic powder
2 teaspoons black pepper
2 teaspoons ground cumin
1½ teaspoons onion powder
1 teaspoon dry mustard
½ teaspoon cayenne

4 cups chopped onions, *in all*
1 cup chopped green bell peppers
½ cup chopped celery
6½ cups defatted chicken stock (page 8), *in all*
5 cups water
3 cups apple juice, *in all*

Day 1: Add enough water to the black-eyed peas to cover them by 3 or 4 inches, and soak overnight in the refrigerator. As the peas absorb the water, they will more than double in volume.

Day 2: Combine the seasoning mix ingredients in a small bowl.

Drain the black-eyed peas and set aside.

Preheat a heavy 5-quart pot, preferably nonstick, over high heat to 350°, about 4 minutes.

Add *2 cups* of the onions, all the bell peppers and celery, plus *2 tablespoons* of the seasoning mix. Stir and cook for 5 minutes. Stir in ½ *cup* of the stock and scrape the bottom of the pot to clear all the brown bits. Cook for 3 minutes, add *1 cup* onions, and cook for 5 minutes more. Add the peas, water, and *remaining* seasoning mix. Stir and cook about 35 minutes, checking the bottom of the pot occasionally for sticking. Add *1 cup* of the apple juice and cook 15 minutes, checking for sticking. Add *1 more cup* apple juice, check the bottom of the pot for sticking, and cook 15 minutes.

Caution: At this point the starches in the peas will start to break down, and sticking will occur more often. It is therefore important to check and clear the bottom of the pot frequently. Add the *remaining 1 cup* apple juice and *2 cups* stock and cook for 40 minutes. Add the *remaining 4 cups* stock and *1 cup* onions. Reduce the heat to medium and cook until the peas are tender, many have broken open, and the liquid is thick and reddish-brown. This may take 30 minutes or more, depending upon how long the peas have been dried and packaged. Taste a couple of the peas—if the flavor is good and they are tender and creamy, the peas are done.

Per 1-cup serving: Calories 187   Protein 9g   Fat 2g
Carbohydrates 36g   7% calories from fat

Lentils and Rice

Makes 8 cups, enough for 8 side- or 4 main-dish servings

 Lentils have a wonderful, distinctive taste and go well with rice—the combination of flavors and textures is a great match.

Seasoning mix

- 2 teaspoons sweet paprika
- 1½ teaspoons salt
- 1 teaspoon onion powder
- 1 teaspoon garlic powder
- 1 teaspoon dry mustard
- 1 teaspoon dried sweet basil leaves
- 1 teaspoon ground cumin
- 1 teaspoon dried thyme leaves
- ½ teaspoon black pepper
- ½ teaspoon white pepper
- ⅛ teaspoon cayenne

- 2½ cups chopped onions, *in all*
- 1 cup chopped green bell peppers
- 8 ounces finely diced turkey tasso or your favorite smoked ham
- 1½ cups dried lentils
- ½ cup chopped celery
- 1½ cups short-grain white rice
- 6 cups defatted chicken stock (page 8)

Combine the seasoning mix ingredients in a small bowl.

Preheat a heavy 5-quart pot, preferably nonstick, over high heat to 350°, about 4 minutes.

Add 1½ cups of the onions and the bell peppers, and cook, scraping the bottom of the pot once or twice to clear it of all brown bits, until the vegetables start to brown, about 5 minutes. Add the tasso, lentils, and seasoning mix, stir, then clear the bottom of the pot and cook 2 minutes. Add the celery and the *remaining* onions, mix, and cook 2 more minutes. Stir in the rice and cook 2 to 3 minutes. Stir in the stock and scrape the bottom and sides of the pot. Bring to a boil, reduce the heat to low, cover, and cook until the rice is done and the lentils are tender, about 35 to 40 minutes. Serve immediately.

Per 2-cup serving: Calories 575   Protein 33g   Fat 5g
Carbohydrates 97g   7% calories from fat

30. Turkey Boiled Dinner
page 174

31. Turkey Rex
page 184

32. Turkey Cutlets in Onion Custard
page 186

33. Turkey Tacos
page 190

34. Turkey Jambalaya
page 192

35. Turkey Meatballs
page 194

36. Round Steak in Onion Gravy
page 198

37. Flank and Greens
page 208

38. Garlic Roast
page 216

39. Roast Leg of Lamb
page 218

40. Bronzed Veal Chops
page 222

41. Maque Choux Thibodaux
page 226

42. Chickpeas Warren (top)
page 234

White Beans Orleans (right)
page 230

Sweet and Creamy Black-eyed Peas (bottom left)
page 236

43. Vegetables as a Main Dish with Brown Rice
page 240

44. Vegetable Pasta
page 245

45. Strawberry Fluff
page 252

46. Buttercup Squash Andrew
page 254

47. Fruity Bread Pudding
page 256

48. Chocolate Yum Stuff
page 258

49. Turkey Jurkey!
page 274

Crunchy Long-Grain Brown Rice
page 263

Chickpea Snacks
page 268

Two-Seed Rice

Makes 8 cups, enough for 8 side or 4 main-dish servings

Pumpkin and sunflower seeds add an exciting crunch to this dish that I think you'll love. The crushed red pepper adds to the excitement, but if you can't stand the heat, just reduce or omit the pepper.

Seasoning mix

2 teaspoons sweet paprika	¾ teaspoon black pepper
1½ teaspoons ground ginger	¾ teaspoon white pepper
1½ teaspoons ground cumin	½ teaspoon ground allspice
1 teaspoon salt	
1 teaspoon onion powder	2 cups long-grain brown rice
1 teaspoon garlic powder	¼ cup pumpkin seeds
1 teaspoon dry mustard	¼ cup sunflower seeds
1 teaspoon dried sweet basil leaves	2 cups chopped onions
1 teaspoon crushed red pepper, optional	4½ cups defatted chicken stock (page 8), *in all*

Combine the seasoning mix ingredients in a small bowl.

Place a 10-inch skillet, preferably nonstick, over high heat and add the rice and seeds. Cook, shaking the pan occasionally to mix, until seeds start to brown, about 5 to 7 minutes. Remove from the heat and set aside.

Preheat a heavy 5-quart pot, preferably nonstick, over high heat to 350°, about 4 minutes.

Add the onions and cook, stirring occasionally, until they start to brown, about 5 minutes. Add the seasoning mix and ½ cup of the stock, scrape the bottom clean, and cook until the liquid evaporates and the onions start to stick, about 4 to 5 minutes. Stir in the *remaining* stock, scrape the bottom and sides of the pot clean, and add the rice and seed mixture. Bring to a boil, reduce the heat to low, cover, and cook until the rice is tender and the stock absorbed, about 25 to 30 minutes. Serve immediately.

Per 2-cup serving: Calories 573   Protein 18g   Fat 17g
Carbohydrates 91g   26% calories from fat

Vegetables as a Main Dish with Brown Rice

Makes 6 to 8 servings

This main-dish recipe was one of the first developed for the book. It has a super combination of flavors, textures, and colors, and even those with hearty appetites will find it satisfying.

Seasoning mix

   2 teaspoons salt
   2 teaspoons sweet paprika
1½ teaspoons onion powder
1½ teaspoons dried sweet basil
      leaves
   1 teaspoon garlic powder
   1 teaspoon dry mustard
   1 teaspoon dried thyme leaves
   1 teaspoon dillweed
   ½ teaspoon white pepper
   ½ teaspoon ground nutmeg
   ¼ teaspoon black pepper
   ¼ teaspoon dried savory leaves

   1 eggplant

   ½ cup apple juice
   2 cups chopped onions
1½ cups chopped green bell
      peppers
   1 cup chopped celery
   2 cups defatted chicken stock
      (page 8), *in all*
   1 teaspoon minced fresh garlic
   4 cups peeled, diced fresh
      tomatoes or 2 (14½-ounce)
      cans diced tomatoes
   3 bay leaves
   3 cups sliced fresh mushrooms
   1 cup medium diced zucchini
   1 cup medium diced yellow
      squash

Combine the seasoning mix ingredients in a small bowl.

Peel the eggplant and slice it into quarters lengthwise. Sprinkle all surfaces of the eggplant with *4 teaspoons* of the seasoning mix.

Preheat a heavy 12-inch skillet, preferably nonstick, over high heat to 350°, about 4 minutes.

Cook the seasoned eggplant in the skillet until browned, about 2 minutes on each side. Add the apple juice and cook for about 6 minutes, turning occasionally, until the surfaces of the eggplant are sticky and caramelized. Remove the eggplant and set it aside.

Combine the onions, bell peppers, celery, and *1 tablespoon* of the seasoning mix in the skillet, and cook, stirring once or twice, until a crust forms on the bottom of the skillet, about 12 minutes. Add *1 cup* of the stock and scrape the bottom of the skillet to clear it of all brown bits. Add the garlic and cook until the vegetables are evenly browned and sweet-tasting, about 5 minutes. When the liquid has evaporated and a new crust has formed, add the tomatoes and scrape the bottom of the skillet to clear it. Add the bay leaves, mushrooms, zucchini, yellow squash, and the *remaining* seasoning mix and stock. Mix together, then return the eggplant to the skillet, submerging it completely in the sauce. Reduce the heat to medium and simmer until the eggplant is tender, about 12 to 15 minutes. Serve with Brown Rice.

Brown Rice

1½ cups long-grain brown rice   ½ teaspoon salt
2 bay leaves
3 cups defatted chicken stock
(page 8)

Place a heavy 2-quart pot over high heat. Add the rice and bay leaves, and brown for 2 minutes. Stir in the stock and salt. Bring to a boil, cover, reduce the heat to low, and simmer until the rice is tender and the stock is absorbed, about 20 minutes.

Per serving: Calories 233   Protein 8g   Fat 3g ·
Carbohydrates 46g   11% calories from fat

Vegetable Rice

Makes about 10 cups, enough for 10 side or 5 main-dish servings

This makes a wonderful accompaniment to roast beef or chicken, and is great as a main dish, too. If someone at your table is a strict vegetarian, use vegetable stock instead of chicken stock.

Seasoning mix

2 teaspoons sweet paprika

2 teaspoons dry mustard

2 teaspoons dried sweet basil leaves

1¾ teaspoons salt

1½ teaspoons onion powder

1 teaspoon garlic powder

1 teaspoon crushed red pepper, optional

¾ teaspoon black pepper

¾ teaspoon white pepper

½ teaspoon dried summer savory

2 tablespoons alfalfa seeds

2 tablespoons sesame seeds

3 cups chopped onions

2 cups chopped green bell peppers

1 cup chopped celery

2 cups uncooked long-grain white rice

1 teaspoon minced fresh garlic

3½ cups defatted chicken stock (page 8)

1 cup large-diced zucchini

1 cup large-diced yellow squash

2 cups sliced fresh mushrooms

1 cup broccoli florets

1 cup cauliflower florets

Combine the seasoning mix ingredients in a small bowl.

Preheat a small skillet over high heat to 350°, about 3 minutes.

Add the alfalfa and sesame seeds and heat, shaking the skillet occasionally, until they start to pop and turn brown, about 5 to 7 minutes. Remove from the heat and set aside.

Preheat a heavy 5-quart pot, preferably nonstick, over high heat to 350°, about 4 minutes.

Add the onions, bell peppers, celery, and *2 tablespoons* of the seasoning mix. Stir and cook, scraping the bottom of the pot occasionally to clear it of all brown bits, until the vegetables start to brown, about 5 to 6 minutes. Add the rice and *remaining* seasoning mix, and cook for 3 to 4 minutes more. Add the garlic and stock, scrape the bottom and sides of the pot, and cook for 10 minutes. Stir in the *remaining* vegetables and the browned seeds. Bring to a boil, reduce the heat to medium, cover, and cook until the rice is tender and the stock is absorbed, about 4 to 5 minutes.

Per 2-cup serving: Calories 400   Protein 12g   Fat 3g
Carbohydrates 81g   8% calories from fat

Sweet and Hot Rice

Makes 8 cups, enough for 8 side servings

This recipe blends sweet rice (see **Note**) and White Grape Syrup with plenty of spices for balance. Serve the rice with main dishes that don't have many heavy spices of their own, like broiled, grilled, or roasted meats and fish.

Seasoning mix
2 teaspoons sweet paprika
1 tablespoon curry powder
1 teaspoon salt
1 teaspoon onion powder
1 teaspoon garlic powder
1 teaspoon dry mustard
½ teaspoon black pepper
½ teaspoon white pepper
½ teaspoon ground coriander
⅛ teaspoon cayenne

2½ cups chopped onions, *in all*
7 cups sliced fresh
    mushrooms, *in all*
4 cups defatted chicken stock
    (page 8), *in all*
2 cups sweet rice (see **Note**)
¼ cup White Grape Syrup
    (page 45)

(continued)

Combine the seasoning mix ingredients in a small bowl.

Preheat a heavy 5-quart pot, preferably nonstick, over high heat to 350°, about 4 minutes.

Add *1½ cups* of the onions and *2 cups* of the mushrooms, and cook until the onions start to brown, about 5 minutes. Add the seasoning mix, the *remaining* onions and *½ cup* of the stock, and scrape the bottom of the pot to clear all the brown bits. Cook for 3 minutes and add the rice. Scrape the bottom clear again, and cook for 7 to 8 minutes, scraping the bottom as the rice starts to stick frequently and a crust forms on the bottom. Add the *remaining* stock, clear the bottom and sides of the pot, and bring to a boil. As soon as the liquid starts to boil, add the *remaining* mushrooms and the White Grape Syrup, stir to dissolve the syrup and return to a boil. Reduce the heat to medium, cover, and cook until the rice is tender and the liquid is absorbed, about 30 to 35 minutes. Serve immediately.

Note Sweet rice is available in some specialty markets. If you cannot find it, use short-grain brown rice.

Per 1-cup serving: Calories 230   Protein 6g   Fat 0g
Carbohydrates 47g   1% calories from fat

Vegetable Pasta

▬ ▬ ▬ ▬ ▬ ▬ ▬ ▬ ▬ ▬ ▬ ▬ ▬ ▬ ▬ ▬ ▬

Makes 4 main-dish servings

The brightly colored vegetable sticks make this dish look like a party. Vegetables and pasta have a natural affinity for each other, I think.

Seasoning mix

- 2 teaspoons dry mustard
- 2 teaspoons dried sweet basil leaves
- 1½ teaspoons onion powder
- 1½ teaspoons garlic powder
- 1 teaspoon salt
- 1 teaspoon sweet paprika
- 1 teaspoon dried oregano leaves
- ¼ teaspoon black pepper
- ¼ teaspoon white pepper
- ⅛ teaspoon cayenne

▬

- 2 cups chopped onions
- 1 cup chopped celery
- 1½ cups apple juice
- 5 tablespoons all-purpose flour, browned (page 7)

- 3 tablespoons tamari (see Note)
- 2 teaspoons balsamic (or your favorite) vinegar
- 5 cups vegetable stock (page 8)
- 1 cup freshly cut corn kernels
- 1 cup peeled carrot sticks, 1½ inches by ¼ inch
- 1 cup peeled turnip sticks, 1½ inches by ¼ inch
- 1 cup zucchini sticks, 1½ inches by ¼ inch
- 1 cup yellow squash sticks, 1½ inches by ¼ inch
- 1 cup broccoli florets
- 1 cup cauliflower florets
- 4 cups any kind of cooked pasta

Combine the seasoning mix ingredients in a small bowl.

Preheat a heavy 5-quart pot, preferably nonstick, over high heat to 350°, about 4 minutes.

Add the onions, celery, and seasoning mix, stir and cook for 4 minutes, checking the bottom of the pot occasionally for sticking. Add the apple juice,

(continued)

scrape the bottom of the pot to clear it of all brown bits, and cook until almost all the liquid evaporates, about 5 to 6 minutes.

Add the browned flour, tamari, and vinegar, and stir until the flour is completely absorbed, forming a thick paste. Spread this mixture evenly over the bottom of the pot and cook, scraping the bottom frequently, for 1 minute. Add the stock, stir until all the ingredients are well mixed, and bring to a boil. Add the corn and the carrots, and cook for 2 minutes. Add the turnips and cook for 2 more minutes. Add the remaining vegetables and cook for 2 minutes. Fold in the pasta and cook just until the pasta is heated through, about 3 to 4 minutes.

Note Tamari is a very rich, flavorful soy sauce, available in specialty markets and the international or ethnic food sections of many supermarkets. If you cannot find tamari where you shop, use any good quality soy sauce.

Per serving: Calories 410   Protein 16g   Fat 2g
Carbohydrates 89g   4% calories from fat

Eggplant and Cream on Pasta

Makes about 5½ cups, enough for 4 main-dish servings

Eggplant is so nourishing that it's good to have ways to serve it besides the popular Italian versions. As you can see, there's not a trace of tomato or cheese!

Seasoning mix
- 2 teaspoons pink peppercorns (see **Note**)
- 2 teaspoons green peppercorns (see **Note**)
- 1½ teaspoons dry mustard
- 1¼ teaspoons onion powder
- 1 teaspoon salt
- 1 teaspoon garlic powder
- 1 teaspoon white peppercorns (see **Note**)
- 1 teaspoon dried sweet basil leaves
- ½ teaspoon white pepper

Creamy mixture
- 1 cup nonfat cottage cheese
- 5 ounces evaporated skim milk
- ¼ cup nonfat cream cheese

- 2 cups peeled medium-diced eggplant, *in all*
- 2 cups medium-diced onions, *in all*
- 2 cups quartered fresh mushrooms, *in all*
- 2 cups apple juice, *in all*
- 1 cup defatted chicken stock (page 8)
- 3 cups your favorite cooked pasta

Combine the seasoning mix ingredients in a small bowl.

Combine the creamy mixture ingredients in a blender and process until smooth. Set aside.

Preheat a heavy 10-inch skillet, preferably nonstick, over high heat to 350°, about 4 minutes.

Combine *1 cup* of the eggplant, *1 cup* of the onions, *1 cup* of the mushrooms, and *2 tablespoons* of the seasoning mix in the skillet. Stir and cook, occasionally checking the bottom of the skillet for sticking, for 2 to 3 minutes.

(continued)

Add *1 cup* of the apple juice, scrape the bottom and sides of the skillet to clear it of all brown bits, and cook, scraping the bottom occasionally, until all the liquid evaporates and a glaze forms on the bottom, about 15 minutes. Add the *remaining* apple juice, scrape the bottom of the skillet clear, add the chicken stock, *remaining* eggplant, onions, mushrooms, and seasoning mix. Stir, bring to a boil, and cook for 10 minutes. Whisk the creamy mixture into the sauce until completely blended, bring to a boil, and turn off the heat. **Caution:** Dishes using these creamy mixtures can "break" or curdle easily if they are brought to a full boil. Therefore, bring the liquid just to a gentle boil, and stir immediately. Add the drained pasta, toss, and serve.

Note If you cannot find separate containers of colored peppercorns where you shop, some stores sell jars with a mixture of pink, white, green, and black peppercorns.

Per serving: Calories 433   Protein 17g   Fat 2g
Carbohydrates 87g   4% calories from fat

Fettuccine with Mixed Greens

Makes 4 main-dish servings

When I was growing up in the country, we picked greens fresh from our garden near the house. If you don't have a vegetable garden, purchase your greens as close to making this dish as possible.

Seasoning mix

2½ teaspoons salt

2 teaspoons sweet paprika

1¾ teaspoons onion powder

1½ teaspoons dried sweet basil
   leaves

1¼ teaspoons garlic powder

1 teaspoon dry mustard

¾ teaspoon white pepper

½ teaspoon black pepper

¼ teaspoon cayenne

Creamy mixture

12 ounces nonfat cottage cheese

1 (5-ounce) can evaporated
   skim milk

3 tablespoons balsamic vinegar

3 tablespoons all-purpose flour

3 cups chopped onions

1 cup chopped celery

1 cup apple juice

4 cups chopped fresh
   mushrooms

4 cups chopped mustard
   greens

4 cups chopped collard greens

4 cups chopped chard

3½ cups vegetable stock (page
   8), *in all*

3 cups cooked fettuccine

Combine the seasoning mix ingredients in a small bowl.

Place the creamy mixture ingredients in a blender and purée until smooth and creamy; set aside.

Preheat a heavy 5-quart pot, preferably nonstick, over high heat to 350°, about 4 minutes.

Add the onions, celery, and *2 tablespoons* of the seasoning mix and cook, checking the bottom of the pot occasionally for sticking, until the vegetables start to brown, about 8 minutes. Add the apple juice, clear the bottom of the pot of any brown bits, then add the mushrooms and the *remaining* seasoning

(continued)

mix. Stir and cook until most of the liquid evaporates, about 7 to 8 minutes. Add all the greens and 3 *cups* of the stock, stir, and cook for 6 minutes.

Add the puréed creamy mixture and stir well. **Caution**: Dishes using these creamy mixtures can "break" or curdle easily if they are brought to a full boil. Therefore, bring the liquid just to a gentle boil, stir immediately, then reduce the heat to low and simmer, stirring occasionally, for 10 minutes. Add the *remaining* ½ *cup* stock, stir, and add the fettuccine. Stir and cook until the pasta is heated throughout, about 5 to 6 minutes. Serve immediately.

Per serving: Calories 392   Protein 23g   Fat 2g
Carbohydrates 73g   5% calories from fat

Desserts

*For everyone who thinks the meal isn't complete
without a sweet finale.*

Strawberry Fluff

Makes 8 servings

 This light, beautiful dessert is so delicious that it makes a big hit with everyone who tries it!

¼ cup apple juice	½ cup evaporated skim milk
1 (0.3-ounce) package strawberry sugar-free gelatin	2 (1-gram) packets artificial sweetener (page 4)
2 cups diced fresh strawberries	2 egg whites
½ teaspoon vanilla extract	3 cups sliced fresh strawberries
½ cup nonfat cottage cheese	

Place a small skillet over high heat, add the apple juice, and bring just to a boil. Remove from the heat, and stir in the gelatin until it dissolves. Transfer this mixture to a blender, add the diced strawberries, and purée until smooth. Stir in the vanilla, cottage cheese, skim milk, and artificial sweetener, and blend thoroughly. Place in a large bowl and refrigerate to keep cool.

Beat the egg whites until stiff peaks form. Using a rubber spatula, gently fold the egg whites into the cooled mixture until completely blended and no trace of the whites is visible. Gently fold in the sliced strawberries.

Divide the mixture evenly among eight 6-ounce custard cups or other serving dishes, and refrigerate until set, about 2 hours.

Per serving: Calories 84   Protein 6g   Fat 1g
Carbohydrates 15g   11% calories from fat

No-Bake Cheesecake

Makes one 10-inch round cake, enough for 10 servings

When we presented this creamy, delicious dessert to the cookbook panel, it was quickly voted the favorite recipe. No one believed (until they saw the list of ingredients) that it was intended for this book.

10 ounces low-fat graham crackers
3 tablespoons nonfat sour cream
4 tablespoons nonfat mayonnaise
4 cups nonfat cream cheese
2 cups nonfat cottage cheese
1 cup unflavored nonfat yogurt
½ cup White Grape Syrup (page 45)
1 tablespoon vanilla extract
3 (1.4-ounce) packages vanilla sugar-free instant pudding
8 (1-gram) packets artificial sweetener (page 4)

Pulverize the graham crackers in a food processor. Add the sour cream and mayonnaise, and pulse until blended. Press the mixture evenly over the bottom and up the sides of a 10-inch round cake pan, preferably a spring-form pan, and refrigerate until set, about 1 hour.

Place the cream cheese, cottage cheese, yogurt, White Grape Syrup, and vanilla in a blender or food processor and purée until smooth and creamy. Add the instant pudding and artificial sweetener, blend in, and pour into the graham cracker mold. Refrigerate until set, about 4 hours.

Per serving: Calories 318   Protein 16g   Fat 2g
Carbohydrates 58g   7% calories from fat

color photograph 47

Fruity Bread Pudding

Makes 8 to 10 servings

All over the country there are many versions of bread pudding. We're proud of this version, not only because it tastes wonderful, but because it's low-cal and low-fat!

8 cups dry bread cubes
   (see **Note**)
4 cups chilled evaporated
   skim milk
1 cup egg substitute
1 cup White Grape Syrup
   (page 45)

1 tablespoon vanilla extract
2 teaspoons ground cinnamon
½ teaspoon ground nutmeg
   Vegetable-oil cooking spray
3 red Delicious apples, peeled,
   cored, and thinly sliced
1 cup raisins

Place the bread cubes into a large bowl and set aside.

In another bowl whisk together the skim milk, eggs, White Grape Syrup, vanilla, cinnamon, and nutmeg until the dry spices are completely absorbed by the liquid. Whip the mixture in batches in a blender at high speed for 1 minute and pour over the bread cubes. Set the bowl aside for 3 to 4 hours, stirring occasionally, until the bread is completely soggy.

Preheat the oven to 350°.

Spray a 9 × 9 × 2-inch baking pan with the vegetable-oil spray. Arrange the apple slices in rows across the bottom of the pan, and sprinkle the raisins evenly over the apples. Carefully spoon the bread-cube mixture over this and bake for 30 minutes. Serve warm.

Note Use day-old bread because it will soak up the egg/milk mixture better than fresh, moist bread. Or dry the bread in a 200° oven for about 15 minutes. Try not to brown the bread—you want it dry, not toasted.

Per serving: Calories 365   Protein 16g   Fat 3g
Carbohydrates 73g   7% calories from fat

Rice Fruit Pudding

Makes 6 servings

Almost every part of the country has its own version of rice pudding, and here in rice-growing country we prepare it a lot of different ways. I think the addition of fresh fruit makes this an incomparable dessert.

4 (1 gram) packets artificial
  sweetener (page 4)
3 medium very ripe nectarines,
  peeled and sliced into thin
  wedges
2½ cups chilled evaporated skim
  milk
½ cup White Grape Syrup
  (page 45)
1 teaspoon cinnamon

1 teaspoon vanilla
4 ounces egg substitute
4 cups cooked long-grain
  white rice
3 cups fresh red seedless grapes
  Vegetable-oil cooking spray

Sprinkle the sweetener over the nectarine wedges, toss, and set aside.

Place the evaporated milk in a blender and add the White Grape Syrup, cinnamon, vanilla, and eggs, and blend until well mixed, about 1 minute. Fold in the rice until well mixed, then stir in the grapes.

Preheat oven to 350°.

Spray a 9 × 9 × 2-inch baking pan with vegetable-oil spray, and pour half of the rice mixture into it. Arrange the sweetened nectarines on top, and spoon the remaining rice mixture over the nectarines. Bake for 45 minutes, and cool 15 to 20 minutes before serving.

Per serving: Calories 351   Protein 14g   Fat 1g
Carbohydrates 73g   3% of calories from fat

Chocolate Yum Stuff

Makes 18 bars, ½ × 3 inches

This delicious dessert should satisfy even the most rabid choco-holic! However, I must confess that it does not meet the guidelines of having fewer than 30 percent of its calories from fat. But I bet you'll agree that the real chocolate is worth the few extra calories. To enjoy this treat without guilt just choose a super-low-fat main course.

½ cup chopped pecans

1 cup unsifted all-purpose flour

¼ cup Prune Syrup (page 46)

¼ cup Apple Syrup (page 47)

½ cup White Grape Syrup (page 45)

1 cup evaporated skim milk

12 ounces finely diced sweet chocolate

8 ounces egg substitute

Vegetable-oil cooking spray

Preheat a 10-inch nonstick skillet over high heat to 400°, about 4 minutes.

Add the pecans, and as soon as the nuts begin to brown, stir constantly for 1 minute. Be careful to avoid scorching. Remove from the heat; the pecans will continue to roast in the skillet. Let cool.

Preheat oven to 350°.

Place the flour in a large bowl and add the roasted pecans; stir together until the pecans are coated with flour. Pour the Prune, Apple, and White Grape Syrups in a circular pattern over the flour and pecans, and mix by hand until the flour is completely absorbed. Add the skim milk and eggs, and stir until thoroughly mixed. Fold in the diced chocolate and mix until evenly distributed.

Spray a 9 × 9 × 4-inch baking pan with vegetable-oil spray. Pour the batter into the pan and bake until firm, about 1 hour. While the cake layer cools, prepare the topping.

Chocolate Pudding Topping

1 (1.4-ounce) package
  chocolate sugar-free
  instant pudding
1½ cups chilled evaporated
  skim milk

4 ounces finely grated sweet
  chocolate
1 tablespoon vanilla extract
4 (1-gram) packets artificial
  sweetener (page 4)

Place all of the ingredients in a blender and process until thoroughly mixed, about 3 minutes. Pour over Chocolate Yum Stuff and refrigerate at least 1 hour.

Per serving (1 bar): Calories 250   Protein 6g   Fat 12g
Carbohydrates 35g   41% calories from fat

Carob Chip Cookies

Makes 3 to 4 dozen cookies

These cookies are not a substitute for something else; enjoy them for what they are: a crunchy treat with a delicious flavor all their own.

1½ cups all-purpose flour
1 tablespoon baking powder
¼ cup Prune Syrup (page 46)
2 tablespoons White Grape Syrup (page 45)
2½ ounces nonfat cream cheese

1 teaspoon vanilla extract
2 ounces egg substitute
½ cup evaporated skim milk
¼ cup roasted sunflower seeds
½ cup carob chips
Vegetable-oil cooking spray

Combine the dry ingredients in a bowl, then push the mixture to the sides to form a hole in the center. Add the fruit syrups, the cream cheese, and vanilla and, using your fingers, work the liquids into the dry mixture until they are incorporated and the dough forms little balls. Add the eggs and skim milk and with a rubber spatula gently fold together until all the liquid has been incorporated. Add the sunflower seeds and carob chips, and mix thoroughly.

Preheat the oven to 325°.

Lightly coat a cookie sheet with the vegetable-oil spray. Drop the batter onto the sheet by rounded teaspoonfuls about 2 to 3 inches apart. Bake for 10 minutes, turn the cookie sheet 180 degrees, and bake for another 10 minutes. Cool for 4 to 5 minutes before removing the cookies from the sheet. Repeat with the remaining dough.

Per serving (1 cookie): Calories 51   Protein 2g   Fat 2g
Carbohydrates 7g   30% calories from fat

Snacks and Munchies

*To satisfy that "in-between" craving, tasty things to nibble on.
Some of the names may sound funny, but try them
first, then see who's laughing.*

Black-eyed Pea Snacks

Makes 8 servings

These sensational snacks retain the distinctive black-eyed pea taste even when they're dry and crunchy. The flavor really lingers on, which generally drives me to eating another handful!

Seasoning mix

2 teaspoons salt
2 teaspoons onion powder
2 teaspoons garlic powder
2 teaspoons dry mustard
1½ teaspoons black pepper
1½ teaspoons dried thyme leaves
1 teaspoon sweet paprika
1 teaspoon ground cumin
¾ teaspoon white pepper

½ teaspoon cayenne

1 (1-gram) packet artificial
  sweetener (page 4)
½ pound dried black-eyed peas
5 cups water
1 cup apple juice
1 cup defatted chicken stock
  (page 8)

Day 1: Combine the seasoning mix ingredients in a small bowl.

Combine *1 tablespoon* of the seasoning mix with the packet of artificial sweetener and set aside.

Place the black-eyed peas and water in a container, add the *remaining* unsweetened seasoning mix, and soak overnight in the refrigerator. As the beans absorb the water, they will more than double in volume.

Day 2: Place the black-eyed peas and the seasoned water in which they were soaked in a 5-quart pot over high heat. Add the apple juice and cook for 20 minutes. Add the chicken stock and cook just until the peas start to turn tender, about 20 minutes. Remove from the heat, place the peas in a colander, rinse well, and drain. Sprinkle the peas evenly with the reserved sweetened seasoning mix and lay them evenly around the dehydrator trays. (See page 10). Place in the machine and dehydrate until beans are crisp and crunchy, about 16 to 18 hours.

Per serving: Calories 70   Protein 4g   Fat 1g
Carbohydrates 13g   6% calories from fat

color photograph 49

Chickpea Snacks

— — — — — — — — — — — — — — — — — — — —

Makes 8 servings

Garbanzos, or chickpeas, are extremely useful and versatile—in many cultures they are simply boiled and seasoned. Here, we've made them into a brand-new form by dehydrating them, and best of all you can snack on them without guilt! Of all the snacks in this book, this is the one I turn to most often!

Seasoning mix

2 teaspoons salt
2 teaspoons onion powder
2 teaspoons garlic powder
1 teaspoon dry mustard
1 teaspoon turmeric
¾ teaspoon white pepper
½ teaspoon black pepper
½ teaspoon cayenne

1 (1-gram) packet artificial sweetener (page 4)
½ pound dried chickpeas
5 cups water
1 cup apple juice
1 cup defatted chicken stock (page 8)

Day 1: Combine the seasoning mix ingredients in a small bowl.

Combine *1 tablespoon* of the seasoning mix with the artificial sweetener and set aside.

Place the chickpeas and water in a container, add the *remaining* unsweetened seasoning mix, and soak overnight in the refrigerator. As the beans absorb the water, they will more than double in volume.

Day 2: Place the chickpeas and the seasoned water in which they were soaked in a 5-quart pot over high heat. Add the apple juice and cook for 20 minutes. Add the chicken stock and cook just until the peas start to turn tender, about 40 minutes. Remove from the heat, place the peas in a colander, rinse well, and drain. Sprinkle the peas evenly with the reserved sweetened seasoning mix and lay them evenly around the dehydrator trays. (See page 10). Place in machine and dehydrate until beans are crisp and crunchy, about 20 to 22 hours.

Per serving: Calories 119   Protein 6g   Fat 2g
Carbohydrates 21g   11% calories from fat

White Bean Snacks

You might never have thought of snacking on white beans, but with this recipe you'll understand just how different and pleasant they can be. Now don't misunderstand, I still love a big plate of steaming-hot beans with rice and some Cajun sausage, but that's a little messy to munch on while I'm driving. Of all the bean snacks, these are the crunchiest and best satisfy the craving to chew. The flavor is terrific, and the satisfaction is real.

Seasoning mix

2 teaspoons salt

2 teaspoons garlic powder

2 teaspoons dried sweet basil leaves

1½ teaspoons onion powder

1 teaspoon white pepper

1 teaspoon dried oregano leaves

1 teaspoon dried summer savory

¾ teaspoon sweet paprika

¾ teaspoon black pepper

½ teaspoon cayenne

1 (1-gram) packet artificial sweetener (page 4)

½ pound dried white beans

6 cups water

1 cup apple juice

1 cup defatted chicken stock (page 8)

Day 1: Combine the seasoning mix ingredients in a small bowl.

Combine *1 tablespoon* of the seasoning mix with the artificial sweetener and set aside.

Place the white beans and water in a container, add the *remaining* unsweetened seasoning mix, and soak overnight in the refrigerator. As the beans absorb the water, they will more than double in volume.

Day 2: Place the white beans and the seasoned water in which they were soaked in a 5-quart pot over high heat. Stir in the apple juice and cook for 20 minutes. Add the chicken stock and cook just until the beans start to turn tender, about 50 minutes. Remove from the heat, place the beans in a colander, rinse well, and drain. Sprinkle the beans evenly with the reserved sweetened seasoning mix and lay them evenly around the dehydrator trays. (See page 10.) Place in machine and dehydrate until beans are crispy and crunchy, about 20 to 22 hours.

Per serving: Calories 104   Protein 6g   Fat 1g
Carbohydrates 19g   4% calories from fat

General Instructions for Rice Snacks

The recipes that follow are for crunchy snacks that are not only nutritious but easy to make. There are a few points I want to emphasize, because they're important and will affect the end result.

1. You really need to use the 10-inch nonstick skillet we call for. The 10-inch size is critical because a larger or smaller surface of water will affect the liquid evaporation rate and, ultimately, your cooking time. If you cannot use a 10-inch skillet, you'll have to experiment with the amount of water and cooking time to be sure that the rice becomes tender during the first stage of cooking.

I don't think you can make these snacks at all without a nonstick skillet. Since for health's sake we're not using oil, the grains would stick to a regular surface.

2. In all of the recipes, the cooking times begin when you turn on the heat, not when the water comes to a boil.

3. The flavor of the rice snacks is dramatically affected not only by the herbs and spices, but by the amount of brown color obtained during the final cooking step. Too dark a brown will leave a bitter taste, while too light a brown means there is too much moisture in the rice which will make it chewy. The color should be a rich brown, or even a red-brown, but no darker than that.

Rice snacks are delicious, and they will remain crunchy in an airtight plastic bag for many days. I enjoy them instead of potato chips or other salty, fattening nibbles.

Crunchy Sweet Rice

Makes 1⅓ cups

Seasoning mix

1½ teaspoons garlic powder

1½ teaspoons dry mustard

1 teaspoon salt

1 teaspoon sweet paprika

1 teaspoon onion powder

½ teaspoon white pepper

½ teaspoon ground allspice

¼ teaspoon black pepper

¼ teaspoon cayenne

1 cup sweet rice (see Note)

¼ cup White Grape Syrup (page 45), optional

Combine the seasoning mix ingredients in a small bowl.

Place a 10-inch nonstick skillet over high heat and add 4 cups of water. Stir in the seasoning mix and rice, and cook uncovered until the rice is tender, about 30 to 35 minutes. If desired, add the White Grape Syrup after the rice has cooked about 25 minutes; this will give it a slightly sweeter flavor. Transfer the rice to a strainer and rinse thoroughly.

Clean the skillet and place it back over high heat. Add the rice and cook about 15 to 20 minutes in all. During the first 5 to 10 minutes, while the starches in the rice are still moist, there will be some minor sticking in the skillet. With a wooden spoon gently clean the bottom of the skillet and turn the rice over. Once the starches dry, the sticking will stop. Gently shake or stir the rice occasionally to ensure that it browns evenly. Continue to stir until the rice turns a golden brown and is crunchy.

Remove the rice and place it in an open container to cool, then cover to store.

Note Sweet rice is a variety of flavorful short-grain rice found in specialty or health food markets.

Per 3½-tablespoon serving: Calories 138   Protein 3g   Fat 0g
Carbohydrates 30g   2% calories from fat

Crunchy Short-Grain Brown Rice

Makes 1⅓ cups

Seasoning mix

1½ teaspoons garlic powder
1   teaspoon salt
1   teaspoon onion powder
1   teaspoon dried sweet basil
    leaves

½ teaspoon ground coriander

1 cup short-grain brown rice
4 cups water

Combine the seasoning mix ingredients in a small bowl.

Place a 10-inch nonstick skillet over high heat and add all of the ingredients. Stir and cook uncovered until the rice is tender, about 30 to 35 minutes. Transfer the rice to a strainer and rinse thoroughly.

Clean the skillet and place it back over high heat. Add the rice and cook for about 20 minutes. During the first 5 to 10 minutes, while the starches in the rice are still moist, there will be some minor sticking in the skillet. With a wooden spoon gently clean the bottom of the skillet and turn the rice over. Once the rice starches dry, the sticking will stop. Gently shake or stir the rice occasionally to ensure that it browns evenly. Continue to cook and stir the rice until it turns a golden brown and is crunchy.

Remove the rice and place it in an open container to cool, then cover to store.

Per 3½-tablespoon serving: Calories 119   Protein 3g   Fat 1g
Carbohydrates 26g   4% calories from fat

color photograph 49

Crunchy Long-Grain Brown Rice

Makes 1⅓ cups

Seasoning mix

1 teaspoon salt
1 teaspoon onion powder
1 teaspoon garlic powder
½ teaspoon white pepper
¼ teaspoon black pepper
¼ teaspoon cayenne

1 cup long-grain brown rice
5 cups water
¼ cup Apple Syrup (page 47), optional

Combine the seasoning mix ingredients in a small bowl.

Place a 10-inch nonstick skillet over high heat, and add all the ingredients except the Apple Syrup. Stir and cook until the rice is tender, about 40 minutes. If desired, add the Apple Syrup after the rice has cooked for about 35 minutes; this will give it a slightly sweeter flavor. Transfer the rice to a strainer and rinse thoroughly.

Clean the skillet and place it back over high heat. Add the rice and cook for about 20 minutes. During the first 5 to 10 minutes, while the starches in the rice are still moist, there will be some minor sticking in the skillet. With a wooden spoon gently clean the bottom of the skillet and turn the rice over. Once the rice starches dry, the sticking will stop. Gently shake or stir the rice occasionally to ensure that it browns evenly. Continue to cook and stir until the rice turns a golden brown and is crunchy.

Remove the rice and place it in an open container to cool, then cover it to store.

Per 3½-tablespoon serving: Calories 119   Protein 3g   Fat 1g
Carbohydrates 26g   4% calories from fat

Crunchy Long-Grain White Rice

Makes 1⅓ cups

Another of the crunchy rice snacks, this one is just different enough from the others that you'll want to make it too, so you can have a variety of flavors. I really recommend you add the sweet Apple Syrup, but then I'm the first to admit I have nothing but sweet teeth!

1 teaspoon salt	3 cups water
¼ teaspoon ground cardamom	¼ cup Apple Syrup (page 47),
1 cup long-grain white rice	optional

Place a 10-inch nonstick skillet over high heat and add all of the ingredients except the Apple Syrup. Stir and cook until the rice is tender, about 17 minutes. If desired, add the Apple Syrup after the rice has cooked for about 12 minutes, to give it a slightly sweeter flavor. Transfer the rice to a strainer and rinse thoroughly.

Clean the skillet and place it back over high heat. Add the rice and cook for about 30 to 35 minutes. During the first 5 to 10 minutes, while the starches in the rice are still moist, there will be some minor sticking. With a wooden spoon gently clean the bottom of the skillet and turn the rice over. Once the starches dry, the sticking will stop. Gently shake or stir the rice occasionally to ensure that it browns evenly. Continue to stir until the rice turns a golden brown and is crunchy.

Remove the rice and place it in an open container to cool, then cover to store.

Per 3½-tablespoon serving: Calories 142   Protein 2g   Fat 0g
Carbohydrates 32g   1% calories from fat

Crunchy Basmati Rice

Makes 1⅓ cups

Seasoning mix

1 teaspoon salt

1 teaspoon onion powder

1 teaspoon garlic powder

1 teaspoon dry mustard

1 teaspoon dried sweet basil
   leaves

½ teaspoon sweet paprika

¼ teaspoon black pepper

¼ teaspoon white pepper

¼ teaspoon cayenne

1 cup basmati rice

4 cups water

Combine the seasoning mix ingredients in a small bowl.

Place a 10-inch nonstick skillet over high heat, and add all of the ingredients. Stir and cook until the rice is tender, about 16 to 18 minutes. Transfer the rice to a strainer and rinse thoroughly.

Clean the skillet and place it back over high heat. Add the rice and cook for about 30 to 35 minutes. During the first 5 to 10 minutes, while the starches in the rice are still moist, there will be some minor sticking in the skillet. With a wooden spoon gently clean the bottom of the skillet and turn the rice over. Once the starches dry, the sticking will stop. Gently shake or stir the rice occasionally to ensure that it browns evenly. Continue to stir until the rice turns a golden brown and is crunchy.

Remove the rice and place it in an open container to cool, then cover it to store.

Per 3½-tablespoon serving: Calories 117   Protein 2g   Fat 0g
Carbohydrates 26g   3% calories from fat

Crunchy Country Wild Rice

Makes 1¼ cups

Seasoning mix
 1 teaspoon salt
 ½ teaspoon ground cinnamon
 ¼ teaspoon white pepper
 ¼ teaspoon black pepper
 ¼ teaspoon cayenne
 ¼ teaspoon ground nutmeg

 1 cup country wild rice
    (see **Note**)
 5 cups water
 ¼ cup Apple Syrup (page 47),
    optional

Combine the seasoning mix ingredients in a small bowl.

Place a nonstick 10-inch skillet over high heat and add all of the ingredients except the Apple Syrup. Stir and cook until the rice is tender, about 40 minutes. If desired, add the Apple Syrup after the rice has cooked about 30 minutes; this will give it a slightly sweeter flavor. Transfer the rice to a strainer and rinse thoroughly.

Clean the skillet and place it back over high heat. Add the rice and cook about 30 to 35 minutes. During the first 5 to 10 minutes, while the starches in the rice are still moist, there will be some minor sticking in the skillet. With a wooden spoon gently clean the bottom of the skillet and turn the rice over. Once the starches dry, the sticking will stop. Gently shake or stir the rice occasionally to ensure that it browns evenly. Continue to cook and stir until the rice turns a golden brown and is crunchy.

Remove the rice and place it in an open container to cool, then cover to store.

Note Country wild rice is a blend of long- and short-grain rices with wild rice.

Per 3½-tablespoon serving: Calories 126   Protein 4g   Fat 0g
Carbohydrates 28g   1% calories from fat

Chicken Jerky

Makes 8 1-ounce servings

Jerky, long strips of sun-dried meat, was originally made with beef. Here we've made it with chicken. You can experiment with other kinds of meat to find the ones you like best. And using a modern dehydrator is surely a lot easier than drying the strips in the sun or smoking them.

Pound the chicken very thin. The thinner the meat is, the easier it will be to eat later. The grape juice and currants give the chicken strips special flavor.

Marinade

¼ cup Purple Grape Syrup (page 46)

2 tablespoons rice or white vinegar

2 tablespoons tamari (see Note)

2 tablespoons white wine Worcestershire sauce

¼ cup chopped currants

2 teaspoons onion powder

2 teaspoons crushed red pepper

4 (1-gram) packets artificial sweetener (page 4)

1 teaspoon garlic powder

6 (2 to 3 ounces each) boneless, skinless chicken breasts

Day 1: Combine all marinade ingredients in a small bowl and mix well to form a paste.

Lay the chicken breasts on a hard surface, cover with waxed parchment paper, and gently pound the breasts until they are about ¼ inch thick. Remove the paper from the chicken breasts, divide the marinade evenly among them, and gently rub on both sides. Refrigerate overnight in a covered container.

Day 2: Drain the excess liquid from the chicken breasts and lay them evenly around the dehydrator trays. (See page 10.) Place in machine and dehydrate until the chicken is cooked and has dried out, about 20 to 22 hours. During this time, turn the chicken pieces over 3 or 4 times.

Note Tamari is a very rich, flavorful soy sauce, available in specialty markets and the international or ethnic food sections of many supermarkets. If tamari is unavailable, use any good quality soy sauce.

Per serving: Calories 148   Protein 22g   Fat 2g
Carbohydrates 11g   14% calories from fat

color photograph 49

Turkey Jurkey!

Makes 8 1-ounce servings

If your idea of jerky is something totally inedible, gnawed on only by cowboys, do we have a pleasant surprise for you! You will need a dehydrator (see page 10), not a major investment, but if you like, see if you can borrow one to try out this recipe before you buy your own. Pound the turkey really thin. The thinner it is, the easier it will be to eat.

Marinade

½ cup Pineapple Syrup (page 48)

4 tablespoons balsamic vinegar

2 tablespoons tamari (see **Note**)

2 tablespoons Worcestershire sauce

12 (1-gram) packets artificial sweetener (page 4)

2 teaspoons onion powder

2 teaspoons garlic powder

1½ teaspoons dried sweet basil leaves

½ teaspoon white pepper

¼ teaspoon cayenne

1 pound turkey breast cutlets, about ¼ inch thick

Day 1: Combine all marinade ingredients in a small bowl and mix well to form a paste. Lay the turkey cutlets on a hard surface, cover with waxed parchment paper, and gently pound the cutlets until they are about ¼ inch thick. Remove the paper from the cutlets, divide the marinade evenly among them and gently rub it into both sides of the cutlets. Refrigerate overnight in a covered container.

Day 2: Drain the excess liquid from the cutlets and lay them evenly around the dehydrator trays. Place in machine and dehydrate the turkey until it is cooked and has dried into jerky form, about 20 to 22 hours. During this time, turn the turkey cutlets over 3 or 4 times.

Note Tamari is a very rich, flavorful soy sauce, available in specialty markets and the international or ethnic food sections of many supermarkets. If you cannot find it where you shop, use any good quality soy sauce.

Per 1-oz serving: Calories 160   Protein 18g   Fat 2g
Carbohydrates 17g   11% calories from fat

Index